SINS
OF THE
FATHER

THE TRUE STORY OF A FAMILY RUNNING FROM THE MOB

NICK TAYLOR

Simon and Schuster
New York, London, Toronto, Sydney, Tokyo

Simon and Schuster
Simon & Schuster Building
Rockefeller Center
1230 Avenue of the Americas
New York, New York 10020

SIMON AND SCHUSTER and colophon are registered trademarks
of Simon & Schuster Inc.

Designed by Diane Stevenson/Snap-Haus Graphics

Manufactured in the United States of America

10   9   8   7   6   5   4   3   2   1

Library of Congress Cataloging in Publication Data
Taylor, Nick.
    Sins of the father : the true story of a family running from the mob / Nick Taylor.
      p.   cm.
    1. Polisi, Sal.   2. Hoodlums—New York (N.Y.)—Biography.
    3. Informers—New York (N.Y.)—Biography.   4. Witnesses—Protection—United
States—Case studies.   I. Title.
    HV6248.P57T39   1989
    363.2′52—dc20
    [B]   89-32508
                                                     CIP

ISBN 0-671-66062-4

THIS BOOK
IS FOR
BARBARA NEVINS TAYLOR

ACKNOWLEDGMENTS

My heartfelt thanks go to a number of people whose assistance was vital to the preparation of this book:
First, to Sal Polisi junior and Joseph Polisi for the insights they shared about their father and about their unique displacement; to Rose Marie Polisi for her patience, trust and candor; to Sal Polisi for his enthusiasm and memory and good humor; and to the entire Polisi family for their courage.

To the Noto family, and especially Phyllis Noto, for her memories of a difficult time.

To the friends of the Polisi family in Port Jervis and Orange County, New York, for their recollections and support of the Polisi family, and especially to Linda Miller for the letters and memories she shared.

To the men who coached Sal junior and Joseph Polisi—Brian Seeber, Joe Viglione and Tom Goddard and more recent coaches who must go unnamed—who recognized, described and helped develop their potential.

To those in law enforcement who knew and worked with Sal Polisi and who contributed valuable information, anecdotes, opinions, recollections and advice; to Dan Russo of the Federal Bureau of Investigation most of all, to John Limbach of the Bureau of Alcohol, Tobacco and Firearms, and also to Lieutenant Remo Franceschini of the Queens district attorney's organized crime squad of the New York Police Department; to Edward A. McDonald of the federal Organized Crime Strike Force for the Eastern District of New York, and to Ethan Levin-Epstein, then assistant U.S. attorney for the Eastern District.

To Dick Babcock at *New York* magazine, where *Sins of the Father* first appeared as an article, for his initial interest and deft editing.

And to many, many others whose names are too numerous to

mention, but without whose contributions *Sins of the Father* would not have been possible.

I thank you all.

Note: I interviewed dozens of people during the preparation of this book. One of them asked that I change his name for the protection of his family, so I did. My subjects almost always were kind enough to share not only their recollections of what happened, but their thinking at the time. These internalized thoughts and feelings, revealed as they are in passages of *Sins of the Father,* are owed entirely to the generosity and candor of my sources.

P R O L O G U E

We were a family to be envied, real Americans. Or so it must have seemed. We certainly tried to put up the appearance of a family that lived a normal life.

This is what people knew: that I was a high-school senior looking forward to a college football scholarship; my brother Joe, just a sophomore, looked like he could be a college player also, maybe even a big star; Mom was a fabulous cook who had been asked to be a substitute home economics teacher at our high school. Dad, the smart, funny guy who everybody liked, was back East, looking in on our jewelry business in New Jersey.

The truth, that fall in 1986, was that my father was in New York City testifying against John Gotti, the most famous mobster in the country. Nobody connected the name of the witness Sal Polisi to our family. But Dad and John Gotti had been friends once, in the old days when Dad was hijacking trucks and robbing banks and nobody knew John Gotti's name, let alone feared him. A few years later, Dad had tried to make a break from crime, but he lost his money and started dealing drugs again, and that got him in a jam. Which was how we ended up where we were.

• • •

We arrived with a vague history, new names and a made-up family tree. Nothing in our past survived our entry into the witness protection program. My girlfriend, Joe's kart racing trophies, Mom's family, even our dog—all discarded on the heap of memory. Nothing survived, that is, except Dad's past. That was our secret that we couldn't put behind us.

Every night on cable while he was away, there was a story about Sal Polisi testifying at the Gotti trial. Sal Polisi the Queens hoodlum turned informant. The convicted bank robber with a history of psychiatric problems. *The gambler. The hijacker. The drug dealer. The witness who said the penalty for witnesses was death.*

Dad came home from New York on a Thursday night. I went to the airport to meet him. He was built chunky and strong, with a round face and curly black hair, and he almost always had a restless sort of energy. But when he got off the plane he was red-eyed and exhausted and all he had to offer was a tired smile. "They took it to me, son," he said. He told me on the way home that John Gotti had pointed a finger at him like a pistol.

"What does that mean?" I asked.

"What do you think it means?" he said.

By Saturday he'd pretty much recovered. The energetic spring was back in his step and he was wisecracking again. He was in my bedroom at first light punching me and saying, "Come on, come on. We gotta go. We're never gonna get there for the kickoff." We were going to the homecoming game at a university two hundred miles away, a big school that wanted to recruit me.

Mom fixed us a quick breakfast, and Dad and Joe and I piled into the car. As we drove, the sun rose to give us a fine October morning. The sky was a high blue, the kind we got in that part of the country. It was warm. You couldn't have asked for a better day.

Dad talked about the game. He gave the edge to the home team because they had a sleeper of a tailback and he liked the left side linebacker. Also, the other team's cheerleaders were dogs. "They just don't make you want to win," he said.

In the old life he would have laid ten thousand dollars on the line to back up what he was saying, for reasons about as good as that. He knew his football though. Knew it and respected it. The game had been his route to fatherhood, his way of demonstrating love. He had coached me and Joe from the time we were midget league players back in Ozone Park in Queens, New York, about a million years ago.

When he took us out of Ozone Park to remove us from the elements that shaped his life, I think he knew that football would be our route to college. And when he got caught that final time, he didn't bet anymore but he still gambled, for higher stakes than money. He gambled for our futures with his life.

"Look at that. Look at that." He pointed excitedly to a car passing in the fast lane. It was full of girls, and they were shaking pom-poms out the window. To us and every car they passed they raised their index fingers in the air. Their wind-snatched voices shouted, "Number one, number one." The pom-poms were the home team's colors. Joe said, "You should definitely come here."

"If they offer me a scholarship," I said.

More cars went by, some with banners streaming, most with rear window stickers from one school or the other in a state passionate about football. Dad waved at the passing game-bound cars. No one would have known from his cheery wave and his wide smile the secrets that his moon-shaped face concealed, or the things we knew together, Dad and me. He looked like another forty-one-year-old grad, taking his two sons to homecoming, not a man shouldering a horrible weight of memory. But the weight was easy now. We were looking forward to the game. It was an old rivalry. The teams were evenly matched, forget about the cheerleaders. As we joined the cars converging on the campus, we felt pulled along into the spirit and fever of the day.

I showed my invitation, and a campus policeman directed us to the athletic center. There were escorts for all the high-school players and their families, and a pretty girl named Paula was assigned to us. She talked in a wonderful drawl, and as soon as she heard us talk, Dad especially, she said, "Y'all aren't from here, are you?"

"No, honey," Dad said, "how 'bout you?"

Paula was from just down the road about forty miles. She showed us around the campus, which was a beautiful place in the autumn sunshine. The brick buildings had a look of age and care and real importance. Students were everywhere, talking, throwing Frisbees to each other on the large quadrangle at the center of the campus; music filtered from dormitory windows; bells tolled on the hour; a festive atmosphere was all about the place. It was like a separate world where nothing could intrude. Paula pointed out the academic buildings, the student center, the library. She was enthusiastic about the school, about the team, about all of campus life. She even showed us the gazebo in the campus rose garden and said it was a favorite make-out place. "Thought you might be interested in that," she laughed. I guess she had my statistics written on a sheet of paper, because she looked at her clipboard and spoke to me, using my name—my new name. "My, ———, you're pretty fast. Are you having a good year?"

I told her I'd been nursing an injury.

"Oh, that's too bad," she said. "I hope it's better in time to play for us next year."

The excitement on the campus grew as game time neared, and soon everybody was heading toward the stadium. Inside, the great bowl of seats was filled to overflowing. The band was playing fight songs with an addictive brassy urgency. Paula led us to a seat behind the home team's bench. I imagined myself standing with the players out there on the field. Dad was going through his program, picking out the names he recognized and trying to find them on the bench. Joe was looking in the direction of the cheerleaders. A network television camera roamed the sidelines. We settled in to enjoy the game on the bright, warm afternoon.

I guess what I noticed was Paula waving. Her face was flushed and eager and she leaned in the direction of the field. I looked to see what she was waving at. I saw the television camera sweeping the stands slowly, moving toward a fix on us, Paula, really. I jabbed Dad in the ribs and pulled him down. "Dad, Dad, tie your shoe," I said.

He pulled Joe down and we sat like that, leaning forward looking at our shoe tops until the camera passed. Someone from the old life might be watching.

Paula looked at us like we were nuts. She'd seen a chance at fame and waved at it, and we'd missed the whole thing messing with our shoes. "What happened to y'all?" she said. "Your shoes all come untied at once? Didn't you see that TV camera?" But she was too much of a host to let us be disappointed long. "Oh, well," she said, brightening at the possibility, "maybe it'll come back later."

That's what it was like.

We had one past beyond recall, and one that wouldn't go away. One, a residue of friends and relatives we'd never see again, a life we couldn't even talk about. The other, an evil pool of memory that threw itself into our faces, or that Dad coaxed up because in his *complexity he wasn't able to give up his criminal past and his memory of it, too.*

The story of how it all happened is really many stories. I can't tell them all, because other people were involved, but they're all included. For my brother and me, leaving one life and living with the other was the price we had to pay for the sins of our father.

O N E

When Dad was arrested in New York City with four ounces of cocaine, things began to change forever. I started growing up. I started to learn about my father, and about myself, the story of his life and what he handed down to me and what his father had handed down to him. Now I know everything, except where the story really ends. But let me start at the beginning.

The cocaine was thirty percent pure. Joe and I watched him cut it in the restaurant at the racetrack we ran north of Port Jervis, New York. We would come home from school and watch him mix it with milk sugar, and after that, with the same nonchalance, he would mince onions and slice green peppers and set them aside for salad garnish. It was purely business, the cocaine. He didn't use it, and we never really thought about it. It was just what we did. You could tell my mom wasn't too proud of it, but that's where our money was coming from, so what are you going to do?

He sold it only because he had spent all our money on the racetrack. The little kart track was our ticket out of New York and Ozone Park, away from the guys like John Gotti he used to hang out with around the Bergin Hunt and Fish Club. He had big plans—karts, stock cars, all kinds of motor racing. But as soon as the pavers and graders and various construction people found out he would pay in cash, counting bills out of Topps baseball card boxes he kept under the sink in what we called the chicken coop, they figured out how to improve what they were doing and charge twice as much. The equipment dealers loved to see him coming, too. He just spent money like it was shredded wheat or something. Pretty soon all the money he had when we left New York was gone, and he went and got a shylock loan from his old friend John Carneglia and started selling cocaine. The night he got busted it was raining.

We went out to dinner first. It was a birthday and anniversary

dinner; he and Mom got married on his birthday in 1967, so we were
going to the Cornucopia to celebrate—me, Joe and Mom and Dad,
Ross Giumarra from the racetrack and his brother Bruce and Bruce's
wife. We should have gone on Monday. That was the date, April 30,
but we were busy at the track and things sort of slid until that
Thursday. It's an easy date to remember, now. May 3, 1984.

I drove Joe and Mom in Mom's Chevette. I was just sixteen,
about to get my license, and I drove every chance I got. The rain
was so heavy it was hard to see, and I scrunched over the steering
wheel and squinted through the windshield where the wipers were
slapping the water back and forth. Mom fidgeted in the front seat.
"God, it's awful," she said. "I hope your father doesn't have to go
to New York tonight."

He had gotten a couple of phone calls earlier. "He'll want to
go if it's like this," I said. "Less people out."

"It's just awful," she repeated.

The lights were on at the Cornucopia, shining through the twilight and the rain. Joe and I dashed across the parking lot, jumping
the puddles and cutting hard left between the spruce trees to the
entrance porch. He tried to cut inside to beat me but I still outran
him by two steps. Mom walked up fast under her umbrella, and we
went in together.

The Cornucopia was a dark, log-cabin brown outside. Inside it
was like the German menu, plain and substantial. Dad, Bruce and
his wife and Ross were at a round table in the corner of the large
back room. We arrived at the same time as the waitress with a round
of drinks. Pretty soon my dad was offering toasts. "To the last year
of my thirties," he said. He was thirty-nine.

"What about to seventeen years of marriage?" my mom said.

"I was getting to that," he said, and raised his glass again.

Then he made a third toast, "To Green Acres."

That was a private joke we had. It had been a big shock when
he decided two years before that we should move to the country from
Ozone Park. Joe and I didn't want to go at first, and Mom wasn't too
hot about leaving her family, who lived next door. He had to try to
keep everybody happy, and when he ran out of all the reasons he
used to throw at us until we were exhausted from arguing, he would

make us sing the song from "Green Acres" on TV. We'd be driving west with the green hills of the Shawangunk Mountains starting to push up, car piled full of stuff from our house in Ozone Park, and he'd start us on the chorus, "Green Acres is the place to be, farm living is the life for me." It got to be funny after a while, and we didn't mind so much. And now it looked like he was right.

My first coach in Port Jervis had switched me from quarterback to running back and I had had a great season the year before. Sal Polisi junior was in all the papers. I gained 853 yards and scored eleven touchdowns in seven games, and Port won the Orange County championship. Joe was getting into kart racing in a big way. Dad had rebuilt an old barn into the house where we lived. He and Mom seemed to be getting along better than I ever remembered. We had a nice family life there. We were happy. We thought his old life was behind us.

Of course, he had to go down to the city a few times a week to sell some coke, but that was just helping the racetrack get out of debt.

About seven-thirty my dad excused himself. "I've gotta make a call," he said.

"I've got to go to the city tonight," he said when he returned. "Ross, why don't you drive down with me? I'm just going in and coming back."

"Oh, Sal, the weather's awful," my mom said. "Can't it wait? Look at it out there." In the twilight you could see the spruce trees swaying in the wind, heavy and slow like they were underwater. Just then a gust of rain rattled on the window.

"Gotta go," he said. A reassuring grin lit up his round face. "Ain't no big deal. I'll be back by one." He always came home the same night when he went to the city, no matter how late it was.

We ate and the waitress brought a cake. We sang two rounds, one of "Happy Birthday" and one of "Happy Anniversary." After that we sat around drinking coffee, and a little after nine my dad got up and said, "I don't want to break up the party, but I've gotta go to my appointment." He never said exactly what he was doing when he left to go somewhere, just that he had an appointment. Even though everybody knew.

*"Please be careful," my mom said. Then he and Ross were gone
into the night.*

• • •

"Jeez, I can't see a thing," Ross said. Sal glanced to see him
concentrating on the road. Ross was a big, toothy guy with a sweet
smile and hair that wouldn't stay where it was combed because it
was starting to grow thin, even though Ross was only thirty-three.
He had the baby blue Chevy locked on seventy, camped in the left
lane, passing the prudent drivers in the two right lanes.

"The sooner we get down there, the sooner we get back," Sal
shrugged. He didn't have a driver's license; it had been suspended
when he was twenty-one and he'd never bothered about a new one.
He loved cars, though. Ross hit a puddle, wrestled the wheel as the
water dragged the car to the left, kept on flying down the rain-slick
road.

They had gone from the restaurant to the racetrack at Cuddebackville long enough for Sal to weigh out four ounces of the coke
on his jewelers' scale behind the counter in the restaurant. Four
ounces was more than Terri had ever wanted before, but Sal didn't
think it was unusual. She was supplying bartenders at neighborhood
bars around Queens, who sold it to their customers. Demand must
be increasing; that was good. Sal suspected Terri was supplying her
own habit, too. He shook the powder into two plastic bags, sealed
them and placed them into a third bag. When he was finished he
ran his fingertip, dusted with coke, over his upper gum. The tingling
sensation felt good, but that was all Sal wanted. Drugs were a business. As soon as they became a habit, you lost sight of business and
things went downhill. He had seen it happen often. Terri was looking
awfully thin. It was getting to the point where her habit would become
a problem, but maybe not yet.

It was nine-thirty when Sal stuffed the coke parcel into a brown
paper bag, wrapped that in a T-shirt from the racetrack and ran
through the rain back to the car. It was ten before he and Ross
reached Middletown and Highway 17, heading for the New York
State Thruway. He'd told Terri he would meet her at eleven.

And didn't make it. The rain seemed to have followed them into

Queens. It let up for a minute when they left the Van Wyck Expressway and turned west on Atlantic Avenue toward Ozone Park, but was coming down in blinding sheets again when they pulled into the lot of the Club Diner at 112 Street and Atlantic at eleven-thirty.

There were a few cars in the lot. Ross parked as close to the door as he could, next to a big, light-colored Cadillac. A guy and a girl were inside, arms around each other, snuggling as they waited for the rain to stop. Sal chuckled when he saw them. He dashed through the rain into the diner. Terri wasn't there, only a few late coffee drinkers. He returned to the car, fidgety, nervous now that the deal was about to go down.

"I tell you what, I'm getting too old for this shit," he said to Ross, who was smoking a Marlboro and fogging the windows.

"Why don't you quit?" said Ross, who was simple and straightforward.

"Need the money. And tell you the truth, I love the excitement."

Ross rolled his window down a crack and tried to flip the cigarette out into the rain, but it fell onto the wet outside of the glass and stuck there. "Well, then, what's the problem?"

"Nothing, I guess." Sal bolted from the car, ran to the door of the diner and looked inside. The same faces looked back at him, turning from the counter to welcome another soul bedraggled from the rain. As he turned back toward the door, he saw Terri walking in, brushing water from the shoulders of her raincoat.

Terri Candido was twenty-eight. She was not Sal's only dealer, but she was the only woman. She had more than one reason for selling cocaine, usually an ounce or two at a time to her bartender contacts. The main reason, she told herself, was to make enough money to help get her husband out of jail. Sal had told her he could help her there; he knew how money, well-placed in the judicial system, could create unforeseen constitutional issues and cause evidence to be misplaced. But the cocaine that was left over when she had paid for Sal's latest delivery seemed to disappear before she could sell it and put the money aside. She always needed more. Sometimes she got a gram or two from Sal when he was feeling horny, but lately he'd been hassling her about putting her profits up her nose. It pissed her off; besides which, she'd been feeling desperate. What the hell did she owe to Sal, anyway? Nothing. She had to remember that tonight.

He started to ask her where the hell she'd been, but she was soaked, and looked tired, so he said, "Can you believe this fuckin' rain? It was like this all the way down. Have you been here? I just got here about ten minutes ago, came in, looked around . . ."

"I was watching for you from the car. I guess I missed you in the rain." She looked over his shoulder at the brightly lighted counter, then back toward the door. Sal glanced sideways, but didn't see anything.

"Did you bring the money?" he asked.

"My friend is out in the car," Terri said.

Sal felt a moment of panic. He fought it down and said, "I told you not to bring anybody over here. I don't want to meet your people. I don't want to know them, or anything about them."

"But he's got the money."

"Well, you go get the money and bring it to me in the car. Don't bring him, just bring the money. I'm in the blue Chevy. I'll pull over against the far wall."

Sal hunched his shoulders up inside his leather jacket and ran through the downpour to the car. The guy and the girl in the Cadillac still had their arms wrapped around each other. A gray-haired guy, with a younger woman. "Send her over here next," he muttered as he yanked open his door to get out of the rain. He fished under the seat for the T-shirt and pulled the paper bag from the folds of cloth, then used the shirt to wipe his face and arms. "She's gonna bring six thousand dollars," he told Ross. "You help me count it and we'll be out of here."

Ross was a good guy, just a friend. He knew what Sal was doing, but it wasn't his thing. Sal felt a little guilty about getting him involved. "Pull back over there, to the far side of the lot," he directed. "We'll do it over there."

Terri came out the door of the diner, peered into the rain, ducked into her coat and ran to Sal's left out of his line of vision. Ross pulled slowly around to the far wall of the parking lot. A moment later Sal was aware of sudden movement in the rain, cars boxing them in, the guy and the girl getting out of the Cadillac, blurred forms taking shape in front of him: a man in a raincoat stood aiming a gun at Sal through the windshield, yelling "Don't move or you're dead!" over the drumming of the rain.

Ross was frozen, with a trapped, wild look. Sal had the package of cocaine in his left hand. He raised both hands and said, "No problem. I guess this party's over."

A few minutes later, Sal stood in the squad room in the basement of Queens Borough Hall, handcuffed and dripping water on the floor, listening to the cops all full of juice talking about how they'd nabbed him in the rain. The guy who had been snuggling in the Cadillac introduced himself as Lieutenant Remo Franceschini. "And this is Peggy Maloney. Detective Maloney," he amended with a smile as he introduced the woman who had been with him in the car.

"Congratulations, both a youse," Sal said sarcastically.

The lieutenant had heard of Sal Polisi. Five years ago there was supposed to be a prostitution ring in Forest Hills operated by Sal Polisi and Dominic Cataldo. Franceschini was in charge of a squad of organized crime investigators assigned to Queens District Attorney John Santucci, and he knew Cataldo was a "button guy," a made member, with the Colombo family. Nothing had ever come of the prostitution tip, and Franceschini had not heard Polisi's name again till recently, during Operation Powder Keg. A woman the police called Terri Rocks, whose real name was Terri Candido, opened up after she was arrested with the cocaine she was selling to an under-cover cop posing as a bartender. Sal Polisi, she said, was her supplier. To make it easy on herself, she agreed to try to lure him to New York with enough cocaine to bust him on a Class A-1 felony.

A cop came up to Franceschini carrying the bag of cocaine the police had taken from Sal. "It's four ounces, all right, Lieutenant," he said.

At that moment Sal realized why Terri had wanted that much coke, and cursed himself for being a fool.

Franceschini nodded. His Italian face with its wide nose and his thick gray hair, combed back smoothly and cut fashionably around the ears, sometimes caused the people he was investigating to mistake him for one of them. His eyes were pale blue, and he fixed them studiously on Sal. "Four ounces, hmmm," he said, "twenty-five to life. Come here a minute, let me show you something."

He led the way into a narrow office at the back of the squad room. A conference table was placed against the front of a desk in a T-shaped arrangement. File cabinets stood along one wall. On the desk was a fancy nameplate of carved wood, R FRANCESCHINI. But the lieutenant directed his attention to the open wall.

There must have been two hundred photographs tacked to a large bulletin board, arranged more or less into five columns but taped and straggling every which way at the bottom where space ran out. The columns were headed with the names Bonanno, Colombo, Gambino, Genovese, Lucchese: the organized crime families of New York. Some were mug shots, others grainy black-and-white surveillance photos, here and there a picture from a wedding and yellowed clippings from a newspaper or magazine. Sal recognized many of the faces. His old friend Dominic Cataldo, under the Colombo column. The Gotti brothers, John and Gene, and John Carneglia under Gambino. Sal scanned the photographs and said, "Very interesting. Who are these guys?"

"These are the people I'm interested in," said the lieutenant. "I know you can help me."

"Oh, gee, Sergeant," Sal said, deliberately demoting Franceschini from lieutenant. "I'd love to help you, Sergeant, but I'm afraid I just don't know any of these people." This dickhead doesn't know who he's dealing with, he thought.

Franceschini shrugged. He lowered himself into a rust-colored chair, the same color as his three-piece corduroy suit that was rumpled from the rain and from pretending to grope with Detective Maloney. "Funny you should be up there with people you don't even know," he said. "Did you miss it there, when you were looking? Look down low, under Colombo. There. That's it, next to your pal Cataldo. Ow, that's an ugly picture, isn't it? Very old. You're much better looking now. It's good you're here. We can get a new one.

"It's lieutenant, by the way. Like I said, I know you can help me. I could probably help you, too."

Sal gave the lieutenant his best Jimmy Cagney routine right out of *Angels with Dirty Faces*. He squared his shoulders and said, "Never. Forgetaboutit. I'll never help you."

Franceschini shrugged again and pushed himself up from the seat. "Maybe you want to think about it for a while," he said.

"I don't need to think about it," Sal said. "Listen, are we about finished here?" he asked. "I'd like to get some sleep."

It was a short ride in a squad car through the rain from the back of Borough Hall to Queens police headquarters for booking. Two policemen took Sal and Ross, handcuffed, in the prisoners' entrance. Sal's clothes were still wet, and as he entered the lockup and heard the metal door clang solidly behind him, he shivered suddenly and uncontrollably.

• • •

I *slept through the night so I didn't hear him come in. When I woke in the morning I lay in my bed under the eaves. The cold rain had left a chill on the house, and I didn't want to get out of bed. Something was missing, some familiar component of the morning, and as I lay there I realized it was the sound of the tractor. Dad was always up early. He was like a kid in the mornings, full of energy, ideas, zinging off the walls. The energy would leave him suddenly. He just used it up. Sometimes he was exhausted and asleep by nine o'clock at night, but in the morning he had to get up and see what was going on. When we moved up to the racetrack, he bought this old blue Ford tractor and by the time the sun was up he was out scraping the dirt stock car track or pulling logs out of the woods, anything he could find to do. He should have been out on the tractor by the time I woke up.*

I went to my bedroom window and looked out. From the second-floor window I could see down across the black asphalt curves and glistening wet spots of the twisting kart track and the buildings, the restaurant and the open pit sheds, that went with it. Dad had gotten into karting just by chance almost ten years ago, when a guy who owed him money paid him with a kart instead. He got hooked. We had gone all over the country kart racing, and then ended up owning the racetrack. The oval dirt track was beyond the grand prix kart course, and then the line of woods that led down to the river where our property ended. The river was called the Neversink. It would be swollen and muddy after the rain, but in another month it would be almost warm enough to swim in. I looked down, to the front of the house where we parked our cars. The Chevette was there, where I had parked it, beside the white Ford pickup. I didn't see Dad's Chevy.

Mom was in the kitchen when I went downstairs. She was stacking up pancakes on a plate beside the stove, and drinking coffee from the mug that said, LORD, GRANT ME PATIENCE, BUT I WANT IT RIGHT NOW. The stack of pancakes was high, which made me know that she was nervous. It was what she did when she was nervous, cook.

Joe came out of the bathroom looking sleepy. "Where's Dad?" I said.

"How should I know?" snapped Joe. He was nervous, too. He wasn't usually that testy, even though he was almost thirteen. The hair on his legs was starting to turn dark and I kept catching him looking in the mirror at his upper lip.

"He stayed in town last night," Mom said, flipping a pancake, "because of the rain."

He hadn't been gone overnight since we had moved from Ozone Park to Port Jervis. I stared at Mom. She was concentrating on the pancakes, and when she brought the platter to the table she didn't look at me or Joe, which made me think that she was lying. She stood against the trestle table in our breakfast nook and looked across it out the window.

"Did he call?" I asked. I hadn't heard the phone ring.

She hesitated. "No. It was last night, at the restaurant," she said, finally. "He said if the rain got worse he and Ross might stay in town."

"I didn't hear him say that. He never stays in town."

"Well, I guess you just weren't listening," she said with an edge of irritation in her voice.

"But did he call?" I asked again.

"It's still too early," she replied, "but if anything was wrong I'm sure we would have heard it by now."

I drove the pickup to school. Mom let me even though I didn't have my license yet, because she wanted to stay home and listen for the telephone. It was six miles from Cuddebackville to the high school and middle school together just outside Port Jervis, and Joe spent the whole six miles chewing on his lip. I parked in the student lot, but before I could open the door he said, "Sal?"

He looked like a little kid sitting there against the door. His books looked almost as big as he was, and his voice sounded high and squeaky. I felt sorry for him, even though I was thinking the same thing he was, that I didn't want to think about.

"Sal," he said, "remember when Dad was, remember two months ago when he was driving us to school, remember, we were . . ." He was talking like he was out of breath.

"Slow down," I said.

He grabbed my sleeve. "No, listen," he said, "he was driving us to school in the pickup and we were talking about him selling drugs. Remember? It was snowing. We said we didn't think it was such a good idea him selling drugs, and he said he didn't . . ." He paused as a kid from the football team walked by, looked like he wanted to stop and then went on, calling, "Better hurry. The bell's gonna ring." Joe continued: "He said he really didn't want to sell them, he knew it was bad and all, he didn't want to do it anymore, but he had no other choice because we were in debt with the racetack and all. Remember that?"

I did remember it. It was snowing and the heater was blasting the frost off the windshield and the wipers were knocking the snow off in big puffs. Dad was driving with one hand on the wheel and the other hammering and sawing in the air, rubbing his face, adjusting the radio and the heater, throwing his nervous energy all over the cab of the pickup. "Yeah, so?" I said.

"So he said, 'There's no way I'll get caught.' Remember?" Joe looked at me. His brown eyes were open wide. He looked a little scared. "Sal, do you think he got caught?" he said.

"No way. He'll be there when we get home this afternoon."

"I hope so," my brother said.

By noon I wasn't thinking much about my classes. After lunch I went to see Coach Joe Viglione. He had given me my chance to start in the third game of the season, against Washingtonville, and after I gained 164 yards and scored a touchdown he told Bill Burr at the Middletown Record *I was "a mature sophomore with pistons for legs." You could stop by his office and just talk. I didn't know what I was going to say: "Coach, I'm worried about my dad." That would be okay. "I think he might have gotten arrested . . ." That would be okay, too, but not the last part, ". . . for selling cocaine." I ended up not saying anything, just sitting there feeling stupid and afraid and Coach, a big bear of a guy, said, "Sal, whatever it is, don't worry about it. It'll pass." Then my sixth period teacher almost gave me a heart attack when she yelled at me for not paying attention. The other kids laughed when she said, "Sal, wake up. What is it, spring fever? You can smell the flowers after school."*

The last bell finally rang. The miles back to Cuddebackville seemed extra long, and the closer we got the more I dreaded reaching home. The pickup bounced as I pulled off the road onto our sloping dirt driveway and around to the front of the house. I looked for Dad's Chevy but it wasn't there. Then Mom came out the door wearing a look and I felt a deep foreboding about what now lay ahead of us.

· · ·

Sal was allowed two phone calls. First he called his mother-in-law in Ozone Park to ask her to call his lawyer to come to his arraignment and get him out on bail. And, oh yes, was she willing to put the house up? Good, because the racetrack was mortgaged to the hilt. Then he called Rose Marie in Port Jervis.

"Oh, thank God," she said when she heard his voice, "I've been so worried."

He got right to it. "Well, I got arrested."

"Was it . . .?"

"Yeah, the drugs. But don't worry," he said. "I get arraigned this afternoon and I'll get out on bail. I've already talked to your mother and she's going to call Capetola about coming down to post bail. It'll be twenty-five, fifty thousand max, no problem. That's all they'll want for six thousand dollars worth of coke."

"You called my mother first?" Phyllis Noto was really Rose

Marie's stepmother, but Rose Marie thought of the little woman with
the elfin face as her mother now after nearly eighteen years of marriage
to her father.

"I had to, to make sure things were arranged."

"I can't believe you would do that."

"Gimme a break, will you?" It was like Rose Marie to get
sidetracked and worry about who he called first when there was only
one real issue. "What we're talkin' about here is getting me out of
jail, not who's the first to know."

"You asked her if she'd put the house up, didn't you?" Rose
Marie asked.

"She offered it. I didn't have to ask her." I just had to hint a
little bit, thought Sal. He hung up the phone feeling good that he
had arranged everything and that he would be home soon.

At nine o'clock that night he entered a second-floor courtroom
in the Queens Courthouse, through a walkway from the Queens House
of Detention where he had been brought earlier by filthy, stinking
bus with the other prisoners who had spent the previous night at
Queens headquarters. He saw Rose Marie at the back of the courtroom
standing with her father. He caught her eye, and she gave him a
nervous smile of encouragement. When his name was called he
stepped forward and stood beside his lawyer, Tony Capetola. The
prosecutor droned on about Sal's bail and he just caught snatches of
it: ". . . criminal sale of a controlled substance in the first degree . . . organized crime connections . . . Colombo family associate, also Gambino . . . a ring supplying bars in Queens . . ."

Blah, blah, blah, Sal thought. Let's get on with it.

"Your Honor, Mr. Polisi has a long record in this jurisdiction."
The prosecutor started reading from Sal's arrest record, charges and
dates that went back to 1965, burglary, assault, gambling, grand
theft auto, bank robbery, on and on. Sal could tell the spectators
behind him were impressed by the way they whispered at each new
charge; he felt like Public Enemy Number One. The back of his neck
prickled and he stood up a little straighter.

"Your Honor, this man is a recidivist felon caught red-handed
with four ounces of cocaine, poison destined for the streets of Queens.

Conviction would carry a penalty of twenty-five to life, and we consider him a threat to run. People request a high bail, Your Honor,
in the amount of one million dollars."

One million? Sal hadn't heard correctly. The impatient look on
his face was supplanted by an expression of disbelief. Rose Marie,
at the back of the courtroom, gripped her father's arm and whispered,
"A million dollars? They can't be serious."

Capetola was protesting: "Your Honor, those were only charges.
There was only one conviction, and Mr. Polisi served his time and
paid his debt. Mr. Polisi has no intention of running."

The judge looked down from her bench and enjoyed the defendant's agitation at the thought of spending another night in jail,
a night, judging from his record, that he richly deserved and more.
She had watched his stocky, powerful body seem to swell at the
recitation of his crimes, most of which he had gotten away with. And
she knew, as the assistant district attorney had pointed out, that
cocaine produced such obscene profits that drug dealers would jump
a fifty-thousand-dollar bail without thinking twice, writing it off as a
cost of doing business. Some guy in California, Falcon or something,
had even jumped a million-dollar bail, but this defendant didn't have
a prayer of raising that. She said, "I think five hundred thousand
dollars will be adequate bail in this case."

Lieutenant Remo Franceschini enjoyed the defendant's agitation, too. From his spot at the back of the courtroom, he could
practically see Sal flinch and his neck flush when he heard the gavel
fall while the words, "Five hundred thousand dollars," were still
ringing in his ears. He watched the bailiff lead Sal toward the door
to the holding room behind the courtroom and thought how persuasive
a little time in jail could be.

Capetola told Rose Marie that night that they'd give the district
attorney a week or two to cool off, then Sal's bail would be reduced
and they could get him home again.

• • •

The following Friday, Joe and I took off from school and rode
with Mom into the city to see Dad.
The parking deck behind the Queens House of Detention was

nasty with grit and broken glass and weeds sprouting up in the cracks in the concrete. The jail itself, across from Borough Hall, was a big white building with a white trailer stuck on its backside like a tumor where the visitors had to enter. Mom had to fill out some papers. Then a big black cop ran us over with a metal detector, like a wand. We went through a door with bars and they stamped our hands with something you could only see under ultraviolet light. We sat in the waiting room for about an hour.

"This sucks," I told Mom.

"Just be patient," she said. "Maybe your father will have some good news about his bail."

Finally we heard our names over a loudspeaker. We went through a door with other waiting families. There was another guard, at a desk, and everybody had to put their hands under a light to show we'd been stamped. On the landing of the stairs up to the visiting room, Mom paused to catch her breath and I noticed how tired she looked.

"You should stop smoking," I said.

"Oh, sure," she said, "now, when I'm calm and relaxed." She looked at me like I'd failed my IQ test.

The room where prisoners met their families was like a big classroom. The white wall tiles were so bright under the fluorescent lights they made my eyes hurt. There were little one-on-one sort of tables around the outside of the room, where just a guy and his wife could talk, and the families had the Formica-covered tables in the middle. A door opened and a whole line of guys came through into the visiting room, looking around and blinking. Sounds of greeting filled the room. I saw my dad. He was wearing a V-necked pullover shirt that showed his gold chain, and blue jeans that Mom had brought him earlier in the week, and loafers, and he looked like he was getting ready to go out to a ball game or something.

My mom stood up and waved. "Sal. Over here, Sal." He came walking over to us, jaunty but cool, smiling like he was really glad to see us.

We all stood up to hug him. Now that we saw him, it was like he was with us again and we could sit there and talk for a while and then we would all leave together, go get a pizza or something and head home. "Boy, is it good to see you guys," he said. "I gotta tell you, I really miss you."

"When are you getting out?" Joe asked.

"Soon, son," he said. "What's going on up at the racetrack? You racing this weekend?"

I had pretty much outgrown karting after driving in the Grand Nationals for six years, but Joe had followed right along and now he was into it. He had finished third at last year's Grand Nationals, which was as good as I had ever done, and we all thought he could win this year. He was a more aggressive driver than I was. He was excited about the season's first big race, at Avon up near Rochester. So he was almost ready to let Dad change the subject, but not quite.

Joe said, "I'm going to Avon. Ross said he'd drive me if you weren't out." Ross had never been in trouble before he was arrested with my dad the previous Thursday night. He had gotten out on bail and was headed for probation. Joe pressed the subject. "Are you gonna be out?"

"That's great you're going to Avon, son. That's a big race. You listen to Ross. He's a good wrench. He'll be a good big brother, too, for the racing." Without pausing he turned to Mom, who was sitting next to him at the table, and said, "Listen, did those guys get up there to paint the lines on the parking lot? And the lines and numbers at the staging area down by the pits? You know where I'm talking about? Did you order enough stuff for the restaurant? You need more hamburgers than hot dogs. I don't know, those people eat a lot of hamburgers. And Coke. They don't like Pepsi, they like Coke. Oops, I guess I can't say that." He laughed, as if he had made a joke. Mom looked troubled. "What about you, son?" He turned toward me. "Have you started working out yet? You know you can't be lazy. You've got to start getting ready for next fall."

We talked a lot, the four of us sitting at the table in that blinding bright room. We talked about everything except the one thing we all really wanted to talk about, which was the question Joe had asked at the beginning. When was he getting out and coming home?

A woman guard stepped into the room and called, "Five minutes."

My mom said, "Sal?"

"I don't know," he said. He pulled his hand down across his face. "The bail's still high. The DA won't go along with a reduction. He told Capetola he still thinks it should be a million. He thinks I'm Public Enemy Number One or something. They've got me tied in with the Colombos, Gambinos, I don't know who all. We're asking for a hearing, but it looks like I might be here two or three more weeks."

When the guard yelled, "One minute," we started our good-byes. He got to me and said, "Take good care of your mother, son." We all hugged him. Then he went with the other prisoners through the door. It still felt like we were just leaving by different exits, and we would meet outside and go home.

At first, when Mom told us he had been arrested, I didn't think about my dad. I thought about what would happen when the kids at school found out. It took the Tri-State Gazette *almost a month to get hold of the story. The* Gazette *quoted the* New York Post, *which said Dad was a member of the Gambino crime family. It said Ross was "reputed to be his bodyguard," like he was the boss of bosses or something. The news got around, and the last few weeks of school were pretty rough. I was humiliated. Not humiliated, but embarrassed, embarrassed to face up to it.*

Some little things happened. Mom was out in the yard planting flowers one day when some rednecks in a Volkswagen bus drove by the house and yelled, "Go home, you buncha drug dealers." She stood up and threw a dirt clod at them.

But nobody ever really said anything to me. I'd hear people talking as I went by at school, or just looking at me, and I knew they were talking about me. But nobody actually said anything to me, to my face, I guess because I was supposed to be a big deal, one of the in-crowd guys, so to speak, a football player and all that. Or maybe they were afraid. They read "Gambino crime family" and were scared shitless. And I just acted like it was no big thing, tried to blow it off.

Friends appeared from strange places. Joe's seventh-grade earth science teacher from the year before told him he was sorry about what happened to our dad, and said he wasn't going to judge him by that. He told Joe it was tough but hang in there.

And Joe knew a kid, he was a stoner, you know, would smoke pot, and it was the kind of deal where Joe would see him and say, "Oh, hi, how you doin'?" and the other kid would say, "Okay, great, how you doin'?" and they would both walk away from each other and say, "What an asshole." Anyway, this kid had a father who got arrested for something. He was being chased for something and he jumped in the river, the Delaware River, and tried to swim from New York to Pennsylvania, but he got caught. This was like two or three weeks before our dad got arrested, and this kid, this stoner, took Joe aside and said, "Look, I know what you're going through. I know your dad's in more trouble than my dad. I know you're closer to your dad than I am to mine. But I know what you're going through and it's not easy. You just kind of lose your dad for a while."

Joe said it made him feel good that this kid opened up to him like that, gave him some understanding.

It was the kid's last concept that we had trouble with. Losing our dad, even for a while, was hard. Ten years ago, when he was in prison, we were both just little kids. Now he was more real to us, more present in our lives, and it made us miss him more. After that first visit we kept hoping he would get out right away, and half expecting to find him there each morning when we went down to breakfast or in the afternoon when we came home from school. Like when you have something you really wish against all hope you're going to get for Christmas, you've dropped a lot of hints and it's really important to you, maybe even when the time comes you don't see it but you tell yourself it's been hidden for a big surprise, and then when all your presents are open and it's still not there, you're disappointed. You're disappointed because you hoped too much.

We hoped less when we got word that Dad's bail was raised to $750,000, but that didn't make his absence any better. I began wondering how we would survive without him.

In the meantime, like Joe's science teacher said, all we could do was hang in there.

T W O

Sal awoke to the sound of cellophane rustling in the wastebasket beside his bed, where he had tossed the wrappings from his bedtime Fig Newtons the night before. He waited to hear familiar sounds: birds, idly barking dogs, the cock that crowed each morning a distance from the racetrack. He heard instead men snoring, the creaking of iron cots and snuffle of bedclothes against a background echo of metal and tile. And the brittle rustling in the wastebasket. What the fuck was that? He raised up on one elbow and peeked over the edge. The cellophane was moving. He put his feet on the hard floor, snatched the basket and looked inside. A small gray mouse, making an irritated squeak, nearly leaped into his face. He dropped the basket and the mouse ran across the floor and disappeared.

When his heartbeat had returned to normal, Sal looked at his watch and saw it was five-thirty in the morning.

The mouse came often in the days that followed to rummage for crumbs among the cellophane. Sal called it Peppy, and when the rustling woke him, Sal sat up in bed and wrote his letters home.

At first he was plaintive, but optimistic. The Sunday after his arrest he wrote, in black ballpoint on a yellow legal pad, "Well, I must say life changes awfully quick. Two days ago (Fri.) I was pretty down—but now I feel somehow things will work out." He was counting on his bail eventually being reduced to a hundred thousand dollars. "Anything more—that's just crazy," he wrote. He asked his family to write, and send envelopes, stamps and paper. He told them he loved and missed them and gave some fatherly instructions:

"Joseph—don't forget the towels in your room.

"Sal—try to read a little more and listen to the stereo a little less."

As the days passed he was comfortable enough. His single cell, a perquisite of his high bail and organized crime connections, was much better than the six-man cage he would otherwise have occupied. Rose Marie and her stepmother brought him clothing and basic toiletries, the few that were permitted. But he was not comfortable enough to make the days go by thoughtlessly, without reflection. He was preoccupied with thinking what would happen to his sons.

The first time he had been behind bars, ten years ago, they were too young to worry about. They were unformed then, just kids, with time to develop; now time was short and every moment counted. He didn't feel the void then he felt now, which was on one hand the lack of freedom and the absence of his family, and also the impossibility of being a father from a jail cell. How feeble it felt when he told Joe in a letter to enjoy his youth: "You are only a young kid—and only once are you 12—almost 13."

Sal junior was no longer a young kid, and with him Sal felt even more strongly the need to give advice.

"Hi, son—I hope everything is OK. I'm feeling better all the time," he wrote on Saturday, May 19, at six A.M. "It was strange to be locked up—after 10 yr. of not being behind bars—it really was odd.

"The longer I am here the more time I have (in my head) to sort all types of ideas out. The first I think you should start to consider (and it's your life, you must think about it), what will you be doing 1 yr from now? Well, you will be just about to start your last year in high school. Then, OK—you have options—Go on to college or get a job—for the *rest* of your life—it's a long time. I must keep saying you must *decide!* And I am not saying now but start thinking about it. And the reason I am thinking about this now is—I would never want you to make any mistakes that I have—(and oh boy did I make a *few*)."

As he wrote Sal felt a need to tell his son more still. Football had been his choice for Sal junior. He had coached the boy from the time he was eight years old, and he had seen him emerge in the past year as a runner with college potential. What would happen to that potential in his absence was what absorbed his thoughts, for Sal knew that getting his bail reduced was only the first of his problems. He wrote urgently without stopping until he had filled five pages of lined white paper.

"Well what I am getting to is you have something special going for you. I never told you—But I think if you wanted to you could go right to the top in college football—But you have to want to—not for anybody else just *you*.

"Think *hard*—Work *hard* on your talent. You have it. Admit it to yourself. The real difference between the great football players of college—is the guys who have it—work, work, work—and the guys who *HAD* it didn't—work, work, work.

"I mean start to give yourself a program—little by little each day—starting soon—I am sure you want it—but you have to want it bad.

"I don't want to preach but—if I could only help you to get that college education I feel I did my job as a good parent—even if I failed a few courses along the way. I know you and Joe still love me—but I feel like I let you down a little. Anyway I am paying the price—just being away from you guys and not being able to talk to you hurts. Do you remember the very first time you raced in Jacksonville, Fla.? You were the youngest kid in the field, and each day that got closer to the race you got faster & faster. Well think about that. We worked and worked—and by race day you went out there and *WON*. Well it all adds up. You have something special. Don't let it go—develop it. I am telling you to. I am hoping for you. Remember all you needed before that Washingtonville game was a chance. You've got it. Take it.

"So what I am saying is do it for you and you'll make me proud to be your father. I would be proud of you even if you never did go to college. But I *know* you got what it takes. So do it.

"Work hard—it will pay. Short cuts only cause trouble like I have. I love you and I know you'll be OK no matter what!!

"Enjoy your self now son. Hug Mom for me. Tell her I said I'll be there soon to create *STATIC*.

"See you soon,

"Dad."

Sal read over the letter and realized the last part was the only thing he wasn't sure about.

. . .

I read that letter and I didn't know what he expected me to do. I thought I might have to quit school and support my mom if he didn't get out soon. It looked like my football career was all but over.

We opened the track for the season at the end of May with Ross, his brother Bruce and another guy who helped, Victor. Victor had been in prison, and my dad kept saying in his letters, "Ask Vic. He knows how it feels." I didn't particularly want to sit down with Victor and talk about being in prison. I was trying to forget about Dad being there. In Port Jervis, we had gotten used to the idea that our lives were different now, that things had changed and jail wasn't in the picture anymore.

Opening the track without Dad there was just another way of finding out how much we all missed him. The karters loved his loud voice and crazy energy, and he had a big name in karting from all the nationals we had raced in and this award he made up, for the best family effort in national competition. It wasn't his name, but it was a big one.

By that I mean he used an alias. One of the few things I knew then about my father's past was that for some reason the first time he had gone karting he registered as Sal Noto, Noto being my mother's maiden name. Maybe it was because he was under indictment for bank robbery at the time. Anyway, he always used Noto in karting and in his other automotive ventures, like his chop shop, Noto Classic Cars. When I raced I was Little Sal Noto, and Joe raced as Joe Noto and the racetrack was called the Noto Raceway.

The Noto Raceway wasn't the same without my father, any more than the Polisi family was. Anger and resentment hung over us in his absence. It had no place to go, and so we struck out at each other.

The racers and spectators, what few there had been, had all left one Sunday afternoon and we had the track to ourselves when Bruce called me and Joe over. "Hey, get your suit back on, Joe. Sal, you suit up, too," he said. "Let's play with the Corsairs; see what we can get out of them if we change a few things around." Bruce was about my dad's age and height, but a little thinner, and the baseball cap he always wore hid the fact that he was getting bald. He had a business of his own, but since Dad had been in jail he'd been giving Sundays not only to helping with the track but to helping Joe prepare for competition.

Joe had raced that day but he was eager. "All right," he said, and trotted off for our equipment. He never had enough of driving the karts. He sensed that this year at last he was going to have an opportunity to surpass my performances. Our house above the race-track was like a trophy case for karting trophies, and most of them were mine, but the more recent ones were his. He saw the chance to finally get out from under my shadow if he could win his class at the Grand Nationals, which was what testing the karts was all about. At the same time he was worried that because Dad was in jail he wouldn't get to go this year and have a chance to prove himself.

The DAP Corsair engine was a one-cylinder, two-stroke little screamer. You could get about twenty-five horsepower out of one, and it would push a kart and driver, combined weight two eighty, close to seventy miles an hour. Which is fast when you're about two inches off the ground. There were little things you could do to make them faster on a particular track on a given day. If you had a course with a lot of turns, for example, you might want better low end acceleration, but if you had straightaways where you could really burn it, you might want top end. Why get technical about it? It was just a bunch of little things, and you were always changing this or changing that to get that extra fraction of a second.

"Sal, you lead; Joe, you follow," Bruce said when we had our flame suits on and Joe had retrieved our crash helmets from the parts trailer. "I'll time you with the radar gun."

We lodged ourselves into identical Emmick karts with the Corsair engines. It was like sitting in a washtub on the ground, with your feet over the edge straddling a broomstick that was the steering column and the engine just outside the seat by your right hip. Joe's kart had a sixty-nine-tooth sprocket on the axle, better for top end; my kart with a seventy-tooth sprocket would get me out of the corners without bogging.

Bruce placed the socket of the battery-powered starter motor over my engine shaft nut and spun it. The engine exploded in an angry buzz. When Joe's started they sounded like a swarm of pissed-off bees.

I hadn't driven earlier. I felt my way along, following the course counterclockwise, easing into the rhythm of the track. From the pits, the course passed below the restaurant and swept up and back into a dogleg that turned left into a long downhill straightaway that ended in a left-hand hairpin turn. From there the course doubled back on itself until it turned right at a ninety-degree angle toward the pits, then left again to pass below the restaurant. Joe stayed on my tail.

When I opened it up, Joe stayed right there.

I was beginning to enjoy the feel of speed again. The air tumbled past, buffeting the folds of my flame suit and pushing my head back. The Bell Star helmet narrowed my vision to essentials. I was aware of the onrushing asphalt of the track, the hay bales covered in black-and-white plastic in a checkered-flag effect, the roller-coaster humps in the midsection of the track, the soft rubber of the tires gripping as I threw the kart into the dogleg and the vista of the long straightaway below me. I jammed the accelerator down and took it up to fourteen thousand RPMs, watching the woods rush toward me from the bottom of the track, then backed off at the last minute for the hairpin, where Ross was standing with the radar gun. There was a rock wall down there just inside the line of trees. Coming out of the hairpin, I watched the steering-wheel-mounted tach until I felt the clutch hook at eighty-nine hundred revs and push me like a kick in the pants up the track toward the right turn and the pits. All the way around the track, which was a little less than half a mile, I kept seeing the front wheel of Joe's kart out of the corner of my eye. Dogging me, the little weasel.

On the next lap, Bruce waved the radar gun to indicate he would time my top speed at the bottom of the chute, then Joe's. I ran through the curves to the pits and started building my speed coming out past the restaurant. Mom had been inside cleaning up, but now she was sitting on the hay bales, watching. I hugged the inside of the dogleg entering the chute and then flared out wide and aimed for the inside of the hairpin at the bottom of the hill and held the pedal down until the wall of woods was almost in my face. Then I backed off and took it around. I glimpsed Joe starting his descent. I slowed and watched him through the hairpin, then let him catch up and we drove around the track and down the straight together.

We stopped, idling, in the middle of the track and removed our helmets. Bruce showed us the results he'd written down, a 67 under Joe's name and a 64 under mine, with a notation about the different gear sprockets on the axles. He said, "Okay, let's go for lap speed now. Sal's quicker off the corners, Joe, so he'll probably be faster around. Stay close to each other, but don't get tangled up."

Joe said, "I don't think so."

"Don't think what?" Bruce was scribbling in his notebook.

"I don't think Sal's faster." I caught him stealing a glance at me.

"Well, it doesn't matter," Bruce said. "We're not racing, just trying to figure the best setup." He wasn't really paying attention, but I heard the defiance in my brother's voice. He wanted to prove that he could beat me. I suddenly realized that it was the first time we had been on the track together, one on one. If he could beat me, he was going to have to prove it.

"Think you're faster now, is that it?" I said to him. "Why don't we check it out?"

He didn't need time to think about it. We pulled our helmets on and started around the track to the start-finish line in front of the restaurant. Then we kicked it in.

The first time down the chute I beat him to the hairpin, took the inside and had twenty feet on him going into the right turn toward the pits. I gained a little in each turn, but I gave him thirty pounds and with his top end he got it back on the straight stretches.

At the bottom of the chute again, Bruce was motioning with his hands, palms down, telling us to stop. But Joe entered the hairpin right behind me, trying to push me to the outside, and we came out of it together racing wheel to wheel. I gained a length on him and cut to the inside of the next turn and he stayed the one length back through the pit row curve.

When we passed the restaurant, Mom was standing up making the same motions as Bruce. For some reason I noticed her hair was tied in a bandanna. When I skidded out of the dogleg, I saw Joe skidding out along the same trajectory, just inside me. I jammed my right foot down hard and felt the howl and vibration of the engine on my hip as the tach climbed toward fourteen thousand. I blasted down the chute on a long diagonal, aimed at the inside of the hairpin. Two-thirds of the way down I saw Joe's front wheels, inching up beside me.

You're supposed to give in the corners if an inside driver has an overlap of half a kart length. He didn't have it. I know he didn't have it and I kept for the inside of the curve. His front wheels were at my hip when I cut the track off and his tire caught on one of mine and flipped his kart end over end.

I skidded to a halt. Joe's kart was lying upside down in the grass on the outside edge of the track and Bruce was fumbling to try and cut the screaming engine off. Joe lay beyond it in the grass. My mother was running down from the restaurant and I knew she was screaming even though I still had my helmet on and couldn't hear her. I tore the helmet off and ran to Joe.

Mom arrived at the same time. She was sobbing for breath and screaming, "Oh, my God. Oh, my God. Jesus Christ, Sal, what have you done to your brother?"

I knelt down beside Joe, lifted his head and tried gently to remove his helmet. He was sprawled out, but nothing looked broken. "Joe. Joe, are you hurt?" I asked. He groaned and fumbled with the helmet and when it was off he opened one eye and said, "I had you." Then he closed his eye again and lay like he was dead.

Mom had pulled the bandanna off her head and was flaying me with it, whipping me around the head with her red bandanna. I was so relieved that Joe wasn't hurt that I just stayed there, kneeling on the ground, and let her hit me. "Jesus Christ, Sal, damn you anyway," she yelled. "Don't we have enough trouble? Your father in jail, and you try to kill your brother. Oh, God, what next? Joseph, talk to me."

He jumped up then and cried, "I had him. I had him and he wouldn't give me room."

"That's bullshit," I said, getting to my feet. "You didn't have nothing." He was almost dancing, like some kind of Indian war dance, and pointing at me triumphantly. It really pissed me off. I threw my helmet at him and he dodged and laughed wildly. His dog Buster leaped and barked and capered, thinking it was all a game.

It was too much for Mom. She gaped at us, speechless, looking first at Joe and then at me. The look in her green eyes was just short of desperation. She pressed the knuckles of one hand against her mouth and turned away from us abruptly. She started walking slowly up the hill back toward the restaurant, leaving us standing there with Bruce, who had shut Joe's kart off and turned it upright and had stayed beside it pretending to fiddle with the engine so as not to notice our discussion. Mom walked in a straight line to the house, and disappeared inside.

"I hate this place," Joe said. "I hate it. Way up here. All by ourselves. Dad's never getting out of jail. I bet he'll be in jail forever."

"He'll get out, Joe," I said. He looked at me and understood that I didn't know that any more than he did, but that our wanting to believe it would have to do until something better came along.

"Maybe you did have me after all," I added.

Dad's letter arrived a few days later, around the beginning of the second week of June. It was dated June 7, a Thursday.

"If that bail isn't down by the time you read this, it might be a few weeks before I get a chance to have it reduced again!!" he wrote. His exclamation points were not encouraging. But then he added, "Well, you keep your head up. Everything will be O.K. You know, I will always find a way."

He would, I knew it. He was figuring out some way to fix the case so he could get out and come home.

Then he returned to the subject of his last, long letter, and this time there was more urgency attached to what he wrote. He was really anxious for me to tell him something, as if what I told him would make things easier for him.

"I am sure that you know what you want in your life. Please try to lay out your plan for the next two years. It's very important for you, and it will help me make an important decision in this

case. It's time for you to know what you want in high school for the
next two years. And if you really want to play ball in college—you
must start to make plans now!! Please answer this letter on this
subject."

He wrote some more, and closed, "STUDY FOR TESTS. I love
you, Dad."

I took the letter into Joe's room that night and showed it to him.
He put his copy of Karter magazine aside and pulled up his knees
to read it in the pool of light from his bedside lamp. "What do you
think it means?" he said.

"He thinks he knows some way to get out." I sat down at Joe's
desk next to the window.

"But what?" he said.

"I bet he's got a way to get the case fixed. Remember the car
case?" A few years ago, before we moved from Ozone Park and my
dad still had the chop shop, Mom and Uncle Lenny had gotten
arrested driving stolen cars that Dad had changed the Vehicle Identification Numbers on. They didn't even know it. He got them off
somehow, and then later was allowed to withdraw his own guilty plea.
He always bragged he fixed the case. He said it cost like fifty thousand
dollars. "He must have figured how he can fix this one," I told Joe.

"Why does he want you to tell him what your plans are?" Joe
asked.

"I don't know," I said.

"What are your plans, Sal?" he asked me then, turning to look
at me. The lamp threw his shadow back against the wall. "What are
you going to tell him?"

There was paper on his desk, and I doodled for a minute while
I thought. "I don't know that either," I said finally. "We don't have
any money. If he doesn't get out of jail I might have to go to work."

"And not play football?"

"How can I play football if I have to work because we don't
have any money? I might not even be in school."

"But he said he figured something out."

"He didn't say that. He said he'd find a way, and then he wanted
me to tell him what I want to do because it would help him figure

something out," I said. "But what if it doesn't work and he can't fix it? How am I supposed to know what to tell him?"

Joe said, "I think he wants you to tell him you're gonna go to college. That's what he wants you to say."

Mom got us another day off from school and we visited him again on the Friday before Father's Day. It took that occasion to get Joe to go down to the city and the Queens House. Joe hated the thought of Dad being in there. He resented having turned thirteen at the end of May without Dad seeing him become a teenager. But even more than his absence, Joe hated seeing him in there and what you had to go through to see him. Like being with your dad was such a natural thing, and it had been for us in the two years we'd been in Port Jervis, and then all of a sudden you had to go through this procedure, being frisked by this electric wand, having your hand stamped, having to stop talking when your hour was up and worst of all, having to go away and leave him there. After the first visit we had gone to Grandma Noto's house and Joe had gone straight to the bathroom and scrubbed the back of his hand for about ten minutes, even though you couldn't see anything there unless you held it under the light. He wanted to get the feel of it off him. That visit had really upset him and he hadn't been back since. He complained in the car most of the way down.

Finally I said, "Why don't you just shut up, Joe."

"Don't start," Mom said immediately.

Joe lapsed into a sullen funk that lasted across the Tappan Zee Bridge, through the Bronx and across the Whitestone into Queens. We parked in the same gritty parking deck. The only good thing you could say about it was the food stand at the entrance. It had great chili dogs.

The heat inside the visitors' trailer entrance was oppressive. "Look at this, a page full of names already," Mom said as she added our names to the sign-in book. "How long will it be before we get in?" she asked the female guard with hollow cheeks and curlicues of hair pasted to her temples.

The woman shifted reluctantly to look at the wall clock behind

her. "If you make it in the next group, half an hour. If not, an hour
and a half," she said.

Joe gave a big sigh to show he was unhappy. When the guard
with the wand ran it over him, Joe stood rigid as a rail and drew
back every time it touched him, like the guy was trying to cop a feel
or something. He submitted his hand to be stamped, and snatched
it back. In the waiting room, we slipped a Father's Day card into
the newspapers we had brought. They had told us we couldn't take
presents in or anything, and we were supposed to mail cards, because
if you took them in that was another route for smuggling, but some
other people had told Mom if you didn't seal the envelope, the guards
wouldn't make much of it even if they caught you. Polisi was the
last name called among the next group of visitors and after just twenty
minutes we were heading upstairs to the blinding bright visiting room.

Even Joe forgot about being unhappy after he saw Dad. He came
out with the other prisoners and we saw each other right away and
he threaded his way among the tables with his big, wide, almost
goofy grin. "How about this?" he said when we sat down around a
table. "The whole family all together." Mom leaned over and put her
head on his shoulder and he reached around and hugged her and
winked across the table at me and Joe.

We talked about racing and football and the job Mom had at
this little gift shop in Port Jervis. It sounded like he was going to be
a part of it all again soon, and I nudged Joe to remind him of Dad's
letter in which he'd said he would always find a way. Then he said
he hadn't. It was some kind of shock.

"Will you be home by the Fourth of July, Dad?" Joe had asked.
"You're gonna be out soon, right? Sal showed me the letter you wrote
him."

Dad frowned, and looked at Mom. She had an expression like
this was something she hadn't heard before. He tried to put some
encouragement into his voice.

"Well, my bail went down," he said. "It's not seven hundred
and fifty thousand anymore."

Mom said, "Oh, Sal, you didn't tell me." She sounded excited.

"It's five hundred thousand again," he said. He took a breath
and looked across the table, first at Joe and then at me. "It's gonna

be awhile. It's not gonna be the Fourth of July, I can tell you that."

Joe stiffened in his chair. His disappointment was immediate. I could see my disappointment on the horizon, dropping out of school to help support my mom and give Joe a chance at finishing high school. Joe stood up abruptly. His chair made an ugly scraping sound that made people at other tables wince and look up for a second. "I want to leave," he said.

Dad nodded. "Go with your brother, Sal," he said to me. "Try and help him."

Joe was already out the door, going down the stairs. I turned back before I went after him. Dad was slumped low in his chair. He looked tired. Mom waved a hand at me: go after him. I followed the squeak of Joe's sneakers down the stairwell. Joe burst into the waiting room, which was full of people who looked up hopeful that the hour was over and it was their time to go upstairs. I came in the door behind him and he turned around. His eyes were full of tears.

"He's gonna be in jail for fifteen years," he said. "We're gonna be old before he's out. It's not fair." He said it louder and his voice broke. "It's not fair."

He started sobbing and I stepped close to him. I said, "Cut it out, Joe."

"I don't care," he said. People in the room were trying not to look at us. I took him by the shoulders to try and calm him down. They were still the narrow shoulders of a little boy and they were shaking as he cried and all I could do was hold him. He cried beyond comfort. His desolation overwhelmed me and I finally stopped resisting crying, too. Both our faces were wet with tears as we pushed blindly out of the waiting room and past the bars and guards to the outside. We stood in the parking lot alone. Cars came and went and no one paid attention to us.

· · ·

The guy named Sonny came to Sal's cell that night and leaned against the door. He was a Puerto Rican Sal had met playing cards in the dayroom. Sal noticed him there and after a minute, when he hadn't said anything, said, "How you doin'?"

"All right. Say, man, I heard you had some visitors today."

"Yeah, my wife and kids came down. What about it?"

Sonny took a little shuffle step and shifted to the other side of the cell door. He was dark, with wavy black hair in contrast to Sal's curls. He looked as if he had something on his mind, but was reluctant to say it for not knowing how Sal would take it.

"Yeah, well, see, my wife came to see me today, too." He paused.

"Oh, yeah?" said Sal. "And your kids. What about your kids? You got kids?" Sal couldn't remember. The guy was in for forgery.

"No kids, man, just the wife."

"Well, that's great, she came to see you," Sal said. "It means a lot, don't it? And it's special when the kids come. I got two great kids, sons. The oldest one's a football player. He's gonna play in college."

In his last letter home he had asked Sal junior to send copies of the stories of his games, which he had bragged about throughout the cell block. "The guys know all about you and your football team," he wrote. "Someday you'll know how it feels to be a father."

"Yeah, well, what it is . . ." Sonny reached up and rubbed his earlobe between his thumb and the outside of his index finger. "My wife was in the waiting room when they came down from seeing you."

"Yeah, they left kind of quick." Sal remembered Joe's angry, disappointed face, and Sal junior's confusion. "It's hard on them."

"So my wife was in the waiting room when they came down, and she said the two of them, you know, well, they were crying, man, and holding onto each other. My wife, she told me she tried not to stare at them. She said everybody was trying not to stare at them, but it liked to make her start crying, too, she said, just to see them standing there, crying and like, like hugging, you know, all broken up. It was sad, man. My wife said, 'Sonny, those people got a real caring family. It's too bad, ain't it?' And I said, 'Yeah, it's too bad.' "

Sonny pushed off the door. He seemed relieved. He said, "Hey, man, you wanna play some cards?"

Sal said, "Tomorrow, maybe. Not right now."

He tried to imagine his two sons crying together in the waiting room. He tried to imagine what his family would do if he was sent to prison for many years. He saw Sal junior and Joseph and their mother back in Ozone Park when he did that. He did not see Sal junior in a football uniform. He did not see either of his sons in college. He saw them leading lives much like his.

Sal thought all weekend about his next letter to Sal junior. Finally, along with his usual urgings that the boy recognize his talent and pursue it, he wrote, "Whatever you do in life—as long as it's legal—I will respect and love you."

He pleaded with Sal junior to shed no more tears on visits. "It makes it too hard on all of us," he wrote.

Finally, the question that was coming to possess him. The boy was all but grown and yet he didn't know him or what he thought. He wrote, "I would enjoy reading some of your own beliefs and ideas. I know I was a stubborn father, but I always wanted you to get a better start in life than me. I think you've got it. But please share it with me—let me know what your plans are."

He asked hoping to break his dire vision. He kept seeing Sal junior back in Ozone Park, repeating history.

Sal kept asking for new bail hearings, and getting one about every two weeks, but there was no reduction. Neither had the case been set for trial. An SOS to his old cohorts had been rejected; John Gotti and John Carneglia sent word there was no way, that everybody was too hot and too jammed up and he'd just have to sit it out. His options were down to roughly zero. There seemed no end to the time that he would spend in jail.

In the last week of June, Sal junior came alone to see him. It was one of his first trips with his new driver's license. They sat at one of the one-on-one tables against the wall of the visiting room. Sal asked the same nagging questions: "What are your plans? Have you started working out for the fall?" He looked fondly on his son's well-proportioned, ruddy face, the darkening down across his upper lip and the fading adolescent blemishes, the stout neck that sloped into broad shoulders, and failed to notice that Sal junior was distracted.

At last the boy broke into his questions. "Can't you fix the case, Dad? This one more time? Can't you get it taken care of and get out of here?"

Sal gazed, astonished, at the boy who sounded so much like himself. He had believed since he was nineteen, just out of the Marines, that only suckers went to jail, that there was always a way out. That's what his uncle Tony said. Then he went in the joint. But it had always worked for Sal except for the fifteen months he'd done at Lewisburg in Pennsylvania. He was Sally Upazz', Crazy Sally, master of manipulation. Crazy Sally, who'd check into a psycho ward before he'd go to jail. He had used inventiveness and his prodigious energy to hustle, con and bribe, and he had always been proud of himself. Yet coming from the mouth of his sixteen-year-old son, the idea of fixing his case sounded obscene. He saw that Sal junior had not understood his urgent letters, had missed everything he had written about having to work, about having to struggle toward a football scholarship. He saw that he had taught Sal junior to rely on shortcuts, as he had. He saw history repeating itself despite everything he'd hoped for, and that there was nothing he could do. He was jammed up, with only one way out.

THREE

John Limbach fingered the message slip thoughtfully. Sal Polisi. Wants you to return his call at the Queens House of Detention. Interesting.

Limbach was thirty-six, slender, with brown curly hair. He had entered law enforcement in 1976 as a probation officer assigned to cases in Ozone Park and Howard Beach, in Queens, before becoming an agent with the Bureau of Alcohol, Tobacco and Firearms. And now one of his probationers, who was in jail, was getting back in touch. Interesting.

Polisi had been a challenging case for Limbach. Sal had come out of the federal penitentiary at Lewisburg, Pennsylvania, in 1976 after serving just fifteen months of an eight-year term for bank robbery. His sentence had been overturned by the Second U.S. Circuit Court of Appeals because the sentencing judge hadn't allowed a competency hearing despite Polisi's history of mental instability. On paper, Polisi looked crazy as a loon, an undifferentiated schizophrenic with sociopathic tendencies. In reality, Limbach concluded, he was crazy like a fox, using his history to frustrate the courts and avoid prison time. He was proud of his nickname, Sally Upazz', or Crazy Sally. When the case was returned to Judge Edward R. Neaher, U.S. v. Polisi had become a minor landmark and the gray-haired, austere judge, who had seen the case bounce in and out of his courtroom for four years, threw up his hands and sentenced Polisi to probation. That's when Polisi had fallen into Limbach's lap. As a probationer Polisi had been hard to manage because he had a one hundred percent veterans' disability pension that meant he didn't have to hold a steady job. Most of his livelihood came from a suspicious auto operation called Noto Classic Cars. Limbach had tried to keep up with Polisi's movements, and wondered all along how Polisi could afford the costs of restoring the vintage Corvettes Limbach had coveted in Polisi's auto shop. Limbach had an old Corvette himself, and he couldn't afford things like the fuel injection system he had seen lying on the shop floor. Then, when Polisi and his wife and brother-in-law inexplicably beat charges lodged by the auto squad in Queens, Limbach had had more suspicions he had never been able to confirm.

So he went to see Polisi the next day.

Entering the room at Queens House where attorneys interviewed their clients, Limbach made sure his handwriting sample book was conspicuous. His cherubic face was well known in organized crime circles; his probation caseload had been full of men involved with the organized crime families of New York, and if he saw one of them or their attorneys, he wanted to have a good excuse for talking to Polisi. The sample booklet would be good enough. Something about forgery in a gun case, he could say. He suspected that what Polisi had in mind could get Sal killed.

He was relieved to see the room was empty. He took a table at the end of the row of cubicles, as far away from the doors as possible, and waited.

Limbach heard a rattle of keys and a door opened. He looked up and saw Polisi entering the room. Sal had the same round face and curly black hair that he remembered, the same brawler's body with thick arms, even the same crooked smile. His greeting was the same, "Yo, John, how you doin'?" But something about him was subdued. He seemed to have trouble looking Limbach in the eye.

They sat facing each other across the metal table, its surface scarred with names scratched in the gray enamel. Limbach realized with a start that he was nervous, and took a deep breath to calm himself. He opened the handwriting sample book and placed it on the tabletop between them, turned so that Sal could make an entry. He handed him a pen. He said, "Sal. I was a little surprised to hear from you again. It's been what, three years? Four? How're the wife and kids?"

Limbach remembered Rose Marie Polisi as a genuinely friendly woman who provided stability and comfort to the family. He had thought at the time that if she hadn't been Italian she would have been the perfect earth mother. An earth mother with a Noo Yawk

accent, he had joked to his wife. Can you imagine it? Limbach hadn't
known the Polisi children well, they had been too young; but it was
they Sal talked about.

"They're doin' great. Joseph, he was just a little guy, remember?
Now he's this tall and driving the karts, could win the Grand Nationals
this year. And Sal junior, remember, I was coaching him at midget
football? Down there in Ozone Park?"

"Yeah, sure." What Limbach remembered most vividly was that
Sal had been the first person he knew with a video camera. He had
the bulky outfit rigged up in a van and was out at the field every
Saturday morning taping the boy's games. He was stealing electricity,
too, from a plug he'd gotten somebody to rig up on a light pole at
the edge of the field.

"He was a quarterback then," Sal continued, "but we moved
upstate and a guy switched him to running back. Man, he gained
nine hundred yards last year and only played in seven games. I think
he can play college ball."

I can keep bullshitting or I can do it, Sal thought.

"Yeah," he said, "they're doin' great." He had been leaning
with his forearms on the table, playing with the pen Limbach had
handed him. Now he raised his hands and let them fall, in a gesture
of helplessness. "Look, it's time for me to make a change," he said.

Sal plunged ahead before he lost his nerve. He had never before
spoken to anyone in law enforcement, not like this. It went against
a lifetime of teaching. "Before I got in here on this drug charge, I
took my family out of Ozone Park because I wanted them to get away
from all that there. This wasn't supposed to happen. And I don't care
about the time, you understand? I can do the time, no sweat. But if
I do, my wife and kids will be right back where they started.

"What I want is to get my family out of here and change everything. Everything. I'm tired, man. I never wanted to be a criminal
all my life. I want to get my kids away from the criminal atmosphere
and give them a chance at something different, where they can be
somebody. I want to get into witness protection and I'm ready to do
what I have to do to do it. I want to meet this guy McDonald."

There. Sal heard his words echo as if somebody else were saying
them, and the person talking was a rat.

Limbach heard the name McDonald and was intrigued. Edward
A. McDonald was head of the Justice Department's Organized Crime
Strike Force for the Eastern District of New York, which included
Queens, Brooklyn and Long Island. He'd be interested in what Sal
could tell him. Whether it would be valuable was another question.

"Why McDonald?" Limbach said. "You know him or something?"

"Nah, I don't know him. I read about him in the papers. He's
a fed, he's into organized crime cases, and he can get us in the
program. That simple. And he's not the FBI. I ain't dealing with the
FBI."

"Why not?"

"I just don't want to. It leaves a bad taste in my mouth. The
bureau's been on my case for years."

"Maybe there's something you can do for ATF," Limbach suggested hopefully. "Go undercover, make cases."

"Maybe. But I want to meet McDonald."

"Why don't you tell me what you plan to tell him?" Limbach
said as calmly as he could. "Give me something to tantalize him
with. I'm not going to ask him to waste his time."

"You were in Ozone Park, come on," Sal said. "You know the
kind of stuff I can talk about."

"Well, I don't think that's gonna do it. The mailman on the
route can talk about that, too. McDonald's going to want something
specific. And if you want me to go to him, you're going to have to
tell me what it is."

Sal fought it for a while. He talked about his drug case. When
he noticed Limbach glancing at his watch, he said, "Okay. I bought
that case in Queens. The auto case. And word on the street is the
O.C. Strike Force is looking at corruption in Queens."

Now we're getting somewhere, Limbach thought. The details of
the case came back to him. Sal, Rose Marie and her brother Leonard
Noto had been arrested in 1980 and charged with auto theft, possession of stolen property and altered Vehicle Identification Numbers.
He sat back and listened to Sal explain how he had paid thirty-five
thousand dollars through his lawyer so that Rose Marie and Leonard

could plead to reduced charges and pay five-hundred-dollar fines. But in Sal's case a guilty plea meant a certain prison term, for he was a convicted felon, and it also meant the violation of his federal probation and the return to prison for the remainder of his eight-year bank robbery term. "So I arranged to take my plea back," Sal was saying.

"That cost me another fifteen thousand. What we did, I had to use two more attorneys, but we filed a writ to withdraw the plea on grounds I was incompetent. We cited my bank robbery case, so the judge would have something to hang his hat on."

"Who was the judge?" Limbach asked.

"Brennan. Then when he gave me my plea back, another judge was sitting in the auto case, and I sent him a gold pocket watch. After that he dismissed a portion of the evidence and eventually the indictment was dismissed. And you know what?" Sal said. "After he got the pocket watch that judge sent word he wanted a gold chain to go with it."

"I tried to violate you on that case," Limbach said. If the auto charge had stuck, he could have sent Polisi back to prison.

"I know you did," Sal replied. "That's what happened."

"Okay," said Limbach, "I'll go to see McDonald."

The next afternoon, Limbach threaded his way among huge concrete planters, strategically placed to prevent terrorist attacks, into the federal courthouse on Cadman Plaza in Brooklyn. An elevator in the IRS wing took him to the third-floor offices of the Organized Crime Strike Force. He was ushered past an ancient lioness of a receptionist down a narrow hall to an office where he told McDonald's two chief assistants, Laura A. Brevetti and Michael A. Guadagno, about Sal Polisi.

"The guy's a piece of work," he said after he explained his history with Polisi. "He may be trying to jerk us around, but he's jammed up and he says he wants the program for his wife and kids, and he's definitely got a street level view of o.c. in Queens. Most of his connections are Colombo and Gambino.

"Oh, yeah," Limbach added almost as an afterthought, "he says he bought this judge in Queens."

Brevetti and Guadagno had been noncommittal to this point. Now both he and Brevetti leaned forward as if they'd been jerked on a string and asked in unison, "Which judge?"

"Brennan."

The two federal prosecutors looked at each other with knowing smiles. Limbach wondered why everybody knew the joke but him.

Brevetti explained that the first tip that Brennan might be corrupt had come to the Strike Force in 1980 from a former cop who was working security for one of the airlines. A case he'd been involved in had taken a funny turn, and the ex-cop had been suspicious. Street talk corroborated the allegation that the case was fixed. But street talk and suspicions were all investigators could come up with. Meanwhile, the Brennan file had moved to the U.S. attorney's office with the lawyer who headed it. The FBI had continued to work the investigation off and on, hoping that somebody like Polisi might come along.

Brevetti said, "There's definitely interest in this guy if he's got something that can help nail Brennan."

Sal had been going to church, of all things. For the last few Sunday mornings, he had gone down to the Queens House gym, which had been filled with folding chairs for the occasion, and sat through Catholic services. On the Sunday before the Fourth of July, which was a Wednesday, he lingered afterward to speak with the priest.

The next afternoon he presented himself at the priest's office in the small area allotted on the seventh floor of Queens House for social services. In the heat of the summer, Father John Wilkinson was wearing a black shirt and slacks, but not his clerical collar. He was a solid, bulky man with world-weary eyes. He shook Sal's hand while grasping his shoulder, a greeting meant to convey openness and sympathy. You didn't need a confessional if you wanted to open your heart to Father Wilkinson.

Sal, seated in a molded plastic chair across the desk from the priest, spilled out essentially the same story he had told John Limbach. He added certain details for the priest's benefit, since unlike Limbach, Father Wilkinson could not have known the extent of

Sal's criminal history. "Father, you wouldn't believe the stuff I've done," he said. "You could just about name it. I've cheated, robbed, stolen, gambled, loan-sharked, hijacked trucks and held up banks. I beat people up and terrorized them. I manipulated the system by pretending I was crazy. I've sold drugs, which is what I'm in here for.

"But I'm ready to change my life." He told the priest about Sal junior and Joseph and his hopes for moving his family. "See, I've got some things to say about the people I did all these things with."

Father Wilkinson didn't want knowledge he didn't have to have. He held up a restraining hand. At the same time he seemed pleased. "That's good, Sal, the Lord wants you to change," he said.

So Sal asked Father Wilkinson to contact Queens District Attorney John Santucci and arrange a meeting.

The talking was going to be easier than Sal had thought. He hadn't actually said anything yet, but he'd covered all the bases by contacting the feds and Queens, too. Maybe he could spin a few yarns from out of his past that showed how organized crime operated in Queens, how it all went together, the gambling and loan-sharking and hijacking and drug dealing and the occasional murder. The fabric of it, that's what Sal could talk about. He could tell stories all day long, just sit there in a room and talk, have them spellbound and rolling in the aisles. He'd sing his song, beat the drug rap and head south. Nobody would even know. It would be different from what he had to say about the judge, but Sal wasn't worried about that. Nobody would kill him for putting a judge away.

· · ·

Dad's last letter had an air of resignation. It was short, one small page, and said, "I hope that in a few weeks I might get this bail reduced again. We'll see."

At the end he wrote, "Be good—and have a nice summer—no matter what."

It was like he had decided to write the summer off. June was over and he seemed to be discounting the prospects for a quick release. A week later, just after the Fourth of July, Mom told Joe and me over supper one night that Dad had been moved to Rikers

Island. "Rikers?" Joe said. "Rikers? I hope he gets out soon, because I ain't never going there."

Dad's absence continued to disrupt our lives, but we did what we could to live as normally as possible. There was a girl, Linda, who was a sophomore at school. She was a jayvee cheerleader. I first noticed her at one of their games. She looked cute with her blond hair and her cheeks daubed with stripes in red and black that were Port's school colors. We got to know each other, and we liked to talk, but she was just a friend, you know. We both were dating other people, and this guy wasn't treating her real well, I didn't think. I guess I wasn't all that happy with the girl I was going out with either. Anyway, we used to talk a lot, I guess crying on each other's shoulders, about our problems we were having with these other people we were dating. That summer, after my dad was arrested and the time till fall loomed like some huge empty space, I took an art class in summer school and she was in it. That was when I started looking at her differently. I had been wanting to date this girl named Donna really bad. But all of a sudden, standing talking to Linda in the hallway, I wanted to grab her and kiss her. It was like my arms had a mind of their own. I would have to remind myself not to let them reach out for her because I didn't know how she would react. I thought she might be completely surprised, and I could see her stepping back and looking at me with wide eyes—blue eyes—full of shock and hurt at my forwardness. What's wrong with you? I thought we were friends, she would say. It would have felt natural to take her in my arms and kiss her, and I wanted to real bad, but I held back because I wasn't sure.

On the Fourth of July, Joe and I went with Mom down to Port Jervis to watch the fireworks over the Delaware River. They burst in whites and reds and golds that glittered on the water and then trickled down to nothing in the sky. Afterward, we saw Linda and a bunch of kids at Brother Bruno's Pizza in the shopping center near the river. There was no school the next day, so we decided to get together and go on an outing.

There were two cars of us. Linda was wearing white shorts and a pink top when we picked her up in front of her parents' green-shingled house in Port Jervis the next morning. Her mom waved and

said, "Be careful." When all the kids were in the car, Linda was
sitting next to me and where our legs touched it felt like a little burn.

We drove down into New Jersey to a state park there, High
Point State Park. Along Highway 23 the trees were heavy with summer, green tufts squatting in their own black pools of shade. A farm
stand displayed baskets of tomatoes and corn on the cob, tilted toward
the road, and a hand-drawn sign advertised FREE RANGE EGGS. "We
should get some, if they're free," said a voice from the backseat,
and Linda nudged me and rolled her eyes to say that was pretty silly.
It was like a little secret. We smiled at each other, sharing it, and
I felt hopeful.

A sign at the entrance to the park said there was a mountain
there that was the highest point in New Jersey—1,803 feet above
sea level. Big deal. Linda's friend Donna said, "Sal, your brother's
friend John gets higher than that." Everybody laughed. Linda touched
my arm and looked at me with sympathetic eyes, and I saw she was
thinking about my dad and worried about my reaction.

The day went like that. She kept catching me looking at her,
and we smiled at each other like we were the only ones who knew
next week's Lotto numbers. Finally, she put a hand on my cheek
and pushed my face to one side and said, "Sal, stop staring. I feel
like I've got a huge zit or something."

"I can't help it," I said, feeling a stab of alarm that I had gone
too far and was scaring her away.

"Don't worry, you'll get over it," she said.

"Maybe not," I answered.

"Maybe not me either," she said. "We'll see. Let's not rush
things."

We spent the afternoon swimming and lying in the sun. The
day softened into a dusky haze and we cooked hot dogs on a little
grill somebody had brought and we all just let the day slip down. At
the end we cooked marshmallows, and that was how we kissed for
the first time, eating a crusty, warm marshmallow together through
the sticky sweetness until we got to each other in the middle, laughing. We held hands in the car on the way home as the sky turned
orange in the west.

One of the best things about that day, I remember, aside from *kissing her and holding her hand and having her hold mine, you know, in a positive way, is that she let me know that the thing with my dad was no big deal to her, but that she cared what other people said.*

One day toward the end of July, Mom went to New York for another bail hearing, and returned to say Dad's bail had been reduced. She then began a process of gathering the one hundred thousand dollars.

Half the money came from a shylock named Ralph in New Rochelle, New York, who lent us fifty thousand dollars on the deeds from two of Grandma and Grandpa Noto's houses. Mom said he made her pay five thousand under the table in addition to charging the New York State maximum of two percent interest a month. Mom had sold the pickup truck and some other equipment from the track, and we had a little money put aside, and she scraped and borrowed until she put it all together. She went to New York on the last Monday of July, expecting to return that night with Dad. Joe and I stayed home and waited.

We were sitting at the kitchen table, attacking a leftover plate of cold lasagna, when the phone rang. It must have been ten-thirty. I picked it up, and heard Dad's voice. "Hey, Sal," he said, "I'm out."

Even expecting it, it sounded too good to be true, which I guess is why I said, "No you're not. Getouttahere. Are you serious?"

"Serious as a heart attack. I'm standing outside looking at the sky. I'm gazing at the stars. I'm drinking in the rancid smell of the East River. I think I'm gonna stop and get me a Heineken."

I held my hand over the phone and got Joe's attention. "It's Dad. He's out." Joe stopped eating for the first time in about an hour. "When's he coming home?"

"When'll you be home?" I said into the phone.

"We're going by your grandmother's for a little bit, an hour or two. Then we're coming home."

It was late, one or two o'clock, and Joe and I were asleep when they returned. Dad came in and shook me awake. He was a dark shadow against the light coming through the door of my room, but

*when he sat on the edge of my bed the light caught his cheeks pushed
upward in a weary smile. I was goofy with sleep. I said, "Hi, Dad,"
and half rose up in the bed and he leaned down and hugged me. He
said, "Go back to sleep, son. We'll talk tomorrow." I remember he
went into Joe's room, and after that he went downstairs and returned
from the shower humming, with a towel around his waist. He stopped
at my door and stood there for a moment, again a dark shadow with
the light behind him. Then he passed away from the door and I fell
asleep until the sun was high the next morning.*

• • •

Sal was free for the first time in almost three months. On the
bus, from the complex of jails on Rikers Island to the main gate
across a long, narrow bridge, Rose Marie had slipped her hand under
his arm and held tight as he chattered happily. The driver glowered
at them in the rearview mirror, irritated at having to turn another
misfit back into society, and in the dead of night. Sal talked on,
oblivious.

"And when the guy calls me down and says 'You've been bailed
out,' next thing he says is, 'All we have to do is verify your identity.'

"I said, 'Who do you think I am, anyway?'

"He says, 'What's your wife's name? Where do you live?' I
finally had to show him the scar on my back from the bullet wound.
Can you believe it?"

Rose Marie was silent. Only when the driver stopped near the
main gate where Rose Marie's car was parked and they climbed down
onto the pavement did she say, "Thank God." They stopped at a
phone booth near the gate to call the boys. Sal insisted on stopping
for a Heineken on the way to Rose Marie's parents.

At his in-laws', whose generosity was half responsible for his
freedom, Leonard Noto, the old man, eyed Sal narrowly and said,
"So, out for a while." He looked like a man who thought he'd parted
with fifty thousand dollars foolishly, having been obliged by blood
and no wish of his own to do so. He had been against his daughter's
marriage. He had resigned himself to being cordial, but Leonard had
it in his mind that Sal would run and leave the fucking shylock in
New Rochelle with his deeds and him with nothing to leave his two

younger children. He was an old man; he liked peace in the family but he worried. Phyllis was cooking; her veal cutlets, fried escarole and hot garlic bread smelled to Sal like heaven.

He ate hungrily, stabbing a cutlet with a fork clutched in his left fist while he sawed at it with the knife in his right. For a time there was no talk, only the sounds of knives and forks clinking against Phyllis Noto's floral china. A kind of dull exhaustion had set in in the aftermath of the release. Then Phyllis said, "When am I going to see those grandsons of mine, now that things are back to normal, more or less?" Sal started choking.

He coughed for several minutes and then sat gasping, tears drying in his eyes.

"Honey, are you all right?" Rose Marie asked anxiously.

Sal coughed again. "Yeah. Yeah, I don't know what it was."

Which was a lie. It had been Phyllis Noto's question. Back to normal? he thought. Nothing would ever be normal again. He could see the future clearly, and everything was changed.

He fell asleep in the car on the way home. Sal junior and Joe were asleep in their beds. They greeted him groggily, and then he took a shower and fell into bed with Rose Marie, who only murmured and stirred and then receded into sleep.

Sal woke up early. His time, the early morning. He went to swing his feet out of bed, but he'd forgotten he was sleeping in a king-size bed and not a jailhouse cot. He tried again and his heels still struck the mattress. He had to chance waking Rose Marie, getting on his hands and knees and crawling to the edge of the bed. The carpet underfoot was a pleasant surprise after the cold floor of his cell.

Downstairs, daylight was beginning to show through the kitchen skylights and the octagonal window over the table. The clock on the stove showed 5:24. Sal made coffee and took the cup outside to the patio of railroad ties that overlooked the racetrack. Ground mist haunted the tree line; it would disappear when the sun rose. There were neighbors who considered the track an ugly scar on the land-scape, and the noise from the screaming karts a voice from hell. To Sal it had been a sanctuary. When his probation had expired at the end of 1981, he'd been free for the first time in years. He had no

charges to answer, no cases pending in the courts, no probation to
restrict his movements, and he'd fled Ozone Park with his family.
He remembered the night he'd made the decision.

He'd had the gold and jewelry stores then. They weren't Tif-
fany's. They were garish yellow with black letters that said, WE BUY
GOLD, SILVER, JEWELRY AND OLD COINS. There were three stores in
Queens, the first at Atlantic Avenue and Rockaway Boulevard, one
on Myrtle Avenue and Fresh Pond Road and the big one, the Great
Atlantic and Pacific Gold Company, on Queens Boulevard. Their
signs were a beacon to thieves and boosters. Sal bought their stolen
wares, broke the metal into scrap for melting down and reset the
gems so the owners couldn't trace them. The beauty of it was the
business was half legitimate. Just before Christmas, 1981, with a
big inventory of gold chains in stock, thieves broke through the roof
and relieved Sal of a hundred thousand dollars' worth of merchandise.
He slept in the store for two nights after that, waiting for repairs,
and in the middle of the second night he woke up with the weight
of his nine-millimeter Beretta on his chest and a revelation forming
in his brain. He thought, What the fuck am I doing here, a thief all
my life, staying here to protect my stolen stuff from other thieves?
He started laughing at himself. The noise of his laughter echoed
through the empty store, and he put the gun away in a desk drawer
and went home to take a shower. A few weeks later he announced
to his family that they were moving to Port Jervis.

He'd hoped that the track would make money. The opportunity
the move would give the boys was more important, but his cocaine
arrest had blown that. Now, looking down across the gentle slope of
land, he felt nostalgic. He would miss the place. He wondered how
he would break this news to his family.

• • •

Dad was awake when Joe and I woke up. Mom was humming
in the kitchen. It was the first time we had heard that sound in a
while.

"Hey, Mom, where's Dad?" I asked her.

She motioned toward the window, and by standing to one side
and looking at an angle I could see him sitting in an Adirondack

chair in front of the house looking out over the racetrack. He sat back in the chair with his legs stretched out in front of him, and his hands clasped contentedly across his stomach.

"Heyyy, look who's here," I said when I went outside.

"Hey, son." He stood up and held out his hands, palms up. I slapped them, and he slapped mine in return. Then we hugged each other. Then Joe came outside and they repeated the performance.

"You guys were out of it when your mom and I got home last night," he said.

"What time was it, anyway?" Joe asked.

"Late. Must have been one-thirty, two," Dad said. "Then I got up at five-thirty to see what the place looked like. I've been sitting here this whole time, just thinking about how much I like it here. I really missed this place. I missed you guys, too. If I had to give up one thing or the other, I mean, this place or you guys, not getting to see you play football and Joe race, man, that would be tough, but I guess I could get used to someplace new."

What he was saying made no sense. It was almost as if he was talking to himself. He had a court date coming up, but it was too early to worry about that. He had told us he could be serving some serious time, but now that he was out of jail, it was easy to believe he would stay out and that the court business would take care of itself. Dad had no business in jail, anyway. He belonged here with us. He hadn't done anything to hurt anybody. That was how I felt, and so what would be served by taking him from his family and disrupting all our lives? I hated the law for doing that. Just leave us alone, I thought, and we'll be all right. Let us live our lives. Now that Dad was back home, things were back to normal and everything would be fine.

Dad stood up abruptly. He said, "Let's go in and have breakfast with your mother."

We sat and ate at the little trestle table in the breakfast nook. Mom was relaxed, without the faraway, distracted look she'd had for these past months.

"Now tell me what you're doing to get ready for the fall, son," Dad demanded.

I outlined the weight-lifting program I had started. "I can already bench two thirty," I said proudly.

"You should be up to two fifty by the time the season starts. When is that, anyway? Just a few weeks, right? What is it, August first already?" And so like that we were indeed back to normal, Dad with his goals for my season and me wondering not only how I'd make him happy, which was hard enough, but how all the news about him would affect things on the team once school started.

"He's got a little girlfriend, too." Joe snuck that in out of left field.

"Is that right, son? Tell me about her."

"Way to go, Joe," I said. "Aw, you know her, Dad. My friend, Linda. We just started going out with each other, instead of other people. It's no big deal." I gave Joe a death look. I had been writing Linda notes almost every day in school. I was crazy about her.

Mom broke in. "She's very nice. She has a nice family."

"Well, that's great, son, really great," Dad said. Then Joe started talking excitedly about going to the Grand Nationals, and the conversation turned to karting as easily as if there had been no three-month hiatus in our lives.

Things were normal for about a week. Dad was up at dawn every morning, and on the second day of his return the reassuring chugging of the tractor was coming through my bedroom window when I woke up. We resisted talking about his return to court. The date loomed over us, sometime in August. We knew our time with him was borrowed. Joe and I guessed he'd get fifteen years; we would be grown men with families before he came out. We didn't know what we would do when he went away, but we didn't want to talk about it either. Not until we had to. I supposed his restlessness had something to do with that, knowing what was coming. He would leave at odd intervals, never for very long, and return with nothing to show for his trip, no groceries or supplies, as if he hadn't been anywhere at all. Then early one evening he called me and Joe over to the old white Jeep Mom hadn't been able to sell. It was a government surplus mail truck. "Hop in," he said. "Let's go for a little ride."

He drove down to the D & H Canal Store first, the little country grocery that stood up on the hill just before the road from the racetrack joined the main road to Port Jervis. He bought a few things, chips, some Gatorade, the usual stuff. On the way back he passed our house and kept driving up the road.

Joe was sitting in front. He pantomimed a left turn and then said, "Hey, Dad, where you going?"

"Oh, we're just going up here and talk a little bit," he said.

He went another quarter mile and pulled into a small campground that I knew about but had never stopped at before. It was pretty quiet during the week. A telephone booth stood by itself at the edge of a clearing, next to the road that led down to the campsites. Dad turned off the motor of the Jeep.

He sat there for a minute looking at the phone booth. You could hear a soft wind shushing through the branches of the pines, and somewhere a woodpecker was tapping on a tree trunk. Joe broke the silence in the Jeep. He said, "What's up, Dad?"

Dad turned toward us, me in the backseat and Joe in front, and said, "I want you guys to know we're going to have to leave here."

That was no surprise. The track was bankrupt, then. He was going into prison and Mom and Joe and I were going back to Queens. I almost didn't hear him add, "I'm working undercover for the government."

A silence ballooned out from where we were and brought back the wind in the trees, louder than before. My face suddenly felt hot and it was not just the August heat. I was ashamed. Of all the things he could have said, that was the most shocking. I had to hear it again before I believed it. "You're what?" I said.

"I'm working undercover for the government."

I had two thoughts. My dad was a rat, and they would kill him. As long as I could remember the government had always been the enemy. The government was the FBI agents who had raided our apartment when I was four, and the judge who'd sent my dad away when I was six, and the law that had harassed our friends and family ever since I could remember. To join the government was to join the enemy and turn against your friends. As a boy I'd learned you never talked. If you saw something, you never saw nothing; Dad had taught me that himself. You never talked, you never turned against your friends, and if you got caught you took your medicine. A boy who violated those principles was branded a rat and pummeled in the schoolyard; a man with a certain kind of friends, my dad's friends, for example, was branded a rat and shot in the head. Joe was silent. I knew he was thinking the same thing.

"I want to tell you why," Dad said.

Joe said, "I don't want to know why. I'm going home." He reached for the door handle. Dad grabbed him by the arm and pulled him back against the seat. Joe was still small then, at thirteen, but he crouched like a spider, angry and ready to fight. Joe is a lot more like my dad than I am. Aggressive. Always pushing. Joe's eyes were full of accusation.

"You're going to know why," my dad said. "Both a youse." He looked at me, challenging me. I was almost as tall and heavy as him then. With his round face and curly hair, he looked like one of those ancient Romans whose faces you see in history books. There was fight in his eyes, and stubbornness. He liked a fight no matter what the odds, and it didn't matter if it was a fight to explain himself to us or a fight on the streets of Ozone Park, where he had almost gotten killed a time or two. He was a maniac and a bully in a fight, and the same with words. They poured out like blows until you were defenseless. You couldn't disagree with him. It was impossible. There were no holds barred; anything was fair. If he couldn't persuade you, he would charm you; he tried to manipulate everyone he ever met, and most of the time he got what he wanted. He wasn't above manipulating me and Joe.

I couldn't hold his eyes. I looked away and looked back and he nodded, satisfied, and looked at Joe. "Just listen to me for a minute," he said. Then he gave us the oldest line in the book. "I'm doing it for you."

FOUR

"See, I never wanted you boys to be like I was," he said, "and this is the only way to change that. I didn't want to do it. They came to me and said you have to or you're never going to see the outside of a jail again. If there was any other way I wouldn't do it, but I messed up and it's too late. I have to do some things, and then we're all going away together, the three of us and your mother, someplace new."

"Go where?" I asked. I felt numb, and a little nauseous and hollow, like you do when you need a sugar fix.

"I don't know. It'll take a long time to find out. But wherever we go things'll be completely different. I mean really different. I know you don't understand it now, but we're gonna have a chance to start over in life. How many people get an opportunity like that? Not many."

"When?" My voice sounded light and distant, not attached to me, as if a loon were calling.

"Well, like I said, I have to do some things. It's gonna be awhile. Not right away. A few months, maybe more. But, Sal, you won't get to finish here. You can just count on that. And you can't tell anybody about this. Don't even tell your mother that you know. You know how she worries. This whole thing bothers her. Just keep it between us."

Just like that, he brought us into the conspiracy.

Then it suddenly made sense. I'm a little slow sometimes. He wouldn't have to go to prison. He had made a deal to give himself back to us.

"So you're not going to have to go to prison, right?" Joe swung around when I said that. Our eyes met and it was like, oh, yeah, and we both looked at Dad. A smile broke over his wide face and he said, "That's ri-ight.

"It's not definite," he added, breaking our astonished silence, "but I think that's what'll happen. I mean, I'm still charged with a crime, but when I do my work for the government they'll tell that to the judge, and most of the time what happens is they recommend suspension of the sentence and most of the time the judge agrees." There was some complicated stuff about the feds taking the drug charge out of Queens, but I didn't catch it. I just heard the important part. Our questions started tumbling over one another.

"Is that how you got out?" Joe asked, as I was asking, "What are you doing for the government?" We stopped, tried to start again at the same time, stopped.

"Hold it," said Dad. "I'll try to explain." He sat back against the door and propped his arm on the back of his seat. "It didn't have nothing to do with my bail getting reduced. That just happened. Which is why I was in there so long. The feds couldn't be getting my bail reduced because that would blow the case. See, remember that case I fixed in Queens, the auto case with your mom and Uncle Lenny? Well, I'm gonna fix this case, too. The only thing different is, I'm gonna fix it and the government's gonna know I'm fixing it and they're gonna help me fix it so they can bust the judge.

"Then we're going to be picked up by the government, and we're going to go away on a secret Witness Protection Program. We'll move to a new place, we'll get new names and everything."

When he said new names, I went, like, wait a minute. "What new names?" I said.

Dad said, "Well, I'm Mr. Edwards at the moment. That's who I say I am when I call this guy, McDonald. I've been calling him from that phone booth. Can you imagine, a phone booth out here in the middle of the woods?"

Joe said, "We're gonna be named Edwards?" I couldn't even see the bottom of his jaw, it dropped so far. It went somewhere out of sight below the seat back. I tried it on for size. Sal Edwards?

"No. No, no, no. That's just what I've been using when I call from here. The operator says, 'A collect call from Mr. Edwards,' and he knows it's me. No. We'll have different names. We'll get to pick whatever name we want. You guys could be Ricky and Rocky, the Balboa brothers."

"Well, what about . . ." I didn't know quite how to put it. I was thinking of my football record, and getting into college. "What if I . . . What about my record? I mean, if I gain a lot of yards and have to change my name, how will anybody know?"

"That's one of the hard things," Dad said. "It's not the only one. Your mother's going to have to give up her family, but she's ready to do that so we can be together. It's going to be hard on you, too, son. It's going to be hard on all of us, but it's going to be hardest on you because of that, because of where you are right now.

"But this is something I've got to do. We're gonna do it as a family. We're gonna be together, and it's all going to work out. It's gonna be better. For now you've got to just live every day the way it comes, and do the same things you've been doing, and when the time comes to make the grand exit, we'll make the grand exit as a family. But I've got to do this, see? It's going forward to keep from going back. And once we're gone from here I ain't ever going back to that old life."

I had a vague idea of what "that old life" was. You couldn't live in Ozone Park without knowing about what some people called "the life." Of course I knew he'd been in prison. Mom had told me and Joe we were going to visit our father in a hospital, but you saw bars and kind of knew it wasn't a hospital. You kind of knew a lot of things. Like you kind of knew the auto shop wasn't just an auto shop, and you kind of knew the jewelry stores weren't just jewelry stores. It was the way he made a living, just like selling cocaine. You kind of didn't think about it.

There was more to his old life before my memory, too.

Not only did we have to think about it then, we began having to relive it, every ugly, fascinating detail. There was no way to avoid it. Once the flow of stories started it was impossible to stop. They came spilling out like kernels from a split-open bag of rice. Dad had to recount his life for everyone. When he talked to one of the government's lawyers, it was a debriefing. When he talked to me and Joe, it was a compulsion to explain why our lives were exploding and also, I think, to cling to his identity, like some old ballplayer who never gets tired of talking about his greatest game. Except there had been a lot of games with Dad.

Were they really in the past? I didn't know whether to believe him, about not going back to his old life, by which he meant his old ways. He hadn't changed yet. We had moved to Port Jervis, and he'd spent all our money and started selling cocaine. When we left Port Jervis and moved to God knows where, what was to keep him from slipping back again? It was what he knew.

But even if a guy does bad stuff, if he's your dad you give him slack. He's your dad first. If he's really your dad, that is, and not just the guy who fucked your mother. And whatever else he had been, our dad had been that. And so we learned on that August afternoon that in order to keep him, we would atone for his past life and trust his vision of the future.

He started the Jeep. "Okay, look," he said, "remember, don't tell your mother that I talked to you guys about this. And don't tell anybody else about it either. That's real important. We're gonna be back down there in Queens from time to time, with your grandmother and them there, and they can't know about this. That could screw up everything. It could be dangerous, too. I don't mind doing this here, because it's the only way to keep us together as a family, but I ain't looking to get whacked out over it."

Dad wheeled the Jeep around in a clatter of loose parts and a chatter of gravel, passing close to the phone booth in the clearing by the edge of the woods. Funny, I had never noticed it before. It was sort of concealed at the edge of the clearing, but still . . . There were a thousand places in the woods where someone could hide and watch a person make a call. I shook it off as paranoia.

• • •

Ed McDonald's calendar for August 8 read, "Mr. Edwards in Yonkers." He looked forward to meeting "Mr. Edwards." So far they had only spoken on the phone.

The first calls had come while Sal was still in jail. It always amazed McDonald that Polisi had the audacity to call him from a Rikers Island phone, but it was nothing compared to the audacity when Polisi wanted to be patched through to his wife upstate. And he would talk to her at length. At first, though, he talked only to McDonald. His buzzer would sound and Shirley's bored voice would come over the speaker saying, "It's Mr. Edwards again." Shirley never gave the slightest indication that she recognized a disparity between the wiseguy voice on the phone and the bogus, forgettable name. That amazed McDonald, too.

Then this crazy huckster would come on, yammering about what a great witness he was going to be and how he wanted to change his life and get away from crime and go into the Witness Protection Program and get a new start for himself and how he was doing it all for his sons. He said, "Listen, I can really help you. I can make great cases. I'll get wired up and go against anybody you say. I'll be a great witness. I'll make Henry Hill look like a nobody."

What egos these guys had. Henry Hill had been a star witness for McDonald, testifying against Lucchese family capo Paulie Vario and hijacker Jimmy Burke and a host of other mobsters he'd turned on after twenty years as a wiseguy on the street. Then he'd been the subject of a book. Now here was another wiseguy jammed up on a drug charge, wanting to be a star. The difference was, Hill knew he was going to get whacked before he talked. Polisi just wanted out of jail. Plus he had this thing about his kids.

Like his two assistants, Brevetti and Guadagno, McDonald had a deep skepticism for criminals who wanted to tell all. So McDonald listened and said, "Well, I look forward to meeting you. If you can get out of jail, fine, but we're not going to do anything to help you get out of jail."

He hadn't, and now he was on his way to Yonkers.

Rose Marie was driving to Yonkers from Port Jervis. She was silent, her eyes fixed on the road, her heart tripping away out of her control. She lit a fresh cigarette about every six miles. Rose Marie was scared to death. She refused to talk to her husband, sitting in the right-hand seat.

She had married Sal against her father's and her stepmother's wishes. "He's in trouble, he was arrested, he's no good, you don't know what you're doing. Look at his uncle, a bank robber. If you marry him you're as crazy as he is," her father had yelled at her. Rose Marie was nineteen then, and nothing in life had been as important as getting out of her parents' house and starting a life of her own. And for the past seventeen years that life had been what she had known.

She had cried when Sal told her he would be working with the government. Even though he said he had no choice about it, that they knew all about him and Brennan and were going to go after her family for fixing the other case unless he cooperated and agreed to work undercover. The day he told her, she actually said to him, "You mean you're going to become a rat?" All her life that had been the lowest of the lows, something to spit on and step on. "Rat or no rat," he had said, "this is something I've got to do." And she was immediately frightened, because she knew what happened to people like that.

In a way it was marvelous, of course. She was smoking so much since he told her that in a week—a week!—she had lost about ten pounds. But even that was no compensation for the fear she felt.

As she drove toward Yonkers, Rose Marie felt that RAT was painted in bright red letters on the side of the car.

"Look," he said, in another vain attempt to draw her out, make her relax, anything to win her endorsement of what he was doing. "Look, I'll say it again. This is the only way. I swear to God. Once this is over and we get out of here, it's gonna be a whole new life. The boys'll have a chance. Both of them can go to college. You know Sal's got the talent, and Joe's gonna have it, too. Think about it. Who in your family ever went to college? Nobody in mine did. And if I go in the joint and youse go back to Ozone Park, that ain't what's gonna happen. I know it, you know it, we might as well admit it to ourselves. This is the only way.

"And I ain't going back no more. Maybe I wouldn't do it if it wasn't for them, but my changing is the only way to give these boys a chance. Look at me, Ro. I've already changed. It's for real this time, I swear."

Sure it is, thought Rose Marie. She said, "Whatever you do, just don't tell the boys. I don't want them to be involved in this until they have to be. At least let them live their lives until they have to know about this." She stubbed out her cigarette and lit another one, blew smoke in the direction of the windshield. She felt lonely as well as frightened; the burden of knowledge was all hers.

Sal felt a momentary pang of guilt. He hadn't been able to keep it from them. It was funny he hadn't been able to tell any of them he had gone to the government instead of lying about how it was the other way around. That way he could save his family and be a martyr both.

"They're going to have to know sometime," he said. "They're going to wonder how I'm staying out of jail."

"Sal's about to start his football season. He doesn't need to worry about his father getting killed."

The streets of Yonkers grew progressively dingier until Rose Marie pulled into the lot of what looked like a welfare motel. It was U-shaped, with parking in the middle of the U. The low buildings with protruding balconies rose oppressively on either side. Shabby curtains flapped from open windows. Children's toys shared balconies with rusty hibachis and broken-down furniture. Rose Marie saw two disheveled Cabbage Patch dolls and at least half a dozen Big Wheels; maybe they were broken, or just unused in the heat. She wondered where the children possibly could ride them. Rose Marie stopped the car and left the engine running.

"Aren't you going to wait?" he said.

"I can't wait here. Look at this place. And I'm not coming in to meet your 'contacts.' " She said it sarcastically, so you could hear the quotation marks.

"So go get a cup of coffee or something. Come back in an hour or two." Sal had to play her along, make it easy for her. If she told her family the whole thing could be over. It would take about twenty minutes for word to get the half block from the Notos' house to Fat Andy Ruggiano's. Fat Andy was a capo in the Gambino family. Fat tub of blubber, you could put him in a thousand-dollar suit and he'd still look as if he slept in the street the night before; fat thick lips, sprayed you all over every time he talked; Fat Andy and Sal had hated each other for years. He'd wanted a piece of Sal's bookie trade, then the Sinatra Club, the illegal gambling joint he ran. He was still nudging ten years later when he went after a piece of Sal's jewelry stores. Fat Andy's son was the father of Sal's six-year-old nephew, but he had never married the boy's mother. Gina, Rose Marie's younger half-sister, had had to raise the boy herself.

Rose Marie drove away. She drove aimlessly, and before she even realized it she was driving into Queens. Familiar territory. She wondered if she should go to see her parents, but how would she explain why she had come to town?

McDonald pulled into the parking lot of the motel between the ominous rise of the buildings and felt a prickle of fear raise the hairs on the back of his neck. Good Catholic curses flooded his mind. Oh, Jesus, he thought. Oh, God. What if this is a setup? If I'm getting set up, it's all over. He looked from side to side for an escape route and saw none. He wondered why Strike Force lawyers didn't carry guns.

Then he saw Joe Kelly waving at him from a balcony and he let his breath out. It's all right, he thought.

Kelly was John Limbach's boss at the Bureau of Alcohol, Tobacco and Firearms. Limbach had gone off for his agent's training in Georgia. In his absence Kelly had contacted McDonald to say Polisi wanted to get together. Kelly had picked the meeting place on the recommendation of a Yonkers detective who was a friend of his. Some friend. McDonald could say one thing for the motel. Nobody in a million years would pick this scumhole as a place for them to meet. It was secure from that standpoint.

McDonald walked up concrete stairs to the second floor. The stairs were open, but they smelled close and musty and like maybe a cat had been looking for a litter box when it found the stairs instead. He emerged onto the common balcony and saw Kelly's blond head, leaning out of a doorway. "Nice place, Joe," he said as he approached, "you come here often?"

"Right. And never once saw anybody I knew. That's why I keep coming back." Kelly, like McDonald, was from Brooklyn, but only Kelly advertised it with his accent.

The heat inside the room was stifling. Kelly could at least have picked a place with air-conditioning in the August heat. McDonald took his blue seersucker suit coat off and slung it on a nightstand. A moment later he picked it up, shook the roaches off it, and put it on again.

"Try the closet," Kelly said. "There's one hanger left and it's only half rusted." He rolled up the sleeves of his white shirt, revealing muscular forearms. Kelly had been with the ATF for fourteen years and was as comfortable on the streets of Ozone Park as Sal.

Sal waited until McDonald was finished hanging up his coat, then he stuck out his hand and said, "Hi, I'm Mr. Edwards."

McDonald looked at him. Nobody McDonald had ever seen looked less like a Mr. Edwards. He saw a craggy, round face full of mischief. Maybe dangerous mischief. But there was more behind Polisi's eyes than you could say for most of the people who had his kind of record, the three printout sheets of which McDonald had seen in his office, beginning with an assault and robbery arrest in 1965. He said, "How are you, Mr. Edwards? I understand the three of us have some friends in common."

Let's see if you're for real.

They began playing the game of Who Do You Know? It was a preliminary to the game of How Can We Help Each Other?

"You oughta ask me who I don't know," Sal said. "See, my uncle Tony Polisi was a bank robber who hung out with the Sonny Franzese gang back in the sixties. We set up a little bookie joint in Queens together and after Uncle Tony went to prison, Dominic Cataldo came in as partners. He got his button with the Colombos when the families opened the books again in the seventies. I knew Freddie No-Nose, Sonny Black, Joseph Broncado, who was the acting boss then. Then me and Dominic and Dominic's brother Joey opened a little joint called the Sinatra Club, on account of that's the only music we played there. Cards, sports betting. You could get a drink or a girl, you wanted to do that. Jackie Donnelly, from one of the Colombo crews, was another partner, and Funzi Tarricone, he was Genovese; my kid was the ring bearer at his daughter's wedding.

"I did a bunch of bank robberies and hijackings in them days, and we'd talk about them all the time around there. Guys would come in from all over, crews from all the families.

"Man, it was funny. You could tell every time there was a hijacking, see, because guys liked to hand out presents and if it was men's clothes, everybody would show up wearing the same thing. Like Leonardi Strassi, Damon knits. Knit shirts? Like this one I'm wearing. You like it? That's prob'ly how I got it. Guys liked that stuff. After a hijacking, they'd all be wearing the same shirts, looking each other over, saying, 'Hey, you wearin' my shirt?' "

McDonald laughed. The guy was a regular comedy routine. He felt a compatibility with him that he had not expected. It made him almost forget about the roaches and the heat.

"You've seen my sheet, right?" Sal continued. "Well, after I got arrested in seventy-two for that bank robbery the year before—that was the only robbery I ever got caught for, by the way—we closed the Sinatra Club and I started hanging out at a place on a Hunnert and First Ave, the Bergin Hunt and Fish Club. They must have got the name from Bergen Street, in Brooklyn, but a sign in the window spelled it Bergin, with an 'i'. Anyway, it was run by the Fatico brothers, Carmine and Danny. They used the names Charlie and Danny Wagner at the club. They were Gambino, old-time button guys, and the up-and-comers in them days were John Gotti and his brother Gene, and Angelo Ruggiero. These were the guys that got the respect.

"I got sent to Lewisburg in seventy-four, the federal pen down there in Pennsylvania. I met a buncha guys in the joint there. That's where I met Johnny Dio . . ." Sal could never think of John Dioguardia without thinking of the evil mission the old Lucchese family mobster with the death's-head smile had sent him to Miami to perform. He gave an involuntary shudder.

"You were there when, in seventy-four? You know John Carneglia?" Kelly wanted to know.

"Are you kidding me?" Sal dismissed the thought of Johnny Dio. "John was like my partner when I had my chop shops. Who do you think I borrowed the money from got me into this cocaine rap?"

"What about his brother?"

"Charles? Yeah. He's still lamming it, I think. There was this court officer got shot."

"You know Banky?" McDonald interrupted.

"Yeah. Banky Frigente? Yeah, Carneglia's partner. Low-key guy. But I heard he whacked Tony Stabile and he's on the lam, too. Nobody woulda thought it.

"Anyway, when I came outta there in seventy-five . . ."

Sal said he stopped hijacking trucks when he came out of Lewisburg. He dealt heroin, often dispensing it to his street dealers from his back door in Ozone Park. Then he started stealing cars, buying wrecks and switching the identification numbers, which led to the auto fraud case he fixed. Then he opened the jewelry stores. When he sold everything in 1982 and moved out of Ozone Park, he took six hundred thousand in cash, a small fortune in stolen diamonds and a wealth of information and illicit contacts. Except for a handful of diamonds and some Krugerrands, the information and contacts were all that remained of his negotiable assets.

"You know Frankie the Eel?"

"Yeah, I know Frankie the Eel."

Sal played the name game with McDonald and Kelly for over an hour.

Finally he said, "Look, I've been out of the picture for a while. But I've been in touch, you know? Because when I started dealing drugs again before I got arrested, I got the money from Carneglia. I been paying him the juice, interest at like five percent a week. So I don't see no problem getting back involved. I could go back there in a minute, wear a wire on those guys. Only thing is, like I told John, I ain't dealing with the FBI.

"So you know what I want, right? I want a shot at the program, get my family out of here. I told you all about my boys."

McDonald sighed. Polisi had told him all about his sons. He said he had started coaching Sal junior's midget football team in 1976. He also said he was dealing heroin in 1976. McDonald's mind formed a picture of Polisi's connections coming to the sidelines to talk drugs and other deals while between the chalk lines the children were playing their game by the rules. McDonald had three children. It was hard for him to fit the kids and the drug dealers into the same picture.

"I got a jones for excitement," Polisi had said, using the street term for a habit. Just the kind of balls you wanted in an undercover operative. McDonald could see a massive sting operation against the organized crime players in Queens, every bit of evidence on tape. Polisi's story about Brennan, fixing his auto case, checked out. Moreover, the guy was no drone or street thug. He was an entertaining, funny guy, clearly smarter than most of the wiseguys McDonald had met. His desire to get into the program for his sons' sakes seemed sincere. McDonald liked Polisi in spite of himself. He made up his mind never to forget the man was scum. Usable scum, though.

"We'd like to work with you," McDonald said, "but we got a couple problems. We can't just go in and steal the case from Queens. You already made contact with those guys, and we're going to have to deal with them some way. Best thing for now is, keep stringing them along. Tell them you know about corruption in Queens generally, but don't tell them about Brennan.

"Second thing is, your mental health record doesn't exactly inspire confidence."

Sal said, "Oh, I was just making all that up."

McDonald and Kelly exchanged looks. Limbach had said Polisi was practically a certifiable lunatic who now claimed it was an act originally put on to get out of the Marines, and later to get out of jail.

"That's what I mean," McDonald said. "I'm supposed to put you in front of a jury and you're going to say you're not really crazy, you were only kidding? Are you still kidding, or what? A good lawyer'll have a field day. Unless you've got evidence on tape.

"Last thing"—he glanced at Kelly—"we're not talking ATF violations here. It's going to be hard to keep the bureau out of what we're doing, so you might have to get used to the idea of working with the FBI. In the meantime, though, you're still an ATF source."

McDonald stood up, signaling the end of the meeting. He retrieved his coat and Kelly's from the closet, tossed the dark coat to Kelly and looked suspiciously at his own seersucker jacket and shook it out before he put it on.

"By the way, where've you been calling me from?" he asked Sal.

"From this phone booth in the woods. At a campground about a quarter mile from my house there. It's weird, this phone booth just sitting out there in the woods."

"Well, in case I have to call you, I want to sound like somebody you ought to know. What's a good name?"

"How 'bout Vito?" Sal suggested. "You look like a Vito."

"Yeah, dat's right," growled McDonald in a wiseguy voice that suddenly resembled Sal's. "So when you get a call from Vito, do the right thing. Talk nice. Unnerstan'?"

The three men left the room together.

From where she was parked under the meager shade of a pair of huddled trees, Rose Marie saw them emerge from the shadows of the open stairway. Sal saw her and started across the parking lot, beckoning the two taller men to follow him. Oh, God, she thought, don't let him bring them over here, but the thought was too late before she formed it, and her husband and the two government men were at her window.

She rolled the window down. "Ed McDonald and Joe Kelly, my wife, Rose Marie," Sal announced. Rose Marie looked up, shading her eyes, and acted her best, like a good Catholic girl from Queens. It was the first time she had met someone from the government who wasn't searching her home or monitoring her husband for probation violations. She felt naked, as if the ghosts of her life in Ozone Park were watching her talking to the enemy and waiting to report the meeting.

When they were safely away from the motel and Yonkers and on the westbound New York State Thruway, Rose Marie said, "That blond guy, was his name Joe? He looks more like a hood than anybody I've ever seen in Ozone Park. I hope you saw his ID."

"Hey, these are great guys," Sal said. "We're gonna get along great. Everything's gonna work out fine."

McDonald and Kelly stood by Kelly's brown sedan and watched Rose Marie and Sal out of the courtyard. "What do you think of this guy?" McDonald asked.

"I think he knows the players. He knows who's into what. He's got the right personality. If he can do twenty percent of what he says, and I think he can, he'll be a great one."

"I see maybe setting him up with a limo service, letting him run it as a front for a card game, wire the place up, let people come to him. It could be perfect. And let him try to get to Brennan, too."

Two days later, Sal and Rose Marie sat in the third row of Justice Vincent Naro's courtroom in the Queens Criminal Court building, Complex One, waiting for his case to be called. Neither of them noticed the man behind them wearing a dark suit and taking notes, or if they did they thought he was a reporter.

"Five-eight, black curly hair, brown eyes, medium build, 170 lbs," wrote FBI agent Dan Russo, who was a little taller and heavier, with straight black hair flecked with gray, gray eyes and a Roman nose he was fond of. He often stroked his nose when he was thinking.

Russo had been keeping detailed notes for years. He had several dozen spiral notebooks squirreled away in the file cabinets of his enclosure in the FBI offices on the twenty-eighth floor at One Federal Plaza on Lower Broadway in Manhattan. His notebooks covered his investigation of the 1975 case that was code-named VAKIL, in which he'd tied the deaths of twenty-six patients at a Veterans Administration hospital in Ann Arbor, Michigan, to two Filipino nurses. They'd been convicted, but a judge ordered a new trial and the government dismissed the case. Russo suspected the dismissal had more to do with keeping U.S. bases in the Philippines than the guilt or innocence of the two nurses. Since the VA murders Russo had been transferred to New York and assigned to public corruption. His efforts so far had been on the white-collar side of public corruption. Organized crime was new to him, but the original agent on the Brennan case was being transferred, and the investigation had fallen into Russo's lap. The first he'd heard about Polisi was from Ethan Levin-Epstein, the assistant United States attorney who himself had inherited the case and been told about Polisi by McDonald. Levin-Epstein wanted to squeeze Polisi for information, even if he was technically an ATF informant. Now Russo wanted a look at Polisi, to check him out and see how he'd do wired up in a sting against Brennan.

Polisi's case was called and Sal swaggered to the front of the courtroom to stand beside his lawyer. Jeez, look at the guy, thought Russo. The way Polisi walked, the smirk on his face, the way he said, "Thank you, Your Honor," when the case was adjourned until September—all suggested to Russo that Sal was a hardcase New York wiseguy who thought the whole court procedure was a joke. Not the kind of guy who would be easy to approach and work with, he concluded. He left the thought out of his notebook.

Russo saw Sal again two weeks later. John Limbach had returned from training and the feds convened within the dungeonlike stone walls of the Officers Club at Fort Hamilton, near the Brooklyn side of the Verrazano Narrows Bridge, to continue to make plans for their newest informant.

Sal loved the attention. He rode into the army base with Limbach and Joe Kelly, who were guarding him like mother hens, and smirked when the guard at the gate saluted. He was still feeling his way among the new names and faces. He acted subdued during the meeting with the two ATF agents, Russo, Tim Dortsch and Gordon Strand of the FBI and lawyers from Ed McDonald's and Raymond Dearie's offices. Dearie was the U.S. attorney for the Eastern District of New York, covering the same territory as McDonald's Organized Crime Strike Force office. Both of them were drooling over the prospects for the Brennan case, now that Polisi had appeared.

Russo listened quietly as Polisi reviewed his dossier for the agents and lawyers as they all sat around a conference room. He wrote, "Mental history. Federal probation, 4, 5 years. Street knowledge—Brennan under investigation. Wants program. Associate John Gotty, Gambino LCN—La Cosa Nostra." Russo had never heard Gotti's name before, as the organized crime squad would have, so he spelled it phonetically when he wrote it in his notebook. Continuing his notes, he wrote "$20,000 and $30,000 loan shark payments owed. Gold theft—narcotics."

Sal's matter-of-fact accounts had the ring of truth. Russo revised his earlier opinion. We're going to be working with him after all, he thought.

Sal described, for what felt like the fiftieth time, how he had fixed the 1980 auto case by giving a total of fifty thousand dollars to his lawyer, Michael Coiro. The money, he believed, had gone to Brennan.

"But that's not evidence," somebody said. "That just tells us what we already know about Brennan and can't prove. We've got to get the evidence."

As the meeting broke up Levin-Epstein approached Sal, put his arm around him and drew him to one side. "Let me tell you something," said the conservatively dressed young lawyer, one of the star prosecutors in Dearie's office.

What the fuck's this? Sal thought. He noticed a college ring on the hand Levin-Epstein had draped around his shoulder.

"You're like a commodity to us," Levin-Epstein said.

"Oh, yeah? Like a pork belly?" said Sal.

"Think of a commodity," Levin-Epstein said, ignoring him. "Sometimes a commodity has no price at all. And sometimes the price skyrockets. It all depends on things happening in a certain way. Right now you're worth nothing to us, but if things happen in a certain way, your price is going to escalate."

"Oh, it's gonna escalate."

"That's right. See, what happened in 1980 with Judge Brennan doesn't make you a valuable commodity. That's ancient history. We've got to make this case now. He's got to accept a direct solicitation. You've got to put the money in his hands."

No problem, thought Sal. The shit I've done, this'll be a piece of cake.

"If we're going to do this," the lawyer said, "it's got to be done right. Then you'll be a valuable commodity."

Sal spotted Russo in the lobby of the Sheraton Hotel near La Guardia Airport five days later. If they hadn't both been there for the same meeting, it would have been Sal's easiest make ever. Russo was wearing a green suit.

A Bob Hope suit, Sal thought. Bob threw it out, you hope it fits. He walked across the lobby to where Russo was sitting. Russo stood up at Sal's approach and introduced himself. They shook hands.

"I was looking for Limbach," Sal said.

Russo looked at his watch. "Well, I'm a little early. Did you meet Gordon Strand?" He introduced Sal to the other FBI agent.

"Well, whyncha come in the coffee shop, meet my wife?" Sal led the two agents into the restaurant where Rose Marie was sitting.

The last time Rose Marie met an FBI agent he had led a party of searchers that burst into her home looking for bank robbery evidence. They had taken away the guns Sal had stashed under the bed, some of his clothes and one of her wigs. She still believed the government was forcing Sal's cooperation. She stubbed out her cigarette—she was up to two packs a day and had now lost fifteen pounds—and said in a rush as she backed toward the door, "It's very nice to meet you but you'll have to excuse me I have some shopping to do I'll pick you up later."

When Limbach arrived ten minutes later, Sal was sitting over coffee with Russo and Strand. They were deep in conversation. Limbach bristled at the sight of the two rival agents plucking over *his* source without having even the courtesy to wait for a proper introduction.

"What's the matter, can't you guys wait ten minutes?" he cried indignantly.

But the forces at work were beyond Limbach's control. Sal had become in the minds of the Justice Department and the FBI the key not only to the Brennan investigation but also a long-running sting they envisioned setting up in Queens. He was a gift. Used correctly, he could make a prosecutor's career. Sal was more valuable than he had ever envisioned himself and, as a commodity, neither he nor Limbach any longer controlled access to his services.

By the end of the meeting, Limbach and the ATF agreed to lend "their" witness to the FBI. ATF would continue to control him; that is, Limbach would be, in effect, his nursemaid. But the FBI would rig him with tape recorders and transmitters to gather evidence as he tried to place a bribe in the judge's hands. The FBI would also use him as a "cooperating witness" to develop evidence in organized crime cases, sending him among his former friends and associates as a human sounding board.

Sal decided it was all the same to him. Which side of the law he was on was immaterial. His jones for excitement was being satisfied.

F I V E

Football saved me from what was left of the summer. After Dad talked to me and Joe out by the phone booth in the woods, things felt awfully shaky. We didn't know what was going to happen, how soon or anything. Nothing was supposed to happen right away, but Dad was going to an awful lot of meetings in New York. I guess he was getting ready to wear a tape recorder and tape people for the government. Joe and I pretended we didn't notice so Mom wouldn't know we knew. I couldn't talk to Linda either. It was just me and Joe with each other to talk to and nothing to say, only questions to ask. Joe went out to the International Karting Federation Grand Nationals in Quincy, Illinois, with great hopes, but he drove desperately and crashed. He tried too hard because he was grabbing at the shadow of his life as it went by. Ask him and he'd tell you, yeah, I was gonna do better than my brother but they took that away from me. He was just starting to get out from under my reputation when everything went into changes on him. It was just, you know, confusion. Like you didn't know how much of your life you had left.

Football practice started the third week of August. For a week we worked out on the freshman field below the school. The moisture rose from Basher Kill, the river that ran past the school toward the Delaware; the humidity crossed the tree line at the river's edge and covered the practice field like a blanket. Sweating through the light workouts was torture, but I liked it. The sweat drowned my worry and confusion.

Football has always been practical with me. It's fun to score touchdowns and win, but really, I play because it has always made things easier. It helps me talk to people and make friends. And now the practices were an obstacle to push against, something I didn't have to think about but just do.

*I wasn't even going to play when we first moved to Port Jervis,
but when we got up there and started building our house out of this
old barn, Dad hired a contractor named Jim Van Horn, who was an
old-timer around Port and his kid Tommy was playing and he told
me about the games and stuff and all the tradition. Like they had
won all these championships. He kind of talked me into it, so I said,
"All right, I'll play." I figured it would be a good way to meet some
friends before school started, so at least when I pulled up to school
I'd know somebody.*

*Brian Seeber was the freshman coach who changed me from a
quarterback to a running back. That was one of the first times I knew
of where my dad lost an argument. Coach Seeber was a short, stocky
guy with a big head, like Mr. Potato Head. The story was that when
he played football at Port Jervis, they had to send off for a larger
helmet for him, but he was a High School All-American at guard,
and a Little All-American when he played in college at Moravian in
Bethlehem, Pennsylvania. And the thing was that big head was full
of football.*

*He said to my dad one day after freshman practice, "I think
Sal's going to turn out to be a running back."*

*Dad said, "What are you talking about? He's always been a
quarterback."*

Coach said, "He's got better potential as a running back."

*Dad wanted to know why and Coach said, "All you have to do
is look at him run. When you see those knees pumping up around
his waist you kind of know."*

*Dad said, "We'll see." But once I started running with the
football, there wasn't any more talk about me being a quarterback.*

*At the beginning of the next week, on Sunday afternoon, I
packed a duffel bag for football camp. It was a week-long deal at
Camp McAlister, a YMCA camp a few miles up the mountain from
Hugenot, which was a little bump in the road between Cuddebackville
and Port Jervis. The other kids rode up in a bus, but I didn't take
it for some reason, and Dad drove me in the Jeep. On the way there,
he said, "Sal, son, I know you're looking for a reason to be motivated
this year. All I can tell you is, whatever you do is going to pay off.
We may not be here and we may not be Polisis, but what you do*

here is going to follow you anyway. You've got to remember that and play like it."

He could do that, just go on like nothing ever happened. Like he wasn't attached to anything. I didn't understand how he could do that. Of course, he was looking at leaving a prison sentence and I was leaving a girlfriend and a football career. I said, "How am I supposed to do that?"

"I can't tell you that, son." He shifted into second for the slow climb around a switchback curve. The trees at the roadside were dusty from the passage of cars; they seemed heavy and weary of summer. "All I can tell you is it's going to work out and we're all going to be better for it. You just have to believe that, and don't let down your effort."

He could do it, I guess, because it was the only choice he had.

We pulled into the YMCA campgrounds. There were three camps there. Dad followed the long road around to the big field before you got to the Camp McAlister cabins. The coaches were standing around in a knot directing players to their cabins and sorting out equipment. We had a new varsity head coach this year, Bob Corvino. Coach Viglione had retired after last year's championship season, even though all the sportswriters went on about how Charlie Wilkerson and I must have made it hard for him to call it quits. Charlie was this black kid who ran like a fish swims; I mean, he was fast and smooth, and a darter. Sometimes it didn't hardly look like Charlie was running at all, but gliding. He was that smooth. We were bad in the backfield together; he gained over a thousand yards the year before, to my eight hundred some. Al DeSantis at the Middletown Times Herald Record wrote that if he were Coach Viglione and he had two sophomore backs like me and Charlie, he'd put off retirement until we graduated. But he went ahead and retired.

Coach Corvino saw me getting out of the Jeep and walked over and shook my hand. "Hi, Sal," he said. At the same time he looked over my shoulder and he got this pained look underneath his smile like he was going to have to do something unpleasant. He moved around me and said, "Hi, Mr. Polisi, how are you doing? Good to see you. Say, you know, we try to keep this just to players and coaches. As much as possible, you know, so . . ."

I turned around and there was Dad, smiling, head cocked a little, so cordial he was threatening. He was a cheerleader, and he was accustomed to being a part of the team and its fortunes. He got along great with the guys on the team; they all liked him, and the year before we had them up at the house a lot, for barbecues and things like that. But you could see Coach Corvino didn't want a drug dealer hanging around his kids.

"Yeah, Coach, fine. How you doin'?" Dad looked around to see what was happening. He didn't look like he was going anywhere. I looked at him, like begging. He just kept looking around.

After a few seconds that felt like a few minutes, he turned back to the coach and said, "Don't worry, I'm not staying."

"It's just a rule," said Coach Corvino, "for everybody."

"I know," said Dad. "Listen. You've got a great team this year with Charlie and Sal. They're gonna do great. Sal, have a good camp and work with the coaches. I gotta go."

He turned when he got to the Jeep and called, "Hey, Coach, the kid's been lifting. He's stronger than ever." Then he waved goodbye. A dust cloud trailed him out of sight.

Coach said, "Sal, I just want you to know that whatever happens with your dad, it won't affect you in any way."

I knew what he was saying, that it wouldn't make any difference in the way he and the other coaches treated me, but for a second there I almost got hysterical with the sudden, sharp awareness of my secret. I just said, "Thanks, Coach," and lifted my duffel bag and headed down toward the cabin he pointed out to me.

Charlie was in there already, lounging on a bunk and listening to the Fat Boys rapping on his blaster. He looked up when I came in and said, "Hey, roommate." I gave him five and took the bunk next to his.

We were tight, me and Charlie. When we lived in Ozone Park I hated blacks. We called them niggers. If niggers came into Ozone Park, it was like an invasion into our neighborhood, and we'd go out looking for niggers to beat up. They weren't supposed to be there.

In Port Jervis everything was different. It seemed like people respected each other more up there, and Charlie and I became best friends. *Maybe it was because we both were sophomores on the varsity, or more likely because his father had had some trouble, too. Some kind of thing, I don't know. Whatever, we hung out together around Brother Bruno's there and over in Matamoras, the town across the river in Pennsylvania, at the skating rink, and we got tight.*

"Your dad bring you up?" *he said.*

"Yeah."

"What did Coach say?"

"Nothing. Just, you know, that it was just players and coaches. *I don't think he wanted him to hang around."*

"I like your dad. Big Saalll," *he said, drawing the word out.* Sometimes when we were together Dad was Big Sal and I was Little Sal.

"Yeah. You can understand it, though."

"I guess. Anybody give you any grief last week?"

"Naw."

"Well, that's great, then," *Charlie said. He jumped off the bunk and started jiving around the room to the rap sounds. He stopped in the middle of the room, stood in one place and shook in time with the music. He closed his eyes and stood there jerking to the rhythm and then he opened his eyes and rapped,*

"Season comes, we'll be on the run,

"We'll be outta sight, gonna do it right,

"So when you see the Raiders, say 'see you later,'

"Cause we'll be the champs . . ."

His voice faded as he searched for a rhyme.

"If we don't get cramps," *I added.*

"Yeah," *he said.* "Did you like that? I just made it up."

"No kidding," *I said.* "You oughta stick with 'Break My Stride.'" *That was this Matthew Wilder song we liked,* "Never Gonna Break My Stride," *or something. We thought it had a special message for us football running backs. I started to sing it, but Charlie broke in.*

"Hey, cut me some slack, man. Anyway, it's gonna be a good season. I can feel it. You're up for it, right?"

"Yeah," I said. And I was. I knew if I could concentrate on football I could forget the confusion, forget what Dad said might happen to us.

For the next week we woke up every morning at five and gathered on the field at five-thirty for our first workout of the day. We did our heavy running then, in the cool of early morning, wearing just helmets, shoes, shorts and T-shirts. We practiced the techniques that would become second nature during the season: stances, starts, ball handling, punting, receiving, all the little skills that are supposed to look easy when you do them right. Doing them, with the coaches barking out cadence, was a comfort. Concentration was a comfort. You wouldn't think a little thing like the three-point stance would take much concentration, but I concentrated on it, the dig of my knuckles in the grass, the lay of my left arm above my knee, the bent knees, the crouch, ready to burst out of the crouch and block or fold the ball into my arms. I was glad to have a routine to follow.

My time in the forty was second fastest in the camp. Charlie's was first.

At ten, after breakfast and a rest, we had full-uniform drills. The first pair of shoulder pads I got was too small and I had to go back and get a larger pair. I guess from lifting weights. Everything else fit. It was modern armor: the shoulder pads, the thigh pads that went inside your pants, the hip pads like a second pair of shorts, the dense neoprene Donzi pads that covered your kidneys. It was just to get used to wearing it again. We weren't doing any contact drills, just going through our plays while the holes in the line opened like magic, the way they were supposed to in preseason. In a real game, the holes wouldn't always open and everything that wasn't padded would get hurt.

We had our third and last workout of the day at two, after lunch and another rest. We put on shoulder pads and jerseys for this one, and then just shorts and shoes and helmets, and ran through plays again. At the end of it we changed and hit the lake, yelling and splashing. The cool water was like heaven.

I was toweling off after swimming one afternoon when I overheard two coaches talking.

"Sal's working really hard," one of them said.

"Kid's got a great work ethic. He's not letting this thing with his dad bother him at all," said the other.

"That's something, isn't it? And you know the old man's gonna do hard time, if what you read is true."

They started moving away and I just heard the second say, "It's really too bad about the family . . ."

At night after dinner we stayed in the big rambling dining hall for chalk talk. We took our playbooks and followed along and by the time it was over at eight-thirty you'd see a lot of yawns. And when the coaches called lights out at nine-thirty, I usually was ready to sleep.

Until the night Linda came up. There were three of us, actually, whose girlfriends got together and said they'd come up and meet us after lights out. On Friday night, our last night at camp before we scrimmaged and broke camp, I went to bed and lay in the dark with my eyes open until the lights had been out about fifteen minutes. Then I rolled out of bed and got dressed.

"Yo, Sal, sneakin' out to meet Linda?" It was Charlie, whispering, but loud. Everybody knew there were girlfriends coming up. Keeping a secret at football camp was harder than finding a dry jockstrap.

"God, Charlie, shut up," I whispered back. The cabins just had screens. I was afraid one of the coaches might be walking by and hear him.

The guy in the bunk over mine started snickering and said something obscene, so I said, "Hey, fuck you, all right? Just somebody answer for me if the coaches do a bed check." I slipped out the front and closed the screen door of the cabin carefully behind me.

From the front of the cabin I could see moonlight reflecting off the lake. There were a few dim lights high in the trees. The row of cabins along the path toward the road from the camp entrance was dark, but you could hear muffled voices. While I stood there I heard a humongous fart in the second cabin over and an explosion of protests and laughter. I turned up between the cabins and took the shortest route to the road.

Darren and Jeff were ahead of me, slipping along the high side of the road staying close to the trees. I followed them. When we got to the practice field we ran across the open space, and at the far end the girls stepped out of the shadows, startling us. Linda was with Donna, Darren's girl, who I'd been hot to date until I fell for Linda, and Jeff's girl, Sheila. It was Sheila's brother Sean who dropped them off.

We all stood around talking for a while, enjoying the summer night and the sense of adventure for sneaking out after lights out. Then we drifted a little way into the woods, just innocent, you know, kissing and stuff.

"Did you miss me?" I asked Linda.

"You know I did."

We found an open spot where we could sit under the canopy of trees, and we maneuvered to put our arms around each other. "How's the camp going?" she said.

"Pretty good. I got the second fastest time in the forty."

"Who was first?"

"Who do you think? Charlie."

"Who else?" she said. "How do you feel about the season?"

I knew she was asking me about my dad, how that would affect me. Everybody just assumed that he would go to prison, I guess. I wanted so badly to tell her, but I wanted not to tell her, too, because if she thought I was going away why would she want to see me anymore? If I had to worry about something, it was better to let everybody think I was worried about my dad going away instead of him working for the government and the whole family having to leave. Or him getting whacked, whatever.

"I'm not worrying about my dad, if that's what you mean," I said. "I mean, I'm worrying about him, but I'm concentrating pretty good. I heard a coach say the other day I've got a good work ethic."

"Mmmm, do you have a good play ethic, too?" The moon shone down through the trees and lit her blond hair and we didn't speak for several minutes. Then she was saying frantically into my ear, "Sal, what's that?"

I looked up to see the beam of a flashlight darting across the practice field. It reached the edge of the woods and started in. The

*light bounced back off a tree trunk and I saw it was Coach Seeber,
short and bulky. We froze, holding each other. He kept poking around
with his beam and then moved in the other direction. From behind
us you could hear some crashing and twigs snapping and then a sort
of clunk and somebody said, "Shit!" in a loud whisper. Then there
was a sound of footsteps running along the road in the direction of
the cabins. The flashlight moved in that direction, too.*

"I'd better get back," I said reluctantly.

"I know."

*We stood up and came cautiously out of the woods. The other
two girls were standing in the shadows and I caught sight of Jeff and
Darren tailing along the edge of the woods back toward the camp.
One of them was limping and hopping on one foot, but staying ahead
of the flashlight.*

*"What happened?" I asked. That would be a kick in the butt,
somebody's off to meet his girlfriend in the woods and he gets hurt
and can't play ball.*

*"Darren ran into a log and hit his shin. Did you hear him say
'Oh, shit'?" Donna and Sheila started giggling.*

"I think I heard him hit the log," I said.

*"You better hurry, Sal," Donna said. "We heard the coach say
they're gonna do a bed check."*

"Okay." I kissed Linda. "See you at the parade, okay?"

*She said, "Okay," and I ran back toward the cabins. I got to
the door and inside just before a group of coaches came out of the
cabin next door and headed toward ours. I didn't even have time to
take my shoes off, just jumped into the bed. When they opened the
door and shone the flashlight around our end of the cabin all four
beds were occupied, but later, when I took my shoes off and went
to bed for real, I didn't need the leaves and dirt that were in there
with me from my shoes.*

*I was trying to brush them out when Charlie said, "I saw you
coming down the hill, man. Best run you ever made."*

I threw a shoe at him and went to sleep.

*We scrimmaged the next morning and broke camp. We had to
leave early because the football team was marching in the Banach*

parade that afternoon. Ed and Lou Banach were two kids from Port Jervis who were on the 1984 Olympic wrestling team, and they both won gold medals. Ed won at 198 pounds and Lou was the gold medalist at 220. Port Jervis was holding a parade to honor the Banachs on September first.

Down in the town, banners hung between the streetlamps and red, white and blue bunting decorated the shop windows. You could feel the pride in the air. The Banachs were twins, adopted and raised by a family in Port Jervis from the time they were four. Now the town was congratulating itself for being a place where kids could grow up strong and do right. It was being repaid.

I was with the team, milling around near where the parade was going to start, when I saw Dad talking to Skip Leon.

Skip was in his twenties, the sports editor and -writer—actually, he was the whole sports department—at the Tri-State Gazette. He'd stopped by a freshman game one day when I was playing and after I came onto the varsity and started doing good, he liked to tell people he wasn't surprised because he'd discovered me. I walked over to say hello.

Dad was saying, ". . . hope you won't let this problem I'm having affect your coverage of the kid."

"Look, I'm a sportswriter," Skip said. "I'm not covering you, I'm covering him. What he does he gets credit for, and it won't have anything to do with you."

"Well, that's great. I think he's gonna have a great year." He noticed me next to his elbow. "Aren't you, son? Tell him about your speed at camp. Sal and Charlie had the top two times in the forty. They should have a year. I look for an undefeated season."

I said hello to Skip. He said, "I talked to Coach Corvino. He said you and Charlie looked pretty good at camp. You know he'd love a championship his first year."

Dad wandered off, and Skip said, "Your dad's worried I might not treat you fairly. Don't worry. The thing with him, it won't have any effect on you."

There it was again. And again I felt like, oh, yeah? Hide and watch. But at the same time, even though Dad was going to a lot of

meetings, our lives had regained a routine. Things were the same as
they had been. Maybe they really wouldn't change.

We wore our football jerseys and jeans or whatever for the
parade, and we marched right behind the red convertible that carried
the Banachs. There were bands and floats; the Deer Park Lions Club
was throwing candy to the crowd. People all along the route were
cheering and waving American flags. I felt lifted by their spirits.
Life seemed fine then, bright and indeed unchanging, with Dad at
home and things real nice with Linda and school starting the following
week and all that and the season to anticipate.

• • •

At the beginning of the second week of September, McDonald
went to see Raymond Dearie on the fifth floor of the federal building
on Cadman Plaza, in the wing opposite the Strike Force offices. His
footsteps clicking through the marble halls punctuated the arguments
he was going over in his mind: since the Brennan case had started
in his office, and since Polisi had reached out to him through Limbach, it was reasonable that the Brennan case be returned to the
Strike Force.

McDonald also knew not to underestimate the power of the U.S.
attorney for the Eastern District of New York.

Dearie waved McDonald to a seat. Dearie himself remained
standing. He had a chronic back problem, and he walked around to
keep his back from stiffening.

"I've talked to this guy," McDonald said. "He asked for me
when he was in jail and I've had a chance to meet him and we get
along real well together. I think he trusts me. I've evaluated him and
I think he's got the potential to be a great, really great undercover
operative. I mean, he's one slick piece of work; he's a fast talker,
he could sell a Honda to Lee Iacocca. We were on our guard every
time we talked to him, and he's bright, he's clever, he's manipulative.
I haven't seen too many guys like him from the wiseguy life. We
could put together major cases with him."

Dearie was prowling around the office, keeping his back loose,
and he picked up a putter to address a golf ball lying on the carpet.

"So since the Brennan case really started in the Strike Force, and since this guy came to me and I get along with him . . ."

Dearie was bent over the golf ball, lining up his putt. He stopped on the backswing and turned to McDonald. With his head bent in the putting stance, he looked as if he were playing peekaboo over his shoulder. He said, "Don't even think about it."

McDonald resigned himself to losing the Brennan case to Dearie's office and Ethan Levin-Epstein. He put on hold his dream of running a storefront sting with Sal. If only Sal could make the Brennan case without being exposed.

Sal adjusted the elastic bellyband, bringing the pocket that contained the slim Nagra tape recorder to the front.

"Put it in back," Russo said. "Most people put it in the back."

"You don't know this guy," Sal said. "Coiro's a guy who likes to slap you on the back. He likes to hug you. He's very touchy-feely. I know he ain't gonna hug my balls, so I want it in the front."

The pocket that contained the recorder hung directly against Sal's pubic hair, its lower edge at the base of his penis. It gave him an electric feeling that was almost sexual. He pulled his pants on before he rose in an erection. Fastening his pants was an event that happened in the shadow of his stomach; he had gained weight during his three months in jail and his forty-four days of freedom, time without exercise and lately with Rose Marie's cooking; he was pushing two hundred pounds. Russo looked at Sal's profile and said, "It'll be out of the rain there, too."

"Hey, you got a big tool, you want a big tool shed to keep it under," Sal replied.

The slender wires ran out of the top of his pants, up his sides and down the insides of his arms where they ended in tiny microphones at each wrist. Although it was September 13 and still warm, Sal pulled a sweatshirt on over the aggregation of equipment. He put a jacket on on top of that. He felt like one of the new toys his six-year-old nephew liked so much; what did they call them? Transformers. That was what he was, a battle toy. With the thought, he caught the excitement of what he was about to do, the same excitement he had felt lying in wait for a truck to hijack, or a loan customer to discipline.

Rose Marie was waiting in the car. She had refused to come into the room at the Viscount Hotel near Kennedy Airport where Sal had arranged to meet Russo, Limbach and Kelly at seven-thirty that morning. Now the three agents climbed into a surveillance van and Sal rejoined Rose Marie for the drive to a meeting with Attorney Michael Coiro. Russo reasoned that if Coiro, as Sal claimed, had gotten to Brennan on Sal's auto fraud case, he could make the connection now.

They reached the rendezvous, the Forge Diner on Queens Boulevard, and Sal said to Rose Marie, "You coming in?"

"I can't."

"Give me a break. What am I gonna tell Mike, that we drove all the way from upstate down here and now you like being in the car so much you just want to stay here?"

"Tell him we had an argument. I'm not coming in."

Sal met Coiro outside the diner, and the lawyer, a short, energetic man who reminded Sal of Phil Rizzuto, engulfed him in a hug. Sal was glad he wore the tape recorder in the front. It was like carrying a gun; at first you think everybody notices the bulge.

"How are you, general?" Coiro said when they had gone inside. It was his standard greeting. "Aren't you a little warm? Whaddayou think this is, wintertime? Whyn't you take that jacket off?"

What a joke, Sal thought. The general's in the van. He took the jacket off gingerly, and hung it on his chair. He started talking to Coiro about his drug case, and how he hoped to get to Brennan. Gradually, as it was when he was carrying a gun, he forgot the wires taped to his body and his arms and the microphones above his wrists under the fabric of his sweatshirt.

Rose Marie could never forget that Sal was wired. She resented with all her heart the incubus below her husband's belt. She tried to imagine the tape recorder, and all she could see was an ember burning red and evil deep within her family, burning away at the life she had known, gradually consuming it. Knowing—even vaguely so she could maintain her self-respect—that he had made his living as a criminal was somehow better than knowing he was living a false life. For one thing she had no one with whom to share the knowledge. Not her sons, because she believed they didn't know; certainly not her family; not her friends in Port Jervis, like the Parkers. She felt terribly alone.

She had begun work the previous spring at Something New, a popular bridal and gift shop in Port Jervis, owned by Arlene Parker and run by Mrs. Parker and her older daughter Dale. After Sal was arrested, Arlene had phoned her and through her sobs Rose Marie had understood that Arlene was offering her comfort. Then after Sal was released from Rikers Island, the Parkers had invited the Polisis to their home for lunch and Rose Marie had been grateful for the support for her the gesture showed. The fact was, the Parkers admired the Polisis as a family; the younger daughter, Jill, was a classmate of Sal junior's and also a Red Raider cheerleader; he had dated her briefly before going steady with Linda. Even Sal's arrest could not undo the Parkers' warmth for Rose Marie, and they treated her like one of their own; when Dale and Jill squabbled after long hours in the store, Rose Marie was always the one to smooth the waters.

Her job at Something New was one of Rose Marie's anchors, just one of the things Sal's role as an undercover informant threatened. Each time Sal met his agent contacts at some motel or other to be outfitted with the tiny Nagra recorder or the insidious T-4 transmitter that allowed agents inside a surveillance van to monitor and record his conversations, she felt not only fear of discovery but threatened with an end to her stability.

There were so many meetings. Agent Dan Russo's spiral notebook contained entries for September 20, 24, 25, 26 and 27. One Monday morning Rose Marie drove Sal to Eisenhower Park near Westbury, Long Island, where Russo and Limbach outfitted him with the tape recorder, then to Coiro's home on the South Shore.

Rose Marie again waited in the car. "I can't do it," she said this time, not angry but afraid. "I'll blow it. Make an excuse."

Sal rang the bell. As Rose Marie watched from the street, Coiro answered the door accompanied by his dog. The dog sniffed Sal suspiciously right where the tape recorder hung, and started barking furiously.

Coiro's wife Stephanie wanted to know why Rose Marie wouldn't come in.

Another argument, Sal said. "She's just going nuts about this case, nagging me. She's driving me crazy. I'm telling her Mike'll handle it, she's worrying anyway. I can't even get no sleep at night."

Rose Marie resented Sal's ability to act. Here she was falling apart, a nervous wreck, down to 120 now with all her smoking, skin and bones, and Sal was getting pleasure out of wearing the wire, feeling the excitement, like he was going out to hold somebody up and knew he would get away with it. When he came out of Coiro's house he would be bubbly and happy-go-lucky, just like when he robbed somebody and came home afterward, flush with the thrill of it, and she was getting sicker and sicker with worry.

Sal's meetings with Coiro were not producing "smoking gun"–type evidence. But there did seem to be a slow, accumulating drip. Coiro was under indictment for obstruction of justice, but he suggested that he could handle Sal's case. All he had to do was get it into Brennan's court. But the drug case remained in the court of Justice Seymour Rotker, who showed no signs either of giving up the case or of being lenient. Meanwhile, Tony Capetola was still Sal's attorney of record. He had been associated with Coiro in the past. The agents began pressing Sal to make a secret tape with Capetola, in hopes of gaining information against Coiro. Capetola was dating Sal's sister-in-law, Gina.

Meanwhile, Sal kept asking his federal contacts, "What's happening with my case? How are you going to work this out?" Finally, Raymond Dearie met with Queens District Attorney John Santucci. They met twice over meals, first at Prudente's in Long Island City, for the second time at the Triangle Hofbrau closer to the heart of Queens in Richmond Hill. Ed McDonald, who attended both meetings, recalled that Santucci picked up the first check, Dearie the second. After that, Santucci agreed to give up Polisi to the feds. He would dismiss the drug charges against Sal, while federal charges were lodged in their place. For the time being, however, the Queens

drug case would remain active as a route to Brennan. Sal got the
better end of the deal; the federal charges would carry a maximum
sentence of three to fifteen years in prison compared with the twenty-
five to life he faced in Queens.

For Rose Marie, the worst day was October third.
She normally looked forward to family events. This was an
especially happy occasion, for her nephew Albert, Gina's son, was
celebrating his seventh birthday. She and Sal doted on the handsome
little boy, who had his mother's good looks and a cheerful, outgoing
personality. When Albert was three, Sal had spent a thousand dollars
to buy the boy a bed in the shape of a race car, an extravagant gift.
But Sal had owned the jewelry stores and auto chop shops then; he
wasn't surviving on government handouts and trying to repay shylock
loans. This year's gift was a more modest ski jacket.
"It's like . . . it's like the Trojan horse," Rose Marie said. "I
don't know what it's like. I can't believe you're doing this." She
tightened the belt of her dress and turned sideways to look in the
mirror. She tugged at the fabric bunched around the belt. "Oh, God,
nothing fits anymore. I can't believe you're doing this," she said
again. "It's really . . ." Words failed her, as they often did, and she
went on. "Anything could happen. My God, what if there's, I don't
know, feedback or something?"
They were in the bedroom of Gina's apartment on the Queens
side of the Whitestone Bridge. Muffled conversation filtered through
the door. Outside in the living room, Phyllis Noto, Gina and her
brother Leonard, and Sal junior and Joe waited for Sal and Rose
Marie to return so Albert could open his presents. Old man Leonard
Noto had stayed home, but Tony Capetola had come to the party.
He was not only dating Gina; to add to the fun Capetola also was
celebrating a birthday. He was the person Sal was really there to
see.
Rose Marie had arrived at the party with the boys. Sal had
driven down alone in order to meet Limbach and Dan Russo in the
ATF surveillance van. Parked at Francis Lewis Park at the foot of
the bridge, they had rigged him for sound and sent him into the
bosom of his family.

All of a sudden there was a banging at the door. Albert cried, "Come *on*, Aunt Rose Marie and Uncle Sal. Come *on*."

"Keep your pants on, Albert," Sal called.

"You're crazy, Uncle Sal," he answered. His voice retreated toward the living room.

"There's no way that can happen. Don't be fucking paranoid," Sal said harshly. He opened his pants and reached inside to shift the recorder in its pouch. He zipped up hurriedly and pulled his baggy sweatshirt down over his waistband. That was all he wore anymore, sweatshirts.

"How do you know?" she demanded. "You don't know how those things work?"

"I do know how they work, and that can't happen."

"You're recording my whole family," she whispered. "It's not decent."

Sal laughed. "Not decent? My whole fucking life has been indecent. You think I give a shit about making a little recording in your sister's living room? Forgetaboutit." He stuck a hand in her face. "I'm recording you, too. Talk into the microphone," he hissed. "Look, something could happen here with Capetola. Maybe he'll say something about Coiro. Hell, maybe he can get to Brennan, or fix my case somehow. Then we're getting somewhere. So far we're going nowhere and this case is getting old."

"I don't know why you can't go to his office."

"I've been to his office. He won't be on his guard here. He's among friends."

"He won't think so when you tell him you're switching to Mike Coiro."

"No, he's gonna be pissed off. That's when he might say something. So just relax and let it flow. Don't even think about it. Nothing's going to happen. Ready?"

Sal opened the door and he and Rose Marie walked into the living room. Rose Marie relaxed as the little party went into full swing. Capetola seemed to like the desk statue of a horse she'd bought for him; he had just begun investing in racehorses with a partner. When Albert started tearing the wrappers off his presents, Rose Marie watched him indulgently. "Oh, boy," he cried, looking down into wrapping paper at a box she couldn't see, "walkie-talkies."

Rose Marie felt a cold hand of fear clutch her heart. Little Albert pulled one of the plastic handsets out of the box and turned it on. Nothing happened.

"Wait a minute," his mother said, "I'll get some batteries."

Rose Marie wanted to run after her and throw the batteries away before Albert could get them into his new toy. Surely now there was reason to fear. The walkie-talkies would pick up the conversation Sal's concealed transmitter was sending to the surveillance van. She was convinced of it. They would cause feedback and something on her husband would start screeching. The humiliation would be too much to bear.

Soon Albert and Joe were talking to each other on the walkie-talkies, testing them in different rooms of the apartment.

"What's the matter, Rose Marie?" her mother asked.

"I'm sorry, what?"

"I asked you if you'd serve the coffee."

She was in the kitchen with her mother and her sister, feeling dazed, waiting for the telltale squawk or screech that would reveal her husband as an informant in his own family. She kept listening for snatches of conversation from the living room, where Sal was finally alone with Capetola.

Sal was saying, "You know it can be done. We did it before. Why can't we do it again?" He had learned to throw the softballs up there, big and round.

Capetola wasn't playing. "You did it," he responded, emphasis on "you."

Sal kept pushing. "There's somebody else involved, I think can help me."

Capetola said he thought switching lawyers wasn't such a good idea. "I know all the games," he said. "I know all the angles. Things don't work out and this guy turns out not being able to help you, you're going to be left high and dry and I'm not going to come back into it and make a fool of myself."

Then Rose Marie heard Capetola say, "Does Coiro have anything to do with this?"

She edged closer to the door. Sal said, "Yes."

"I think you're a real fucking jerk," said Capetola.

"Why?"

"I just think you are. You and him both." His voice was filled with disgust. Capetola loathed Coiro, who he suspected of undermining him with clients.

His furious entry into the kitchen startled Rose Marie. "Happy birthday," he said. "I'm not Sal's lawyer anymore."

"What do you mean?"

"He wants Coiro."

Gina turned to Rose Marie with a mortified expression. Rose Marie did her best to look surprised and mystified. "I didn't know," she said. Her eyes pleaded with her sister. Gina turned away.

"Nobody knows anything," said Capetola sarcastically.

Sal was saying hurried good-byes. Coming into the kitchen, he said, "Hey, I'm getting outta here. Tony's not too happy with my choice of lawyers. Hey, Tony, happy birthday anyway. Ro, you and the kids stay as long as you want. I'll see you back at home."

Rose Marie was giddy with relief when he left the apartment. She hardly heard the angry accusations that followed Sal's departure. She left the kitchen and found Albert. "Here, Albert," she said, "let me try that walkie-talkie." She found herself talking to Sal junior in the other room. "I think the party's over. Your father told Tony he was getting a new lawyer. So let's get ready to go home. Over and out."

The reply was just a garbled screech. It could have come from anywhere.

SIX

Leonard Noto followed Sal downstairs and caught him as Sal was getting into his car. Leonard was a handsome kid, with light eyes, black curly hair and a beard that, though he shaved every day, made each afternoon look like the next morning on his jaw. Leonard's biggest problem in life was that he idolized his older brother-in-law. When Sal had sold cocaine, Leonard had been one of his dealers. But Leonard had failed to treat drugs strictly as a business; he sniffed up his profits and lately, seemed to Sal always to have the glazed look about him of a cokehead. It was a good thing, Sal thought, the kid didn't like needles. Sal felt no responsibility for Leonard's drug use; hadn't he always told the kid not to mix business with pleasure? When Leonard climbed into the front seat beside him, Sal knew immediately that the twenty-three-year-old had drugs on his mind.

"Hey, listen," Leonard said. "Listen, I heard you tell Tony you were going with Mike Coiro. What are you going to do for money?"

"Well, for starters, I'm selling everything I've got. There's a guy I think wants to buy the racetrack." Sal hoped that would put an end to it.

"Yeah, but then what?" Leonard was sincere, trying to help. "I know this case is gonna cost you serious money. But you know there's serious money to be made out here. I got connections, I can move a lot of powder. With that Colombian connection you got, we can get great stuff for less. We'd make serious profits. What about it?"

Sal felt the tape recorder acutely in his crotch. For the first time he regretted wearing the recorder and transmitter at the family gathering. Leonard was incriminating himself on tape, and the feds were listening.

"Hey, forget about it, Lenny. Look, I gotta go."

"What do you mean, forget about it? This is big profit I'm talking about here. Just get me half a key and I'll do the rest. Or if we can get some good H, I can move that, too."

"No, look, Lenny." Goddamn it, how could he make the kid shut up? He couldn't do anything about the recorder. Even if he could turn it off or pull out the microphone wires, the transmitter would still send the conversation to Russo and Limbach in the surveillance van. He crossed his arms and tried to bury the microphones in his armpits. Maybe it would come out UI, transcript shorthand for unintelligible. "Lenny, I just don't think I need to do that yet."

"Yeah, but . . ."

"But nothing." Sal's mind was racing. Maybe he could get Lenny to back away from incriminating himself. "I thought you were staying away from that shit now. You ought to stay away from it."

"Look, you need the money, right? You got the connection, introduce me to the Colombians. What's the difference? Why not do it?"

Sal remembered the footnote to his Colombian connection: he still owed the men he had met in Washington Heights near the Manhattan side of the George Washington Bridge fifteen thousand for the cocaine he had bought before he got busted. Even if he wanted to, introducing Lenny to the Colombians would be awkward at best.

"No," he said, "I'm selling the racetrack, so the money's gonna come from there. I'm just too hot to fuck with dope no more. The city's got me. The feds are gonna be coming after me. I don't need the aggravation. You don't either. You really ought to give it up. Whyn't you get a job or something?"

Lenny looked at him carefully. His eyes were green, like Rose Marie's, and they had a feverish sparkle even in the dim light that came from a streetlamp half a block away. It had been twilight when the birthday party started. Now it was dark. Lenny said, "This don't sound like you no more. It's like you changed or something."

"Hey, it's all this time I'm looking at, twenty-five to life, it scares me. I'm trying to be careful." Did the kid suddenly suspect something? "Look, Lenny, I gotta go, okay?" He started the car and shifted into gear. "If I change my mind I'll let you know, okay?" He was pulling out of the parking lot when he stopped and leaned out the window and called back. "Hey, Lenny. Thanks."

Lenny waved him off and walked back toward the building.

Sal pulled into a strip shopping center four blocks away. Metal shutters were pulled down over most of the storefronts. In the light that spilled from the window of a coin laundry, he could see an overflowing trash can dribbling food wrappers onto the sidewalk. The white surveillance van with the dark windows arrived a minute later. Sal knew the agents could see him through the windows of one-way glass. Shit, they could even videotape him if they wanted to, with the little periscope lens concealed within the pop-up vent that rose from the center of the roof. He walked straight to the van without bothering to look around. Limbach was behind the wheel; Russo and the other ATF agent, Kelly, looked up from panels of sophisticated taping gear when Sal climbed into the van.

Sal pulled his sweatshirt off and tugged at the wires leading to the tape recorder. He snatched the transmitter off the small of his back and opened his pants to get at the belt that held the tape recorder. It occurred to him to pull out the cassette and smash it, but the cassette decks in the van already had the conversation from the transmitter.

"I don't know what you're gonna do with that last there," he burst out when the recorder was finally turned off. "That kid's my brother-in-law. I been around him since he's a little kid. I don't want to get him busted. You got to bury this fuckin' tape. You got to leave him alone."

"Relax a little," Russo said.

"Relax, hell."

"Hey, did he say anything about Brennan?" Russo asked.

Sal looked at Limbach to express his impatience with the question. He was still Limbach's source, and Limbach remained the buffer between Sal and the FBI. It was his job to keep Sal happy, and with the program. Limbach was only slightly more comfortable with Russo than Sal was. They were still feeling their way in the relationship.

"Did he say anything about Brennan?" Russo asked again.

"I don't think so." Sal spaced the words sarcastically. Kelly coughed politely.

"Okay, then," Russo said.

"What the fuck does that mean?"

"It means I didn't hear much we could use."

"Is that a promise?"

"As much of a promise as I'm allowed to make." It was important to the Brennan case to keep Sal happy, but Russo also knew that he would use the tape in a second to squeeze Leonard if he had to. He didn't think he'd have to, but he would.

Sal bunched up the wires and recording gear and plopped them onto a console in the back of the van. "I'm going home," he said. He felt drained. His plan to tell the feds about fixing cases and committing crimes and then go away to a new existence had gone wrong. He didn't know quite how, only that he had not planned on getting evidence against Leonard down on tape. The kid was like his little brother; the only other brother he had had was dead. He'd coached Leonard at football before Sal junior had been old enough to play. Now he wondered if, one way or another, he hadn't ruined him.

• • •

By Albert's birthday Port Jervis had a two and one record.

In our first game against Valley Central over in Montgomery, near West Point on the Hudson River, Charlie was just untouchable. He carried the ball thirteen times, gained almost 150 yards and scored three touchdowns. I gained 98 yards on twelve carries and scored the other TD, the defense was awesome and we won 27 zip.

No big deal. Coach said things went according to plan and Cha and I "did just what was expected."

The next week we busted Middletown 26 to 7. They were the only team to beat us in 1983, and beating them it looked like we were rolling. I ran for 131 yards and scored two touchdowns, and picked up an interception on defense. Cha had two interceptions and ran for 109. You could have driven a truck through the holes our linemen opened up for us.

Beating Middletown was the next best thing to winning the Orange County League championship. There was a prize that had been around about a hundred years, this bell called the Erie Bell from a canal boat, or maybe an engine from the old Erie & Lackawanna Railroad. Like a lot of places Port used to be a railroad town.

Anyway, winning meant we got it back. A bunch of us painted that sucker a nice, bright, Red Raider red inside, so that the next time Middletown got it back they'd know who had it last. And all the next week I couldn't help but put my number—23—down in all the notes I wrote to Linda when I should have been paying attention in trigonometry.

We let down against Washingtonville a week later. The Wizards were a team we should have beaten. Charlie got almost ninety yards, and I scored our only touchdown on a forty-six-yard run, but after that their defense tightened up and held us to seven yards in the second half. We kept turning the ball over and finally got beat on a last-minute field goal, 9 to 6. I guess we were flat after beating Middletown.

The bruises were still tender on my back and shoulders when we went down to Gina's for the birthday party. Sometimes, at home after a game, Mom would make me take my shirt off so she could put alcohol or Heet ointment on the places where I'd taken hits. She could identify each bruise and scrape with a play of the game. "Oh, my God, Sal," she would say, "that's an awful bruise on your side here. Can you feel it?" Her fingers would be pressing gently, and I would try not to wince. "That must have been where their linebacker hit you and knocked you out of bounds. In the second quarter there." It was these sessions that made Joe start saying he wanted to play defense. "I'd rather hit than be hit," he would say.

We didn't stay long after Dad walked out of the birthday party after arguing with Mr. Capetola. Dad was the one everybody blamed. Little Albert couldn't understand why his party was all of a sudden over. I hated to leave him there with nobody to talk to on his walkie-talkie, but the accusations were getting pretty strong about Dad going back with Mike Coiro. Grandma Noto and Gina and Mr. Capetola were talking about how Dad was going to try to fix the case and it was going to backfire and be worse than ever and what a jerk he was. Mom had been acting nervous all night anyway. The last thing my mom would ever do is be not nice to somebody. At first she was all apologetic about Dad firing Mr. Capetola, but after a while she got insulted. That was when we left.

She slammed the car door and sat there for a minute just gripping the steering wheel and staring straight ahead. "Come on, Mom, let's go," Joe finally said.

She started up and we rode in silence across the Whitestone Bridge and halfway across the Bronx before she said, "It makes me so mad."

Joe and I were so glad to hear her speak we both said, "What, Mom?"

"Your father has this case hanging over his head and everybody blames him for wanting to switch lawyers."

"Why'd he do that, anyway?" I asked.

"It didn't have anything to do with Mr. Capetola. He just thought it would be better." She groped around on the dashboard and pushed in the lighter, then started feeling in her purse for the cigarette pack.

"That's passive smoke, Ma. You're gonna kill us," Joe said. His health class had been studying smoking. Mom ignored him and lit up. Joe rolled his back window down as far as it would go and the air roared in, pungent with road fumes. She raised her voice a little.

"Your father's just doing what he has to do. I don't see why everybody has to be so nasty."

Something struck me about what she said. Back at Gina's Mom acted like she didn't know what was going on, and now she did. I thought all of a sudden maybe Dad was doing undercover work on Mr. Capetola, and Mom knew it and couldn't say anything. For the government to make you wire up on your own family, that was pretty sad. The government was sure acting like it could make Dad do anything it wanted, just make him go out and do stuff. He didn't seem to mind, though. Maybe he got off on it. Maybe he didn't even care.

We played at home the following Monday afternoon. It was a holiday, Columbus Day. Normally we played on Saturdays. Our home field was about half a mile from the school, closer to downtown Port Jervis, between two rows of pine trees. Glennette Field. You could get, I don't know, maybe a thousand people in the bleachers. It was like, very small town, very American. I mean, you could smell burning leaves it seemed like every time we played a game there, and through the pines you could see the fall colors on the distant mountainsides.

The Port fans would come early and park together in the parking field, where they'd have their pregame tailgate parties. Then after the game some of the parents would stay around until we showered and changed, and we'd go back over there and resume the party. It was part of the Port Jervis tradition.

Dad wasn't about to let a little thing like his drug arrest interfere with tradition. He was too much of a football fan for that. He and Mom were right there with everybody else, eating cold cuts and potato salad, talking about the team. Some people stayed away from us, on account of the drugs and all. But a lot didn't. They'd figure, hey, the guy had some trouble but he's out here rooting for the team, so he can't be all bad. Mostly the talk was about the team, or about football in general, which were my dad's two favorite subjects. Now and then somebody might ask about his case, in a roundabout way, like, "You doing okay? Everything working out okay down in New York?" He'd say, "Oh, man, forget about all that down there. I was in the wrong parking lot at the definitely wrong time. I got set up. I didn't have nothing to do with that down there. Believe me, it'll all come out in court." That was what people wanted to believe, most of them anyway, so they'd nod and seem real pleased. Maybe if I'd been a scrub they wouldn't have forgiven him so much. But they did for my sake, and Joe's and Mom's.

Not everybody just kissed off his arrest. The Tri-State Gazette one time ran a picture of one of the tailgate parties. Dad was in the shot. He was wearing his big grin, having a good old time. Skip Leon said after it ran that somebody called the paper to complain about them running pictures of drug dealers at our football games.

The Columbus Day game against Monroe-Woodbury was my game to block. My man Charlie was the star. He scored from five yards out in the first quarter. They tied the score at seven in the second, and on our next series Charlie gave the crowd something to remember.

Coach sent in Red One Sprint, a sprint draw play to the weak side. The key is for the tailback to be far enough back to read the blocks and adjust, and Charlie could adjust like a rabbit. He took the handoff. I went through right tackle with him behind me. He cut to the outside. I stayed between him and the rest of the field and headed downfield with him, looking for somebody to mow down. Finally there wasn't anybody left but the strong safety. He had an angle and was coming fast. I saw him shifting his stride a little, thinking about how he was going to get around me and get to Charlie. He just thought too long. When he made his move I aimed my shoulder pad right at his gut and knocked him back about five yards, and when Cha scored it felt almost as good as if I'd done it myself. A sixty-one-yard touchdown. We high-fived it in the end zone.

"Great block, Sal," Coach Corvino said when we got back to the bench.

I heard Mom yelling in the stands. She was up there with the Parkers, jumping up and down and waving a red handkerchief. Up behind her in a corner of the WDLC radio booth, Dad was just taking his eye away from his videotape camera. He'd always videotaped my games, even back in Ozone Park. He would use the tapes to coach with, until the league said it was an unfair advantage and made him stop. Sometimes the Port games were on a little local cable channel, Channel 6. When they weren't, he'd tape them himself. Ralph Zelno, the radio announcer, let him use the booth as long as he stayed quiet. It was difficult for him, being quiet. He was giving me a big thumbs-up sign and just waving and pointing at the camera, like, "I got it. I got the shot."

In the third quarter, Charlie took a pitchout from Mike—Mike Lamoreaux, the quarterback—and headed right again. The Monroe-Woodbury guys are thinking, screw this, this guy ain't gonna break another one. So here they come, up to stop him. And Charlie stops and throws a pass downfield to Jeff Gray who turns it into a seventy-yard touchdown. There wasn't anybody in the same county with him.

We scored one more time and it ended 27 to 7. We were three and one after four, which wasn't where we should have been but where we still could save the season.

There was a lot of shouting and towel snapping in the shower after the game. When we got back to the parking lot, all the parents and the hard-core fans were there, gathered around in a rough circle of cars and pickups, with all the food laid out, Mom's baked lasagna and Mrs. Simmons's knockwurst and German potato salad and thermoses of coffee and hot chocolate.

Linda was there with her parents and her two crazy sisters, who were drinking toasts to Cha's pass and Jeff's catch and my block. I realized all over when I saw her how beautiful she was. She came up and hugged me. "You were wonderful," she said, "even if you didn't score."

I kissed her and pulled her against me and ran my hand down her back and cupped it over one of her cheeks. I used a word I'd heard the teacher use in our art class, talking about the Mona Lisa. "Mmmm," I said, "exquisite." Of course, he hadn't been talking about the Mona Lisa's butt.

She pulled away and said, "Not here in front of everybody."

"Why not?" I said. "Everybody knows we're going out."

"Not everybody thinks we should be going steady."

"Like who?"

"Darren thinks I should go out with other people."

"Other people like him. Who cares what Darren thinks? We're always with him and Donna anyway. And Staci and Marc. I wish we could spend more time together by ourselves."

"Well, don't you want to be around Donna?" she said tartly.

"I stopped thinking of her a long time ago."

"She hasn't stopped thinking about you."

"I don't care what she thinks. I only want you. I'd never do anything like cheat on you. I'd never even think about it. Linda, Linda, I . . . I just want to be alone with you."

"We've been alone," she said. "What about that night at football camp, when we met up on the mountain?"

"That was different. I mean, that was like . . . just making out. Besides, there were six of us. I mean, just spending time with you, without everybody else around." My words were starting to get tangled.

"What's on your mind?" she said. The way she said it, well, it grabbed my heart and twisted it. She gave me a little smile to go with it. "Never mind, I can guess," she said. She tossed her head and her hair caught the late sunlight.

I was helpless. I was in love and I told her so. I blurted it out, "I'm falling in love with you. I mean, I love you. I love being with you. I don't want anybody else but you. I never will."

"Never's a long time."

"I don't care. I want to be with you."

"I want to be with you, too," she said gently. "Soon." She squeezed my hands and I realized they were sweating, and then she gave me a kiss that was hard and soft all at once and over before I wanted it to be. "Let's get back," she said.

We walked back to the group hand in hand. I have never felt better. The soreness of the game descended comfortably upon my body, like if you could wear satisfaction that's what it would feel like. Harold Schoor, this guy who was a great Port Jervis fan and a friend of ours, saw us and walked in our direction. I'd dated his daughter Colleen when we first moved upstate, and his wife Joan and Mom were friends. He said, "Sal, Sal, great game you played today. That was a killer block." He grabbed my hand and shook it. We joined the small crowd standing in the circle of cars, and it was just easy to be there. So easy. It was like being home.

• • •

Sal stopped into Tenke's auto parts and used-car place in Huguenot one morning to pick up a tire, when he heard the worst cracker accent he had ever heard. You could cut it with a knife. He hadn't heard anything like it in a long time. He had to go all the way back to 1963 and Marine boot camp at Parris Island, down in South Carolina where they had this stuff looked like mohair hanging from the trees. What was that fucker's name? The little banty drill sergeant. Striker. D. W. Striker. Yeah, but this guy's accent was even worse than Striker's.

The guy had the original beer gut. It hung out over the waist of his rump-sprung variety-store jeans, which were dark with grease and improbably supported by a pair of narrow hipbones. He was fiftyish with lank gray hair. He was leaning on the counter talking to Tenke, a razor slice of a man with a sharp, pointed face and rotten teeth. They both could have just climbed up out of the grease bay.

Sal walked up and the cracker looked up and down at his wiseguy casuals—his leather jacket, Damon knit shirt, slacks and Gucci loafers. Sal shook his gold bracelet down his wrist. Then he picked at the side of his nose so the cracker could see the diamonds in the bracelet that spelled "Sal." He gave an extra pick in case the cracker hadn't seen his diamond ring. "Yo, Tenke," he said. "Listen, I want to get a spare for that bomb I got from you. I looked and it ain't got no spare." He had bought the car from Tenke knowing it wouldn't last long. It wouldn't have to. They weren't going to be here anyway. It was just something for Sal junior to drive to football practice in the meantime.

"Sure." Tenke jerked his head toward the back of the shop. "Go out back, there's another one out there like it. It's got a spare. Just take it."

Sal tiptoed through the cluttered lot to protect his Guccis until he found a blue Horizon. He opened the hatch and pulled out the worn spare, carried it around to the front of the building, holding it out away from his clothes. Tenke and the cracker were waiting for him. As soon as he stowed the tire they approached.

Tenke said, "Sal, this is a guy you want to meet. Sally Upazz', this here's the Rebel."

The cracker looked at Sal and then at Tenke. "Sally what?" he said.

Sal greeted the man with a curt handshake and went back to wiping his hands on the towel he'd taken from the trunk. "Upazz'," he said.

"What's that mean? That your name? Weird fuckin' name."

"No, man, it's a nickname. It means crazy. U'pazzo. Means 'crazy man' in Italian. Sally U'pazzo. Sally Upazz'. But I'm not so crazy anymore, so most people up here just call me Sal. Polisi."

"Oh, yeah," the cracker said. "Julius Leonard's my real name. They call me the Rebel on account of I come from West Virginia. Been up here now a few years though. Me and m'wife and kids. Talking to Tenke, I thought me 'n' you might have some friends in common."

"You're kidding," said Sal. Not a chance in hell, he thought.

"No. There've been a couple've Italian guys I knew from down around New York. Like Banky Frigente."

Sal couldn't believe his ears. Banky Frigente, the name first thrown at him by the head of the Organized Crime Strike Force for Eastern New York, now by a West Virginia cracker called the Rebel.

"And John Carneglia."

"Jeez, I was in the joint with Carneglia. We were kind of like partners down in Queens. You know him and Banky? That's amazing." Sal didn't mention that Carneglia and a punk named Richie Inguardia had started pressuring him for the fifteen thousand he still owed Carneglia from his cocaine stake the previous November. Since his arrest, he hadn't been able to pay the juice, let alone the principal.

They stood in front of Tenke's and talked for half an hour. They talked subjects both knew well, like hijacking. Sal slowly remembered what he had heard about the man called the Rebel. He had been a switch driver, a guy you'd throw into a truck to drive it off once the up-front guys, the guys like Sal who used the guns, got it under control. Sal was seized with inspiration. "What about guns?" he said. "You know anybody who's got guns up here?"

"I might. Why?" said the Rebel.

"Well, Tenke must of told you about me getting arrested. I know these Colombians, man, they're looking for everything. Guns. Exotic shit. Machine guns, assault rifles, night rifles, laser scopes, you name it. Bombs."

"These fellas, they got money, right?"

"Are you kidding? Coming out the wazoo. They don't care what it takes, long as they can get what they want."

"Say they want bombs?"

"If they can get 'em. They're hard to find."

"Well, some people can make 'em. I made 'em when I was in Korea. Did some demolition over there."

"No kidding," said Sal. "Isn't that something?"

"We should talk some more," the Rebel said. "Come up to the house the next few days, maybe we can do some business."

Sal was trembling with excitement when he was back in the car on his way home. Colombians, he thought. The Colombians who were going to want to know about this were Limbach and Kelly. He drove past the house and went straight to the phone at the campground.

• • •

When we lost to Warwick, Skip Leon wrote, "Inconsistency has been the enemy of the Port Jervis football squad throughout the first half of the season."

We just couldn't get on track. Charlie got our only TD, but it was nothing spectacular like the week before, just a push over from the two in the fourth quarter when it was too late. We each lost a fumble and neither of us gained a hundred yards even though we had a lot of carries. It was Coach Corvino's fifth game, and Port fans were yelling, "Bring back Viglione."

The next week at home, we spotted Goshen sixteen points before Cha broke two touchdowns in the second quarter to wake us up. One was a seventy-one-yard punt return. In the locker room at halftime, Woody and Skin—that is, Darryl Wood and Rich Padgett, who we called Skinhead on account of his haircut—went around quietly pumping people up. They were both seniors, both linemen, both monsters, Woody on defense, Skin on offense, and they were saying, "Get in the game. Get pissed off. Get pissed off. You gotta believe."

Whatever that quiet talking did, it worked. We took the second-half kickoff to our thirty-four. Mike called the "six," which hadn't worked last week, but in the huddle there was this kind of, like, knowledge that wasn't there before, that this time it was going to. It was my play. I took the handoff and broke off left tackle where the line had cleared a path, cut back right and ran.

In memory a run like that is like a dream, in slow motion. The obstacles come at you but it's like they aren't there, you're past them before you even think about it. You're moving like a freight train, passing trees and houses, or maybe the cars on a road running alongside. They're moving, too, but they fade behind you and you enter an open space where you're all alone, running for the joy of it.

In the end zone I gave the ball my little trademark point-down spin before Cha caught up and hoisted me in his arms. My sixty-six-yard touchdown put us on top for good. We scored again on a *pass after their guy shanked a punt, and then we had an interception and I scored for the second time, this time with a twenty-nine-yard run. Same play, the six, off-tackle. Three touchdowns in seven minutes.*

It was just a great half of football, all around. The defense gave up zip in the second half, about fifty, sixty yards. My second-half totals were 143 yards on ten carries, compared with 8 yards on six carries in the first half. Go figure. Anyway, we won 42 to 16.

Mom took a great picture of me breaking a tackle. I wrote on the back, "I love you more than I've ever loved anything in the whole world. I'll love you more and more each day forever and ever," and gave it to Linda.

We won our next three games. I broke a few good runs and scored in every game, and blocked for Charlie who broke more and scored more, living up to the nickname Skip Leon had given him: "Smooth As Silk Wilk." We faced undefeated Marlboro in the last game of the season.

· · ·

The undercarriage of Sal's car kept scraping on the hump between the dirt tracks and he wondered if he would still have a transmission when he made it to the Rebel's. After about a mile, the road opened onto a community of trailers, barking dogs and rusting bikes and cars. He recognized the car he'd seen at Tenke's and pulled in beside it with a snarling cur snapping at his tires.

Julius Leonard emerged from a double-wide trailer set on concrete blocks. Behind him, the November wind whipped shreds of woodsmoke from a toppling stovepipe on the trailer top.

"How y'all doin'?" the Rebel greeted Sal. He was wearing overalls and a pair of stiff-looking work shoes. His moon-shaped face had just been shaved. He smelled of Mennen Skin Bracer and tobacco, and there were stains between his first two fingers where he held a lighted Camel.

"Doin' all right," Sal said, almost imitating the southern mountain accent but stopping himself. "I came up to see the 'merch,' like we talked about."

"Come around back, then." The Rebel led the way around the

trailer to a makeshift garage. Inside were workbenches strewn with tools. Amid ancient pipe wrenches and wood-handled screwdrivers were kitchen pots set on propane hot plates, the water boiled out, leaving white calcium striations. "Got me steam heat in here," Julius said.

He bent down and pulled a bundle wrapped in a white Holiday Inn towel from under a bench. Pushing some tools aside, he set the bundle on a bench top and unwrapped it carefully to reveal a World War II–style hand grenade and three lengths of two-inch galvanized steel pipe, capped at both ends.

"Shit, look at that," said Sal, admiring the pineapple-shaped grenade. He could see John Wayne pulling the pin out with his teeth and lobbing it into a bunker full of gooks. Except it didn't seem to have a pin. "Where d'you get a thing like that?"

"Surplus store," said Julius. "You buy 'em, they're defused and empty, just the shell. Here, feel it. See? It's light. I fill 'em with powder and re-fuse 'em. I can fix that one up, you're interested."

Sal said maybe. "I'll stick to these right now," he said. He picked up a length of the steel pipe and hefted it. It was about ten inches long, and had a satisfying weight. Packed with blasting powder and ignited in any of a variety of ways, a pipe bomb that size was a deadly weapon. The exploding powder would turn the metal casing into shrapnel and its heat would light a fire. It would demolish a car, if you just wanted to send a message. Or put it under the driver's seat and rig it with a pressure switch, if you wanted to kill somebody.

"D'you bring the fuse?" Julius asked.

"Got it right here." Sal fished out a length of fuse he'd bought at a gun shop fifty miles away. "I got a little powder, too, left over from some blasting I did up at the track."

"This should get you fixed right up then," Julius said. "You say you're gonna want all three?"

"Yeah, I'm pretty sure."

"What're they gonna use 'em for?"

"Who knows? Colombians, you figure it. They got all this drug shit going on, they're blowing people up back home. What's the difference?"

Julius rubbed his shiny jaw and his forehead wrinkled in a

frown. After a minute or two he said, "Yeah, it's their business, right? I mean, what the hell. I can fix 'em up in a couple of days. You want 'em Saturday?"

"No, man. I got my kid's last football game of the season to go to Saturday. How's Monday? Thing is, I've gotta have 'em in New York."

"Why's that?" Julius wanted to know.

"Well, for one thing, I ain't got a driver's license, and if I get stopped I'm subject to a search. Other thing is, that's where the customers are, and I got to get the money from them."

"Well, then, I reckon that's no problem. Where you want to meet?"

Julius agreed that his wife and daughter would bring the three pipe bombs to the World's Fair Marina near Shea Stadium in Queens the following Monday.

• • •

The morning of the Marlboro game Dad took me aside for one of his little talks about motivation. It was cold; Thanksgiving was coming up and the red-gold fire of the mountains had faded to the color of a dust ball in the corner. "Hey, son," he said, with the old mail truck parked out front, "let's go chop a little wood."

"Dad," I said, "I gotta protect myself. Did you forget we've got a game today?"

"Come on, it'll loosen you up," he said.

"No, it won't, it'll make me tired and weak."

He laughed. We were playing a game. "Okay," he said, "I'll chop and you watch. That's fair. Then later I'll be watching while you work."

I followed him out the door and almost turned around and went back in, it was that cold. But I climbed into the Jeep and he drove down to the bottom of our land along the river. There were the remnants of a Boy Scout camp on a flat bluff maybe thirty feet above the river, and a tree house Joe and I had built. We had been pulling fallen trees from there and chopping them up for firewood ever since we moved to the racetrack almost three years before. There always seemed to be more. With the leaves off the trees now, you could see the water frothing over the gray rocks of the Neversink. Down below us was a pipe that tapped a spring; there would be ice around its mouth now.

Dad got the ax from the back of the Jeep. I helped him pull a couple of pine logs into the clearing and he took a few halfhearted swipes at them, cutting off the smaller limbs for kindling. Then he laid the ax down and said, "Son, this game today's real important to you."

"I know it is, Dad," I said. "It makes a big difference in our season."

"Aw, forget that, I mean to you. You have a good game today, you could gain a thousand yards for the season. That's going to follow you no matter what happens."

"You mean we're still leaving?" I had almost forgotten. In fact, I had come not to believe it. Part of me didn't want to believe it. And nothing had happened to make a move seem likely. Dad kept going to court, and meetings in New York, and coming home. Like a guy with a new job, not a guy planning to pick up and move. He told me and Joe about some radicals he met, mad bombers he called them, and he was going undercover on them for the government. He was no closer to the judge, though. So things were just going along, and the prospect of leaving seemed remote. If we did leave, I figured it would just be for a while, not forever.

"We're still leaving, son," he said. "I still don't know when. Not tomorrow, or next week. Maybe not for a long time. But if you have a thousand-yard season, that'll be something you'll have with you. And you've got to be motivated to do that no matter where we are next year, no matter how many people know you got those yards. So far you've worked real hard, but I just want you to work extra hard today to get those extra yards."

I was going to have to have one hell of a day to get 1,000 yards. Charlie already had his, but I had about 860, 859 to be exact, and it didn't take Albert Einstein to figure out what it would take to break 1,000. A lot of work. And luck.

I said, "I'll try, Dad. But don't hold your breath. Marlboro isn't Goshen." All of a sudden the gray morning got to me and I felt cold.

"Let's go back," I said. "It's cold, and I've got to be ready to go soon."

Dad threw the ax and the few sticks of kindling into the Jeep. I was getting into the passenger seat when he grabbed my arm and swung me back against the side of the Jeep. He startled me. His eyes were angry. "Don't ever think like that," he said.

"What do you mean?"

"Don't ever think you can't do something. Just go out and do it. Then if you can't, at least it won't be because you quit before you start."

For an instant I hated him. "If we were going to be here next year at least I'd have another chance," I said.

He had only hit me once in his life, once when I had lied to him. He wanted to hit me now, but he didn't. He just said, "Leaving is the only chance we're going to have."

We drove back to the house without talking.

Well, Marlboro wasn't Goshen. It was bitter cold and blustery in Marlboro that afternoon, with the wind coming off the Hudson River. Not that many fans were there. I gained 94 yards on fifteen carries and wound up with 953 for the year. The thing was, I had a 30-yard run called back on a clipping penalty, and a couple more on holding, 50 or 60 yards altogether. So I really had the 1,000. It wasn't all that important since we lost, 22 to 0, the first time we'd been shut out all year.

No. 23. In the locker room afterward, I looked at the soiled jersey in my hands and thought for a moment of hiding it away. If I needed a memory someday I would have it. Just then the student trainer came around, collecting the equipment to load on the bus home. "Good game today, Sal," he called to me. "But they were tough. Hey, throw me your jersey, willya?"

I did, and watched it disappear into the hamper.

SEVEN

Two or three sea gulls wheeled overhead, gray and white as the roiled November sky the Monday before Thanksgiving. Sal could hear their harsh cries when the thunder of the jets subsided between takeoffs from La Guardia Airport a mile away across the water. The few boats that were left at the World's Fair Marina had been mothballed for the winter, their lines neatly coiled and their cabin windows blank. The white van was parked a hundred feet away, inconspicuous among a scattering of cars and an itinerant Airstream trailer huddled in the parking lot.

Sal leaned back against the fender and shoved his hands deeper into his pockets. He thought idly that if he still had his "sporterized" carbine he'd take a shot at one of the gulls. He wondered if the FBI still had the .30-caliber rifle locked away somewhere. Sporterized. It had a pistol grip, a cooling baffle and a banana clip. A real sporting weapon. That was what he'd told the agent who'd led the raid on his Ozone Park apartment on a cold and misty April dawn twelve years ago. "Hey, I like to hunt," he'd said.

"Sure you do. And fish like to play baseball." Agent Lawrence T. Sweeney was a wry man with great patience. He needed it, because Sal then made faces while his mug shots were being taken and smudged his fingerprints.

That was the week after the raid, when Sal had turned himself in to be arrested. He had escaped the raid itself by blundering across it. He'd been on his way home from the Sinatra Club when he saw the men in white raincoats jimmying his car trunk with a crowbar. Then he saw the cars converging on his house. Rose Marie told him later that she heard banging on the downstairs door. She opened the door of their upstairs apartment to see men rushing at her, two steps at a time, with pistols drawn. She woke Sal junior and with an urgency she had never used with him before she said, "Go next door to Grandma Noto's. Now!"

"But I'm not dressed," the sleepy boy had whined. He was four then.

"Just go." She put a robe and slippers on him and pushed him out the door. Then she changed ten-month-old Joseph and sat him in his high chair and spooned oatmeal into his mouth while the agents and detectives tore the house apart around her.

Sal had called her while the raid was going on. He grinned remembering it. "Is anybody at the house?" he'd asked.

"I really can't talk to you right now, there's somebody here," she said, like people were always dropping in at six A.M.. She was trying to protect him. That had been one of the moments in which he'd loved her deeply. There had been few enough of them.

"Put them on," he'd said. He'd had to insist, but she had done it.

When the agent in charge came on the phone, Sal screamed, "Who the fuck are you and what the fuck're you doing in my house?"

A soft, steely voice came back, "I'm Agent Lawrence Sweeney of the FBI. We have a warrant for your arrest for bank robbery."

On Monday, Sal had gone with Mike Coiro to FBI headquarters in Manhattan and turned himself in. He was charged with robbing the Franklin National Bank on Horace Harding Boulevard in Queens the previous May. The FBI had taken the carbine in the raid and part of a sawed-off shotgun, some ammunition he'd had hidden in the basement, a suit and shoes and one of Rose Marie's wigs. Neither the weapons nor the wig were the ones he'd used to rob the bank.

The raid had been his family's introduction to the FBI. And now he was working with the bureau. The thought stirred in him some sympathy for Rose Marie. It tempered his impatience. She was still reluctant to believe he was doing the right thing. When he told her that morning he was going to New York to buy pipe bombs for the ATF, her face had frozen in horror.

"Bombs?" she said. "Bombs?"

"Bombs," he said.

Tears appeared in her eyes for no reason he could figure out.

She had simply turned away, and when it was time for him to leave she didn't say good-bye.

A small, mud-spattered, foreign car slowed and turned into the marina lot. Showtime, thought Sal. He looked casually in the direction of the van. The pop-up vent was open and he mugged at it. "You guys are looking good," he said into his sleeve. Limbach and Russo would be watching the videotape monitor. The ATF and FBI agents had submerged their interbureau rivalry; they were getting along so well they'd scheduled Sal in tandem. First he would make the bomb purchase for the ATF, then he was due at a meeting with Mike Coiro, who still was thought to be a conduit to Brennan. The agents wouldn't even have to unwire Sal, just change the cassette in the tape recorder that dangled in his crotch.

The car moved across the parking lot in Sal's direction and stopped beside him. Four large people were inside the little car. Sal recognized Doris Leonard, her daughter Cynthia and one of her two sons. The other guy must have been a friend of his. They would have made a couple of good bodyguards.

Doris rolled her window down and Sal leaned on the door with his wrists stuck inside. "You got it?" he said. He was eager to get the pipe bombs from her car into his, but Doris looked around the lot and said suspiciously, "Who's in the telephone truck?"

A New York Telephone truck was parked facing the water. Its driver was eating a sandwich and staring out in the direction of the airport. It was a little after noon. The planes were lifting off every few minutes and banking right, over the marina and Shea Stadium.

"Who knows? I don't know him. Let's go," said Sal impatiently.

"You sure?" Doris said, her eyes narrow in her heavy face.

"I just came here. There's nobody here," he said.

Satisfied, she showed him a plastic bank bag containing the three pipe bombs. "They're all ready," she said. Sal lifted the bag gingerly and opened it. It was heavy. The capped lengths of pipe had been drilled, fuses inserted and the openings sealed with wax. The three together, blunt metal shapes invaded by the sinuous fuses, were dull and evil-looking, just like—now that Sal thought about it—the sporterized carbine. He took one from the bag and noticed the stock numbers had been ground from the end caps. "Did he say how long that fuse would last?" Sal asked. He thought it was an important thing to know.

"He didn't tell me," Doris said.

"But they're all ready to go?"

"Just light it up and that's it."

Sal counted out nine one-hundred-dollar bills. "I'll see you tomorrow," he said. "Tell him that they want them other things." He had told Julius Leonard the Colombians might want other bombs as well. Doris nodded her assent and said good-bye. Sal followed as she exited the parking lot. He circled around when the other car was out of sight and joined Limbach and Russo at the ATF surveillance van. The transaction had been recorded perfectly on audio and videotape.

• • •

Ever since I could remember, my mom's family had come to our house for Thanksgiving and we had gone there for Christmas. Even after we moved to Port Jervis, Grandma and Grandpa Noto, and Leonard and Gina and little Albert, would come up for Thanksgiving dinner.

This Thanksgiving the hard feelings lingered over Dad's dismissing Tony Capetola, and it was just us there at the racetrack.

Mom fixed a turkey with all the trimmings. Normally we would have set up one big table in the living room, but we ate around the kitchen table. Before we started Dad did something he'd never done before. He said, "Let's say grace." Before anybody could be surprised, he ducked his head and said, "Lord, we thank you for this food before us and ask you to deliver us from evil, amen."

Mom looked shocked. Joe caught my eye, like, what's this? Dad saying grace was nothing short of weird. "That was very nice," she said. "Now pass your plates down here, and I'll start the sweet potatoes."

There was too much left when we were finished eating. Mom kept saying, "Have some more," but there weren't enough of us. I called Charlie, and he came up with a couple of friends and we played a little football in the yard as the sun went down.

You hate to let go at the end of a season. You want to keep on playing, so you can fix what you did wrong. You want another chance to convert a busted play: anticipate, cut a little sharper or kick a little higher to avoid a tackle, grip the ball harder to keep from being stripped. The good plays you can replay as they happened, but you always want to redo the others in a way that might have been even if it's just a touch game in the yard. So we played, and produced some new images to spend the winter with, and at the end we managed to reduce the leftovers.

And then Christmas was upon us.

The red and green decorations went up in downtown Port Jervis. The gift shop where Mom worked grew busy with the Christmas rush and she worked into the evening almost every day.

I saw an awful lot of Linda. She wore my class ring and I spent my first period trig class writing her notes about how much I loved her. Now and then when I was with her I'd see her mind was somewhere else and it would drive me crazy and I'd say something I was sorry for. Then I'd end up writing her a note. One day I wrote, "I'll try to stop bringing up his name but every time I hold you I keep thinking that you're thinking of how it was. And then you said that you care about him a little and I got mad and didn't understand but now I do. All right. So don't worry about nothing. Alls I need is you and I got you, so I ain't got to worry about nothin', right? So do you want to go see the big X-mas tree in Manhattan soon?"

At the bottom I drew our names: Sal-n-Linda, and wrote "Don't let anyone forget it!!" You can't relax even for a minute when you're in love.

I felt I should tell her something about what might happen. The way I saw it we might have to be away for a while, a few weeks, and she should know so she would wait for me. I didn't want to just disappear and come back to find her going out with someone else. I could hear her saying, "Well, what was I supposed to do?" I kept looking for the right moment to let her know.

On the Saturday before Christmas we did go down to see the big tree at Rockefeller Center. We parked across the river in New Jersey and took a train into the city. We were getting off into the crowds at Penn Station when she caught my hand in a death grip and said, "Hold on to me no matter what. I've never been here before. I'm afraid of getting lost." Her first trip to Manhattan. I could hardly believe it. But I loved it. Hold on to me no matter what.

We jostled and pushed our way upstairs and onto Seventh Avenue. The crowds were thick as far as you could see. Everyone was friendly, but she held tight to my hand. It took us half an hour to walk to Rockefeller Center, because we had to look into every one of Macy's windows.

We waited on line to rent skates at the Rockefeller Center rink. The ice was crowded, and the promenades around the rink were crowded, too, with frost on everybody's breath. One couple skated like the Ice Capades in and out of all the rest of us. Linda and I just managed to get around the rink. She was a good skater, but it was all she could do to hold up both of us. Once we went down in a tangle of arms and legs and I just wanted to lie there with her and melt the ice beneath us, but then here came the Ice Capades who showered us with ice shavings before we could scramble out of the way.

Afterward, sitting with hot chocolate and admiring the big tree that rose in a pyramid of lights against the buildings overhead, I blurted out, "I have to tell you something."

"You can't skate," she said. "You meant to tell me before we rented skates, but you forgot."

"No." I reached out for her hand. "No, this is something serious, and I'm not supposed to be telling you and you can't tell anybody else."

She pouted. I was taking away the carefree feeling of the day. "Okay, never mind," I said. I regretted mentioning it, but it was too late. She took her hand back, stared into her hot chocolate and looked up. "It's Donna, isn't it? You want to go out with her again."

I was relieved for about ten seconds. "No, it isn't Donna, it's about my dad."

She got a concerned look then, and it encouraged me to go on. "It's about all of us, really."

She said, "Oh, Sal, I'm so sorry. He's going to have to go away, isn't he?"

I lost my nerve. "Yes," I said. "I'm not sure when."

She reached out and took both my hands in hers and her eyes

were pure and kind. "What will happen?" she asked. "You'll still be in Port Jervis, won't you?"

"I'm not leaving you for anything," I said. "That's all I know. I don't know when he has to leave or anything, except it won't be until next year. We're just waiting now. Please don't say anything. I just had to tell somebody." I felt like a dog turd for not telling her the truth, but then I figured, half of the truth was better than none. I could tell her the rest later. To have made the first step, and to feel her concern pouring out for me, it made me fierce with love.

"I love you," I said. "Nothing will change that. Ever."

"I know," she said. Her face was beautifully flushed from the cold and from skating, and I listened to her with growing happiness. "I love you, too. Sal, whatever happens, I'll be there. I just want you to know that. I'll always be there for you. I know it will be hard without your dad, but you can always lean on me. That won't ever change. Not ever."

We walked back to Penn Station bumping through the Christmas crowds, arm in arm in our own joy, teenagers with all our lives ahead of us, and I believed in those giddy moments that something would happen and we would never have to leave Port Jervis.

• • •

Christmas Eve without her family was unthinkable, but Rose Marie was working so hard she hardly had time to think at all. The gift shop was crowded with last-minute shoppers through the weekend. Christmas fell on Tuesday, and inevitably, half the population of Port Jervis still had shopping to do on Monday, and gifts to wrap, and trees to decorate.

It was only when the shop had closed and she had wished the Parkers a Merry Christmas and told them good night and was riding home with Sal and the boys, who had come to pick her up, that Rose Marie felt desolate and guilty.

Joe said, "Ma, we got the tree all decorated. You know where we got it? At the edge of the woods down where the road goes to the river. Remember the one we thought about last year? The one we decided had another year to grow? It was just the right size. It looks great."

Rose Marie said, "You know, this is the first time in my life I haven't been at home on Christmas Eve."

Sal's voice was sharp. "We're going home now."

"You know what I mean. We've always gone to my family's house on Christmas Eve. It's the first time we haven't been there."

"We talked about that," Sal said. "It was gonna be too late."

That had been the excuse. By the time Rose Marie got off work it would be dark. There would be too much to do at the last minute, baking, wrapping presents. Driving the hour and a half from Port Jervis to Ozone Park would be too much. "We'll come down the next morning," Rose Marie had told her stepmother, who had acted disappointed at this breach of family tradition. The truth was she felt too nervous to be around her family. Since Sal had fired Tony Capetola, her stepmother and sister had spoken of him bitterly and with suspicion. They sensed something wrong. Privately, they were convinced that Sal was going to jump bail and disappear, leaving Rose Marie and the boys to fend for themselves and the Notos to give up the houses they had mortgaged for fifty thousand dollars of his bail. But Rose Marie feared the unguarded moment when she would say something to expose the truth. She missed her family, but she wanted as little time with them as possible. Her husband was an actor who enjoyed the excitement of performing, but Rose Marie simply didn't trust herself to lie.

She said, "I'll have to learn to live without them anyway."

Joe spoke quickly to console her. "That's okay, Ma. We'll all be together. That's what counts, isn't it, Dad?"

"That's right, son. That's what counts."

The last stragglers were making their way home in the early evening darkness. The highway was almost deserted. Lighted windows beckoned. Sal turned onto Oakland Valley Road and they approached the racetrack.

Rose Marie said, "Wait a minute. Joseph, what did you say?"

"I said, 'We'll all be together.' Sal, leave me alone. Quit digging me in the ribs." Joe squirmed away from his brother.

"It's okay, Sal." Sal junior looked up and saw his father's eyes in the rearview mirror, saw him give a slight nod. "They know about it, Ro," he said. "I told them a long time ago. I thought you'd worry."

"Worry? Oh, boy. Worry? With you running around . . . How much did you tell them? Did you tell them everything?"

Sal turned into the driveway and stopped in front of the house. He killed the engine. "Yeah," he said, "I told them all about it."

Rose Marie opened her door and gathered packages into her arms. "Did you tell them about wearing a tape recorder? Buying bombs?" She addressed the boys climbing out of the backseat. "Did he tell you about that? Did he tell you about taping Tony Capetola at Albert's birthday party?"

Sal said, "Don't get hysterical."

She walked around the car to an Adirondack chair left sitting on the patio and fell into it, ignoring Buster nosing at the packages she carried in her arms. "Hysterical? Worry? Oh, my God." She kicked her legs up into the air and threw her head back to look at a clear and starry sky. Sal and the two boys were staring at her. "You thought I'd worry? I've got too much to worry about to worry about that," she cried out through the stillness. "This is a relief. This is the best Christmas present I could have. Thank God. At last I've got somebody to talk to."

"Well, that's good," Sal said after a moment. "We can all talk about it now. And you're right, we're all gonna have to learn to live without them. Now let's get these packages inside."

Rose Marie was washing dishes. The boys were back at school and the holidays had gone quite well, considering. She felt more a part of her family since Joe's blurted words on Christmas Eve had made her realize they all shared the same secret. She had been so relieved, both by the revelation and the fact that Sal had not been wired, that Christmas Day at the Notos' house in Ozone Park had actually been fun. She'd been able to ignore the unspoken suspicions directed at her husband. The thirteen of them around the dinner table, including her aunt Dolly, Phyllis's sister, had done justice to the turkey and side dishes of baked macaroni and lasagna and her specialties, the pumpkin pie and chocolate swirl cheesecake she had baked the night before. Her father, who had not been well, was gruff but cheerful. The gifts of clothing she had exchanged with Sal and the boys had an additional purpose: to be portable. No one had thought they were at all unusual.

And yesterday had provided fresh evidence of her husband's transformation. There had been a time when he'd bet ten thousand dollars on a New Year's college bowl game. And lost. It was the 1973 Sugar Bowl, held on New Year's Eve, when Notre Dame beat Alabama 24 to 23. He had been so angry that he'd ripped off his tuxedo and said, "Forget about going out tonight. I just lost ten thousand big ones and I ain't going nowhere." An hour later he had changed his mind. "Fuck it," he said. "Get your clothes back on. We're going out." They'd gone to the Pan American Steak Pub on Queens Boulevard. The New Year's celebration was in full swing. Balloons, noisemakers, hats, confetti, a din of talk and music. Their closest friends were there, men with whom Sal had hijacked trucks or gambled or dealt drugs: Jackie Donnelly and Dominic Cataldo and their wives, Dominic's brother Joey and Joey's wife Louise. Sal entertained them by ordering eleven daiquiris and lining up the drinks to resemble the wishbone formation used by Alabama and Notre Dame and drinking every one. This year they had stayed home on New Year's Eve. As far as Rose Marie knew, Sal had not placed a single bet. Perhaps it was true that he had changed.

A car pulled into the driveway and she went to the window. John Limbach was getting out, carrying a briefcase. Another agent, one she didn't recognize, tall and balding, was with him. She went to the front door.

"Hello, John," she said warmly, "come in. I haven't seen you in a while."

"Rose Marie," he said, a little surprised at her relaxed greeting. When Limbach had been Sal's probation officer, she had given him a bottle of cologne for Christmas and he had been embarrassed to have to turn it down. She had wanted nothing to do with the other agents when Sal began cooperating. Limbach had been the one exception, he supposed because she knew him. Cool at first, over the months she'd dropped her guard until now, the first time he'd been to their home in Port Jervis, there seemed to be no barriers between them. "Let me introduce you to Paul Lettis," he said. The other agent's face was wrenched in an expression of perpetual distaste, and he greeted her with a wan smile.

"What brings you up here, John?" she asked. Before Limbach could answer, she said, "You like our log cabin in the mountains? It's a lot different than Ozone Park, isn't it? Let me show you. Would you believe we built it all ourselves? It used to be a barn. We've been so happy here, until this last thing with my husband. Can I get you something to eat?"

"You were always trying to feed me, Rose Marie."

"I'm an Italian mother, what can I say?"

Limbach followed Rose Marie as she pointed out features of the living room. Three windows looked out over the sinuous racetrack and the dense forest beyond it. The back corners of the large room were occupied by a coal stove and a heating fireplace. The room was snug and warm. "This is really something," he said, "country comforts."

"I've got a pot of soup on the stove," Rose Marie offered again.

Lettis brightened. "That might be just the thing," he said. "Soup's about all I can eat."

"Oh, good." She ushered them into the kitchen, where the windows were steamed and the aroma of minestrone rose from the stove.

"Yo." Sal came down the stairs with his usual greeting. "You guys all ready? What's this?" He stood in the doorway of the kitchen. "John, you would never eat with us before."

"We're on the same side now, more or less," said Limbach. "Times change, Sal."

"Yes, they do," said Rose Marie.

"Now that I've had your minestrone, Rose Marie, I'm sorry I waited so long. It's wonderful." Limbach put his soup bowl aside and spoke to Sal. "Well, we've got to get you wired up here." He opened the briefcase and took out the elastic bellyband and recording gear. "We're going to try and make it work without the van today. Recorder and transmitter." He glanced sheepishly at Rose Marie.

She looked less betrayed than wistful. "I'll just let you go ahead, then. It's good to see you, John. And nice to meet you, Paul. Come back when . . . when you can stay for supper," she said, and retreated from the kitchen.

A few moments later Rose Marie watched from the window as Sal left the driveway in his car, followed by the two agents in the car Limbach was driving. She tried to think what could possibly go wrong.

Limbach pulled to one side of the dirt road while Sal continued to the Rebel's trailer. Julius emerged at the sound of his car and motioned Sal to come around to his workshop in the back.

"I got what you ordered," he said. On the workbench were two wooden boxes, painted green, about four inches thick and one foot by eighteen inches long. The top half of a windup clock protruded from a cutout in each box. Julius lifted off the top of one to reveal a juice can filled with black powder nestled in a bed of foam rubber. Thin wires connected the clock to a battery-operated switch affixed to the outside of the box.

"Looks good," said Sal.

"All I got to do here is put a bead of solder on the wires. Then you wind the clock, throw the switch and when the hour hand gets around to where you see the post there, that completes the circuit and you best be somewheres else."

"Whoa, now. Things'll be cool as long as this switch stays off? Is that right?"

"Yeah. Which is this position right here."

"These Colombians, you know, I gotta explain it to 'em very carefully," said Sal, "because if something happens they're gonna be asking me about it. You know?"

"Well, like I say, I got to solder the leads here. Then ain't nothing gonna happen unless that switch is on. And they got to wind the clock and move the hour hand around to here." Julius dropped the top back on the box. "You want 'em tomorrow, is that right?"

Sal said, "Yeah, around eleven. Is Doris gonna bring 'em?"

He heard her voice behind him. "You want 'em the same place, Sal? At that marina."

Sal said yes.

Doris said, "I'll bring 'em. Me and Cindy. But I sure hope they ain't gonna use 'em to blow up any children."

When Sal pulled into the driveway followed by the agents in the second car, Rose Marie realized with a start why she had felt afraid. Of course. One of the bombers could follow them home. Home to her house. They would realize that Sal was working with the agents. They made bombs, and they knew where her family lived.

"Don't be ridiculous," Sal said, when Limbach and the sour-faced agent had gone. "Nobody followed us, and what difference does it make if they know where we live? They don't have any idea I'm bugging them."

"How do you know that?" Rose Marie went to the window and began closing the blinds, dimming the room.

"That same way I knew it was gonna work every time before. I just know. Because I'm not paranoid." Sal went from window to window, raising the blinds to the window tops. "See. There's nobody out there."

"Please," she said, "indulge me. You know I worry. It's not just me. It's the boys. How long can this go on?"

"As long as it takes to get to Brennan," Sal replied.

She sank down onto the ottoman in front of the reclining chair. "But these bombs. This is ridiculous. What does this have to do with anything? Why do you have to do that?"

"Look," he said, "the more I do the better chance we have of getting in the program. I'm doing it for all of us, so when we do go . . ."

Rose Marie interrupted him. "When, when, when. When? I'm ready to go now. I don't know about the boys, but I'm ready to go. Can't we just go and get it over with? Get away from all this undercover stuff? I know you love it, but I can't stand it. It makes me nervous. You get excited, I get nervous." She stopped to light a cigarette. "You see this?" She crushed the empty box and tossed it weakly toward where he stood silhouetted in the window. "Three packs a day. If something doesn't happen soon I may die of cancer first."

"Hey, but you look good," he said. "What are you now, about one fifteen, one twenty?"

"Why won't you touch me, then?" she said with bitter anger.

Sal let a sigh slip out and out, like a magician pulling scarves out of his sleeve. She was right, it had been months. And there was no reason for his reluctance to make love to her, except that she was the mother of their children and he loved her that way but not in the other. He moved toward her but he couldn't bring himself to hold her. He sat on the edge of the recliner facing her. "Hey, I've had a lot to think about, okay?"

"So have I," she said, "and all that time you didn't tell me that they knew, when I couldn't talk to them."

Sal stood up before she could take his hands. "It'll be different when we move, I promise. We're trying. We're moving as fast as we can. We're not getting any closer to Brennan, is the problem."

"We," she said scornfully. "You'd think you were an agent yourself. You ought to be. I hope you get close to him soon, because we, meaning your wife and family, can't wait much longer."

Dan Russo was frustrated, too. Sal was chasing a third-rate bomb case for the ATF, but the FBI's main object remained Justice William Brennan. Sal's meeting with Coiro following his purchase of the pipe bombs had been more of the same. Coiro had told Sal again not to worry, that things were going to be fine. Russo read into these assurances a devious connection between Rotker, who still had Sal's case, and Brennan. But the connection refused to develop, because it simply wasn't there. Sal's case remained before Rotker. With Queens District Attorney John Santucci on board with the federal investigation, his prosecutors were acquiescing in postponements sought by the defense. Rotker fumed and demanded an end to the seemingly endless delays. Meanwhile, Ethan Levin-Epstein was on the phone to Russo every other day, wanting to know about the progress of the FBI's sting against Judge Brennan. Russo finally concluded that Rotker was not compromised and that Coiro was not reaching out to Brennan. He sought another route.

Russo remembered a story Sal had told, that Jackie Donnelly and Dominic Cataldo once had sent Brennan on a trip and picked up his expenses. Russo then learned that Donnelly and the Cataldo brothers had been regulars at the Pan American Steak Pub, the same restaurant where Sal had taken Rose Marie to ring out 1973. The restaurant was owned by Brennan's good friend Andy Bruno. Bruno had since left New York for Florida, where he operated the Runway 84 restaurant in Hallandale near the Fort Lauderdale Airport. But he stayed in touch with Brennan.

Russo felt that he was agonizingly close to a discovery. Then

Sal happened to mention one day that Joey Cataldo was his *compare*.

"Your what?" said Russo.

"My goombahta," said Polisi. "You know, goombahta. My good friend. Joey and his wife Louise baptized my youngest kid, Joe. I named him after Joey."

"You mean he's your son's godfather?" Russo asked, incredulous. Debriefing Sal was full of surprises. He had known since the summer that Sal's connection to the Colombo family was through Dominic Cataldo, but this was his first inkling that a close—and possibly exploitable—friendship was involved.

"Yeah, I go back a long way with Cataldos. I knew Dominic before he got his button with the Colombos. We were partners in them days." Sal spun out in detail the history he'd only hinted at with Ed McDonald.

In 1968, Sal said, he was running a luncheonette on Atlantic Avenue in Ozone Park. He and his uncle Tony had bought the little storefront a year or two before from a woman who'd won the Irish Sweepstakes and returned home on her winnings. Shanahan's Candy Store became Sal's Luncheonette, but the menu of sandwiches and sodas was incidental. Sal and Anthony Polisi ran a horse-betting book from there, and Sal bought stolen coins, jewelry and small appliances. Uncle Tony was the person Sal admired most in all the world. He was a short, dapper little man who wore a kiss-my-ass mustache and a diamond pinky ring and the best suits you could buy off the rack. He drove Cadillacs and liked to have a blonde at his side. Sal admired him because he'd chosen a different path in life than Sal's father.

Frank Polisi had had his brother's opportunities, but he had reined in his criminal instincts when he'd begun a family. Sal had always resented the hard life his father's carpenter's wages had provided. He turned to Uncle Tony, who hid Sal at his motel near the Aqueduct Race Track when Sal was wanted for forging checks after he got out of the Marines in 1965 by pretending to be crazy. Uncle Tony helped Sal fix that and an earlier assault case, convincing Sal that only suckers went to jail. Uncle Tony also hid Sonny Franzese's gang of Mafia-connected bank robbers at the Aqueduct Motor Inn, whose entry foyer floor was strewn with bills and coins set under a clear coat of polyurethane. The gang hung out at the motel lounge, called the Diamond Room, and when they were arrested Sal hid their guns in a laundry hamper. In those days, before high counters and thick Plexiglas windows and silent alarms killed the bank robbery profession, Uncle Tony robbed a bank now and then himself. He robbed the Central Queens Federal Savings and Loan on July 7, 1965, and when he went to prison for it two years later, he left Sal with the luncheonette and a pawn ticket for a diamond pinky ring.

Sal was sitting in his back booth, near the wall phone and the hole in the wall behind the seat back that was there in case he needed to ditch some betting slips, when Dominic Cataldo entered his life.

"He was a trim little guy," Sal said to Russo. "Straight black hair, sharp features, about five-seven, in his early thirties. I was maybe twenty-three. I remember he was wearing a leather jacket and a pair of alligator tassel loafers. He walked straight back to where I was sitting, and he knew my name.

"He said, 'Sal Polisi, I'm Dominic Cataldo. We go back.'

"Cataldo's family," Sal continued, "lived in East New York on Essex Street, which was two blocks from where my grandfather ran a bar at Elton and Glenmore and where my family lived when I was born. Cataldo's father Sammy and my father had grown up together in the teens and twenties. My father was wild in them days. They called him Upazz', too, you know? Oh, yeah. He was crazy. Sammy's uncle had a funeral parlor, and my father was the only boy who would crawl into a coffin and play like he was dead, or sleeping. Later he hauled moonshine in a horse-drawn wagon between New York City and Long Island for some people that Cataldo knew. He backed away from all that when my sister Rosemarie was born, even though he was still fascinated with crime. He used to tell me bedtime stories about Al Capone and Murder Incorporated. But my uncle Tony stayed close to the Cataldos.

"It turned out that Dominic had been in prison, for some kind of paper crime, and he'd met Uncle Tony in the joint.

"We're talking, and he says, 'Your uncle Tony told me what you got here.'" Sal described Cataldo smoothing back his hair and brushing something off his jacket sleeve. "And then he says, 'I'm going to build a big book. You can get your own sheet, and we'll be partners.'"

As Sal described his blossoming friendship with Dominic Cataldo and then his brother Joey, Russo decided that he had found Sal's route to Brennan.

"Ah, where the hell did all these years go?" Sal was standing in a hallway of the Queens Criminal Court building with Joey and Louise Cataldo. He could still feel the pressure of Mike Coiro's hand on his back, just above the transmitter, as the lawyer ushered him out of the Forge Diner after their meeting. Sal's trial date was right around the corner and once again Coiro had told him not to worry. They'd crossed the street together, huddled against the January winds, and in the court building met the Cataldos, whose son Sammy, Coiro was defending on an assault charge.

Sal had met Joseph Cataldo through his partnership with Dominic. He and Rose Marie were a young married couple then, and so were Joey and Louise, a wisecracking niece of Albert Anastasia. They had had some times together. Joey and Louise had stood with Sal and Rose Marie when Father Joseph Greenfelder baptized Joseph Polisi at St. Elizabeth's Church in Ozone Park. A few months later, in the fall, Sal lay in Jamaica Hospital with a bullet in his back. A policeman had shot him. It was a reasonable act; Sal had narrowly missed the cop driving at seventy miles per hour on Atlantic Avenue in a Corvette prepared for drag racing. The Cataldos' visits with platters of baked macaroni and peppers and eggs and cannoli eased his recuperation, and one day he was talking with Joey about what he would do next.

"Hey, *compare*," he said. "*Compare*, what am I gonna do? I can't steal because my back's laid up. The FBI is laying all over me on this bank thing. How'm I gonna make a living?"

"I don't know," said Joey. He rested his prominent jaw in the palm of his hand and thought for a moment. "You're gonna have to lay low."

"Tell you what," Sal answered, "I've got some fruit I stashed from that bank job. Why don't we do something stupid and open up some kind of joint?"

And that was the beginning of the Sinatra Club.

It was a hole in the wall on Eighty-seventh Street just across

Atlantic Avenue, one block over and one down from the Polisis' apartment at Ninety-fifth Avenue and Eighty-eighth Street. The one-story stucco building, with its windowless facade, might have been a tiny warehouse but for the peephole in the metal door. They chose for the inside a nautical decor—fishnets hung from the ceiling with corks and starfish dangling in the strands. A tape player and a stack of tapes with every song Frank Sinatra ever recorded gave the place its name.

The game started out small, Friday night gamblers betting a quarter or fifty cents a card at poker while Sal or Joey fetched prewrapped sandwiches and beer and sodas from the refrigerator behind the bar that stretched along the wall. One table grew to three or four, bets increased and soon the Sinatra Club was open all week long, practically around the clock.

By the beginning of 1972, mob crews from all over the city were coming to the Sinatra Club to gamble.

The "shallow" players, mailmen, salesmen, factory workers from the neighborhood, had a couple of tables near the door. The middle-level games went on in the corner near the TV set, which was always tuned to sports. The heavy hitters had the green felt table in the back. Often they were drug dealers with money to burn. They ballooned the game so the house cut of five percent on small pots and less on larger ones was pushing two thousand dollars a night. Dominic Cataldo, who by then headed a Colombo family crew, came in as a partner, and so did Funzi Tarricone from the Genovese family and Jackie Donnelly, who was called "Beans" and who also was attached to the Colombos. The conversations were all about hijackings, stick-ups, numbers, sports betting. A customer could get whatever he wanted. Italian food. Mixed drinks from the bar. Hookers. Sal had a deal with some girls who worked out of the Surfside Three motel on Cross Bay Boulevard; he gave them the club's business, and they'd kick back to him with a quick throw or a blow job. He was a horn in the night.

Gene Gotti started gambling at the Sinatra Club. So did Wilfred "Willie Boy" Johnson. Gene was John Gotti's younger brother and Willie Boy was his friend. Both, like John, were part of a Gambino family crew. John was in prison then. Gene and Willie Boy were waiting for John to get out to tell them what to do next.

Gotti was thirty-one, black-haired and powerfully built when he came out of prison and began to frequent the Sinatra Club. He'd walk in, and always wait for somebody to take his velvet-collared Chesterfield overcoat. Sal kept boxes of Gotti's favorite Italian stogies, DiNobilis, under the bar. His charisma was like a magnet to the other wiseguys who gambled at the club. With them it was, "Yes, John. No, John." His favorite word was homage. Homage had to be paid where it was due. John Gotti was beginning to accumulate power at the beginning of 1972.

Sal yawned and stretched. The feel of the tape tugging at his arm hairs brought him back to the Cataldos and the present. In January 1985, Dominic Cataldo was in prison and Joey was trying to dodge a case by pretending he was crazy. Sal's *compare* was disheveled, shambling and wearing a sweatshirt with the hood pulled over his head. But his speech was lucid. Eventually, the memory-freighted conversation turned to what was really on Sal's mind.

"I've got so many problems," he moaned. "Forget about it. They're offering me six to life." Indicating Coiro, he said, "I'm gonna go bye-bye if he don't do the right thing here."

Moments later, after Coiro had departed for the courtroom with Sammy Cataldo, Sal said, "I'm gonna reach out. He can't do nothing. Remember that guy who owned that Pan Am, Joe?"

"Yeah."

"You know him good?"

"Yeah."

"Andy Bruno."

"Yeah."

"I heard he's down in Florida."

"Yeah, he lives in Florida."

"I heard he knew some people over here in Queens."

"Yeah, yeah."

"You know him good, right?"

"I know him good."

"All right. In case I need a phone call . . . Because I don't think he'll remember me, but he'll remember you."

E I G H T

Dad was bursting with energy when he hung up the phone. He rubbed his hands together and said, "Okay, okay, okay. Now we're moving. Now it's happening."

"What's up, Pop?" I said.

"Don't Pop me, I'll pop you." He danced across the living room, feinted and tapped the side of my head with his right hand before I could set the popcorn bowl aside and get up from in front of the TV. "That was Russo," he said. "Brennan's going to Florida on his vacation to see Bruno, and he thinks now is a good time to make contact. He wants me to go to Florida. Then if everything goes right we'll be saying 'Bye-bye,' to Port Jervis."

I felt my face go numb. "Are you sure?" I said.

"Sure, I'm sure. Once this caper's over we'll be history. Bye-bye, P.J. Bye-bye, Polisis."

"But, Pop . . ." He feinted at me again and I ducked back. I didn't feel like playing with him.

"But nothing." He came at me, grinning and playful. I felt the edge of the sofa behind my knees and flopped over backward. I scrambled to sit up to cover my embarrassment.

"I can't go," I said.

"You what?"

"I can't go." That was it. I simply couldn't. I don't know why I hadn't thought of it before. "I have the wrestling team. There's only a month left in the season. How will Coach Seeber get another manager now? And Linda. Dad, I . . . You go. You and Mom and Joe. I'll stay. I can stay with Linda's parents. Or Charlie. Maybe I can stay with him."

He stood there looking at me. "What did you think?" he said. "Did you think that this was never gonna happen? I been telling you for months. It's gonna happen. It's gonna happen soon. I told you to be ready for it."

I thought about the months of waiting. I said, "We've just been sitting here, and nothing's happened. In all this time. You told us to act like nothing was different. Now you're saying it's all going to happen all of a sudden and everything's different. When are we supposed to leave? Tomorrow? I can't leave tomorrow."

"Not tomorrow."

"So when?" A date would have helped convince me.

"Next week, two weeks, I don't know. But you'll be ready. We all will."

"What am I supposed to tell Linda, that I'm going to just disappear?" I demanded. "I can't just go and not tell her anything."

"Son, you think you're in love. You're not in love. Tell her you're going away for a while, a couple of weeks. She'll get over it. It'll be in the papers. She'll understand what happened. You'll get over it, too."

He just had no understanding. "I can't do that. It's not fair," I said.

"Son, listen to me." He walked over and turned the television off, came back and sat down on the sofa. "You knew this was going to be hard. I told you. It'll be better in the end. Better than me going in the joint and you and your mother and your brother going back to Ozone Park. I told you we had to get away from all that back there. That's why we came up here, but I made a mistake and this is what we've got to do about it."

I couldn't look at him. "I didn't do anything," I said.

"What do you mean?"

"I didn't do anything. I didn't make any mistakes." I could hear my voice rising. "I didn't, and Joe didn't. And Mom didn't either. Why do we have to go?"

He didn't say anything for a long time. I looked at the wall, where the karting trophies were lined up, until my vision blurred. Finally, he said, "Because I made so many mistakes it takes more than one person to pay for all of them. Someday I'll tell you all about it." He paused again. The ticking of the wall clock grew into an echo. "And because we're a family, son. We're a family and we have to stay together as a family. And because it'll be better for you and all of us. Believe it or not, it's gonna be better."

He got up then, took his parka from the coat tree and walked to the door. "I'm going to pick your mother up," he said. "If your brother comes in from sledding you can tell him what we talked about."

I was sitting in the darkening living room when Joe came home. I could hear him stomping around outside to knock the snow off his boots. Then he came in and started turning lights on and was headed for the kitchen when he saw me sitting on the sofa. "Hey, Sal," he said, "what're you sitting in the dark for? Where's Dad?"

"He went to pick up Mom. He said we're going to be leaving."

"Where we going? Out to dinner? I got to change."

"No, leaving. Like, leaving Port Jervis and going in the program. Like, soon, he said."

"Get outta here," Joe said.

"No, really. He has to go to Florida to bribe the judge, and then we're going to be leaving."

"When?"

"He didn't know, a week or two."

"Oh, boy, no school," he said. "Do you believe it?" he asked me.

"I don't know. I did before, but then nothing ever happened."

"Right. Is there anything to eat?" Joe was like me. He didn't really believe it. He turned and walked into the kitchen, and came out a minute later with a handful of Fig Newtons. He turned the TV on, plopped down in the recliner and started switching channels with the remote. The "Never Gonna Break My Stride" video was on MTV. I wondered if I'd ever have another friend like Charlie.

• • •

The plane banked in off the ocean and Sal could see the lights of Fort Lauderdale reflected in the water. It was Wednesday night, January 30, 1985. Nine days had passed since he had run into Louise and Joey Cataldo at the Queens Criminal Court building and told

142 SINS OF THE FATHER

Joey he needed to get in touch with Andy Bruno. The operation was about to move into high gear.

Outside the terminal the air was warm and soothing. Sal took off his leather jacket and carried it over his suitcase. "Ain't this wonderful?" he said, taking a deep breath. "Beats the shit out of New York this time of year. I'm sure glad this Bruno don't own no restaurant in Alaska."

"Yeah, well, keep in mind that this is a working vacation." It was the blue suit talking. The other agent wore a gray suit. They'd been waiting for him at the gate when he'd walked off the plane with the other winter-shocked New Yorkers. Every other pale, sweater-clad arrival lugging a heavy coat had been greeted by tanned men and women wearing ice cream colored polo shirts: pistachio, raspberry and black cherry. Everyone was smiling: the relieved smiles of winter's escapees were met by the proud grins of the inhabitants of the perfect winter climate. Only these two guys were grim and wearing suits.

"I used to come down here all the time this time of year," Sal said. "Course, I never thought I'd be down here on the government."

"No, the maximum-security prisons are all farther north," the blue suit said.

"Hey," said Sal, grinning, "you'll like me when you get to know me."

The Holiday Inn at Fort Lauderdale Beach rose between the Intracoastal Waterway and the Atlantic Ocean. At the desk in the lobby that was studded with potted palms and huge pink vases lush with flowers, a clerk who looked like an airline flight attendant found Sal's reservation. She smiled a professional, noncommittal smile and made statements that sounded like questions. "You'll be with us for a week, Mr. Polisi? And you'll be paying cash? You realize we'll require a deposit?" When he'd counted out three hundred dollars in twenties, she said, "We have you on thirteen, Mr. Polisi."

"No way," said Sal.

"I beg your pardon?" said the clerk.

"No thirteen, no way I'm staying on thirteen. Give me something else." Sal ignored the looks from the two agents. He leaned over the counter. "Give me twelve."

"Sal," said blue suit with a juicy chortle in his voice, "Sal, I didn't know you were superstitious."

"That's quite all right. That's a common request," said the clerk. She pressed a key on the keyboard below a computer monitor and waited as the information on the screen scrolled upward. "Twelve-oh-three? Is that all right?"

"Fine."

Sal was at the elevator with his key before he turned around. The agents were standing at the counter where he'd left his suitcase. "Oh, aren't you coming up?" he said. He returned and lifted the bag as if it were a great burden to carry it himself. "Well, just tell Russo I'm here then, willya?"

The hotel was built in a way that gave all the rooms a view of the ocean. Sal stood at the window looking at the wide beach and the white lines of surf curling up from the Atlantic and disappearing on the sand. The Breakers, which called itself a suite hotel, stood nearby across busy U.S. A1A, the Main Street of the Florida Gold Coast. Russo was somewhere in The Breakers. Sal was being kept apart. Limbach and Joe Kelly were coming down to watch him, but his cover depended on the appearance of having come to Fort Lauderdale alone to speak to Bruno. He picked up the phone and dialed the racetrack.

Sal junior answered.

"I'm here," Sal said.

"Hi, Dad, what's it like there?" Sal was glad to hear the kid sounding normal again.

"Oh, about eighty degrees."

"That's great. We're snowed in up here."

"Snowed in? You're kidding."

"Well, it's snowing now, real hard, and I don't know if we'll be able to get to school in the morning."

"Don't miss school unless you have to," Sal said. "You're gonna miss enough school as it is. You and your brother, too. Is your mother there?"

"What's the use of going to school, Dad, if we're leaving any-way?" Resignation and bitterness welled up in his voice.

"Don't worry about it. You go to school. Let me talk to your mother."

"She's right here," said the boy. "Nobody's going anywhere tonight."

Rose Marie came on the phone cautiously. "Can you talk?" she said. "Oh, good," she said when he replied. "I didn't know if you were in a room full of agents or not. So, how is it going?"

Sal told her what he knew, that he would make contact with Bruno as soon as Joey Cataldo made the introductory call. "Then Brennan's supposed to be here and we'll see where we go from there."

"So you don't know when you'll be back?"

"No. Hey, I just got here."

"I know, but I'm anxious."

"Well, sit tight. I'll let you know when to start packing."

When they'd finished talking, Sal went downstairs and returned with two cold beers. The room phone was ringing. Limbach was on the other end. "I just checked in," he said.

"Come on up. Twelve-oh-three. I've got an extra beer."

They both were seated near the window, feet up and chairs tipped back, when Sal said, "I used to come down here a lot in the old days."

"Not when you were on probation," Limbach said. "You couldn't travel."

"Oh, ho, don't you believe it," Sal said. "It was mostly before that. But I came down twice right after I got out of the joint. They were quick trips though, for this guy Johnny Dio. You never missed me?"

"Never," said Limbach lazily. "What'd you do?"

"Well, one time before I went in the joint . . ."

"You said after," Limbach interrupted.

Sal ignored the question. "Before I went in one time, Ro and I came with the Cataldos, Joey and Louise, and Joey's sister and her boyfriend. We went on the spur of the moment. It was like Wash-ington's Birthday, real busy, and we couldn't rent a car big enough for all of us. We had to settle for a dune buggy, and later we got a compact. But I liked that dune buggy. I was up driving it every morning before anybody else was up. Louise was ten weeks pregnant at the time, and she and Joey were shopping for houses. And one day I told Louise I'd seen some houses I wanted to show her.

"What I really wanted to do was scare the shit out of Louise, so we'd have something to talk about when we got home. So we took a ride somewhere off the beaten path, and I found this area where they were building a couple of houses, kind of hilly terrain, and all of a sudden I just whipped that dune buggy right off the road.

"We go through trees, we go up in the air, we come down. She's yelling, screaming, 'Upazz', you're crazy. You're a sick motherfucker. I'm having this baby.'

"I said, 'You wanted to see the houses. I'm taking you to see the houses.'

"Meanwhile, Ro and Joey're following us in the compact rent a car, all around in the grass and hills and weeds. Louise is laughing and crying at the same time, holding her stomach. We're bouncing up and down. And when we stop, we look at the front of the dune buggy and it's fiberglass, it's totally destroyed.

"There was only one thing to do. I said, 'It's got to get stolen.' Sure enough, I ran it off the side of a hill, flipped it over, broke off the key in the ignition. We called up the guy who rented it to us and said, 'The dune buggy was stolen from the hotel. This is very inconvenient.' And he called back to say we didn't have to pay, and to come pick our deposit up.

"We went back to New York and laughed for years about that."

Limbach tipped his chair upright. "That's a good story. I bet they'd be tickled to death to know what you're doing down here now."

"Hey, they know what I'm doin' here. I'm here to try and bribe a judge."

"You know what I mean. I'm hittin' it. Talk to you in the morning." Limbach left the room and closed the door behind him.

Sal spent the next day lounging in the sun and buying designer sweat suits at Brooks Brothers and Saks Fifth Avenue at the Galleria Mall. He used more of the cash the government had given him to make the purchases, reasoning that to do the government's work his wrists needed to be stylishly concealed. He called the Cataldos in the evening and learned Joey was asleep. "He's supposed to call that guy for me," he said. "All he's got to do is say, 'Hey, my friend is down there, Sally Upazz', my *compare*,' and that's it."

When he called back at eight o'clock, Louise said, "He's expecting you tonight."

Runway 84 was on State Road 84 north of the Fort Lauderdale Airport. It was constructed to resemble an airport control tower, and airline logos decorated the outside. Sal walked from the landscaped parking lot to the front entrance, where a glass case displayed enthusiastic reviews of the restaurant's New York Italian cuisine. There was a photograph of Andy Bruno. He seemed heavier than Sal remembered him from the Pan American, with sagging jowls and rubbery lips, and thinning hair combed straight back on his head.

Sal walked in the front door and stood for a moment, slightly amazed. The airline theme had been carried to the ultimate in gray and burgundy. Booths in the bar were set off from the dining room by little porthole windows, which from the dining room seemed to be set into the exterior skin of a DC-10. A waiter glided by, wearing a white shirt with pilot's epaulets. Sal entered the bar to the left of the entrance. He ordered an Amaretto, straight up. He drank it down, ordered another and asked for Andy, then sat down at a booth close to the piano player, whose baby grand was stationed between the bar and the dining room.

Bruno took several minutes to appear. He was a big man, about six-four, casually dressed in a blazer, slacks and a dress shirt open at the neck, the uniform of the Gold Coast impresario. He greeted Sal with guarded familiarity. "Sally. Yeah, I got a call about you."

For a few moments they felt each other out, swapping the names of mutual acquaintances, before Bruno abruptly said, "What's your problem? You got a problem or something?"

"Yeah, I got some problems there."

"What do you got?"

"I need someone to talk to . . ." He paused for a moment. "I don't know . . ."

Bruno said, "I don't know if I can help you, but . . ."

Sal threw Jackie Donnelly's name into the conversation. "Years ago, I was really close," he said. He talked about cases he believed Donnelly had fixed. Then he said, "I got a case in Queens."

"Your timing is good," said Bruno.

"Why?"

"The head man's coming down to see me."

Dan Russo, monitoring the conversation from a rental car in the parking lot of a nearby Waffle House, burst into delighted laughter.

Sal explained that Mike Coiro "took care of my case years ago before an Irish judge."

"Brennan?" Bruno asked.

"Yeah, Brennan."

Bruno now seemed eager to help Sal. Sal said he had a court date the following week and Bruno reacted with concern, asking him if he could get a postponement. He said he expected Brennan on Saturday. "It might work out perfect. I can sit you down with him," he said.

"Yeah? Because Jackie used to drink with him, you know."

"I introduced them," Bruno said. "How do you think they met? That was through me. They all meet him through me."

"Hey," Bruno said a moment later. "You don't object to changing lawyers if I tell you to? If I tell you to do something . . ."

"I'll do it," Sal agreed.

"I won't steer you wrong," Bruno promised. Offering Sal an old menu, he said, "Write everything down here, all the information I need." Sal wrote on the back, behind last Thanksgiving's specials, his name, his room number at the Holiday Inn, the names of the lawyers Coiro had told him to retain and that his drug charge before Judge Rotker—he misspelled the name "Rotka"—was a repeat felony. Bruno lumbered off to call the Pan American Hotel in Miami Beach to confirm Brennan's Saturday arrival. Sal waited, tapping his foot as the piano player eased through a repertoire of lounge standards. He smiled to himself imagining that the entire recorded conversation would be played in court with "New York, New York" in the background.

Bruno returned. "He's due in Saturday," he said. They started swapping names again. Bruno recalled that Dominic Cataldo had hired a chef away from him when Cataldo opened an Italian restaurant in Ozone Park. "Rosario. Rosey Rosario. He's here. Do you know him?" Bruno asked.

"I think so." Sal searched his memory. More importantly, would Rosario remember him? The phone call had gotten his foot in the door, but Bruno wanted to be sure. By now Bruno was leading him into the kitchen, calling, "Rosey, where are you?"

Rosario appeared from behind a row of copper pans hanging from a ceiling rack over one end of a butcher block counter. In front of him, a row of long-bladed kitchen knives bristled from a slotted holder. "Remember this guy?" Bruno asked.

"He worked for Dominic," Sal said. He recognized the cook, but he wanted to drop as many hints as possible. He stuck out his hand. "How are you? Sally. How're you doing?"

"Oh, yeah. Sally," Rosario responded after a long look. Sal felt as if he'd passed an important test.

In the bar again, the talk returned to Sal's earlier case before Judge Brennan.

"I don't know how much you gave these lawyers," Bruno said. "I hope you didn't give them too much."

"You know, Mike Coiro last time, took me for like seventy-five thousand." Sal figured it wouldn't hurt to inflate the bribe.

"Oh, my God," said Bruno. "Jesus Christ. I never handled anything that big." He advised Sal to stay away from lawyers. "Lawyers kid you. Judges don't get nothing."

Bruno's last words as Sal left the restaurant, deserted now except for the two FBI agents who were laughing as they secretly watched from across the bar, were, "We'll work it out. Don't worry about it."

Ethan Levin-Epstein was asleep at his home in New Rochelle, New York, when the phone rang at two in the morning. Dan Russo was on the other end. "Listen to this," Russo said excitedly.

Levin-Epstein heard piano music in the background and a voice, not Polisi's, saying, "Your timing is good. The head man's coming down to see me." He said, "Dan, that's great. That was worth waking up for. Listen, is that a copy of the tape?"

"No, that's the tape. That's the original, right from the Nagra."

"That's our evidence," Levin-Epstein screamed. "What if something happened to it?" He didn't sleep any more that night.

Sal returned to the Runway 84 the next evening with an attractive blonde. He introduced her as "A friend of mine from here, Melinda."

"Melinda. Melinda. Mindy," Bruno greeted her with a restaurateur's ebullience.

It was busy, a Friday night. "Sit right here," said Bruno, indicating the house table, the first table to the left inside the dining room. Sal ordered an appetizer of Italian seafood and a bottle of Pouilly-Fuissé. Mindy conveniently excused herself to go to the bathroom, and Sal and Bruno moved to the bar for a huddled conversation. Bruno said he'd telephoned Brennan with the information about Polisi, but he was less optimistic about putting Sal together with the judge.

"He may not want to talk," he said. "He may not want to sit down with you, but he'll tell me, and I'll deliver whatever has to be done to you. You know?"

"Whatever," Sal replied.

"Look, I don't like to put you in a spot," said Bruno. "If it's hot he may not want to, you know. He figures you're out on bail, you could be followed, who the fuck knows, you know?"

"No problem."

"Wait till he comes. He may think you're wired. Today they, they're so fuckin' scared."

"You can't blame him, you know," Sal said reasonably.

Russo, listening in his rental car in the Waffle House parking lot, chuckled with appreciation.

"Whatever can be done, will be done, that I can tell you," Bruno offered.

Sal said, "Whatever it costs, let me know. I don't care about the money. See this broad over here." Sal's date had returned and was sitting at the table. "She got money. She got big money."

Bruno said, "Have faith in me."

Sal returned to the table. Later, he and Bruno talked about people and cases they had known in New York. Mindy joined the conversation now and then. They talked about the pitfalls of greed. "Nothing like that greed, boy," Sal said. He used Jackie Donnelly as a for-instance. "You know how much money he made in seventy-nine to eighty-three? I'll tell you, what he had, he could fill that whole room up over there."

"What are you going to do with it? How many cars can you drive?" said Bruno philosophically. "How many Cadillacs?"

"That's okay. We're working on Sal. He's going to turn around," said Mindy Meyer.

Russo thought he detected a wry note in her voice as it came over the transmitter. He shifted in the seat to stretch his legs, caressed his nose enthusiastically and had another quiet laugh. It was good, he thought, for an FBI agent to have a sense of humor.

. . .

One afternoon when Dad was in Florida that first time, and Joe had gone off with Mom to buy groceries, a car pulled up in front of the house and a big guy got out. It was somebody I'd never seen before. I left my homework on the kitchen table and went out. The guy said, "Hey, is your dad at home? I've got something here to show him." He had some accent in his voice, like from down South.

He didn't wait for me to say Dad wasn't home. He ducked back into the car and came out with a hand grenade like you see in the movies. Like a little dull green pineapple. Or a toilet tank ball. You see toys, like Albert had, but something about this one you could tell it was real. You could tell it had weight the way he handled it. I thought, Oh shit, this is one of the bombers. They found out Dad's working for the government. I backed up about three steps and the guy just laughed. "What's the matter, kid?" he said. "I ain't gonna throw it at you. I just brought it t' show your old man. Where's he at?"

He saw me swallow. He got this smirky look and he raised himself up on the balls of his feet once or twice.

"He had to go to Florida. On business," I said. "I don't know when he'll be back."

The guy hawked and spat. "Well, in that case I ain't got time to wait," he said. "I was just passin' by anyway. I reckon he can see it later." He got back into his car and threw gravel going up onto the highway. I felt a sudden urge to go to the bathroom and went back in the house.

Mom and Joe came home from shopping and the first chance I got I took Joe aside. I said, "You won't believe what happened."

"What?" he said. He looked over his shoulder to make sure Mom was still putting away groceries in the kitchen.

"A guy came here with a hand grenade."

Joe got this look, like, oh sure.

I said, "No, I'm not kidding. It must have been one of those bombers Dad told us about. Remember?"

"Sure, I remember. A hand grenade? For sure?"

"Yeah."

"What'd it look like?"

"What do you mean? It looked like a hand grenade."

"What'd he want?"

"He said he wanted to show it to Dad."

Just then Mom came in from the kitchen and I grabbed one of the karting trophies off the shelf between the coal stove and the fireplace. "Remember this race, Joe?" I said. We stared at that trophy like we had X-ray vision. Mom gave us a funny look. She said, "What are you two up to?"

"Nothing, Ma. Just talking."

"Sure you are," she said, and went upstairs.

"Are you gonna tell Mom?" Joe asked me.

"I don't know. She worries about the bombers finding out about Dad and blowing the house up."

"Well, they can't find out when he's down there," Joe said. "Can they?"

When Mom came downstairs again Joe and I were standing together nervously. He poked me in the back and I said, "Mom, a guy came here with a hand grenade."

She stopped in the door to the kitchen and said, without turning around, "What did he say?"

"He said he just wanted to show it to Dad."

"That was all?" she said.

"Just that he was passing by and it wasn't no big thing, that Dad could see it later."

"What did you tell him?" She had turned around and was looking at me carefully. "Did you tell him your father was in Florida?"

"Yeah, I did, Ma. Why?"

"You told him we were alone here?"

"So?"

"Oh, my God, Sal, what's wrong with you? We have no idea what's going on where he is, or who these people know. What if this judge finds out and lets everybody know, and they know somebody he knows? They'll know he's working against them."

"I don't know, Ma. This guy didn't look like he knew any judges. Except maybe like Dad does."

"I don't care," she said. "I just wish you didn't say he's away. I'll worry every night until we're out of here."

She lit another cigarette, coughed and went into the kitchen. I slunk away outside. Joe came in a minute and we stood there and didn't say anything to one another. Light clouds streaked the sky and past the woodline to the west, the sky was starting to get red. After a while Joe said, "Sal, are you worried?"

I looked at him and he didn't look like a little kid anymore. I could see he was going to be bigger than I was. "Not like Mom is," I said.

"No, I mean about what's going to happen to us."

I couldn't imagine what was going to happen. From the first moment Dad had talked to us, I had tried to see into the future, and it was blank. I saw us in a rowboat without oars in a stormy river, and other times in a space capsule floating in space, but where we were going was never revealed to me. Wherever it was, though, we were going there, and it looked as if there was nothing we could do about it. So I said, "No, I'm not worried. Are you?"

And Joe said, "No," too.

We were by the woodpile. Dad's ax was chunked into the stump where he split the logs into firewood and I pulled it out of the stump and hefted it. I balanced a dry log on the stump and tapped the ax blade into the end of it, lifted it and brought it down. The log split neatly. I did it again, and again, until a pile of split wood littered the ground around the stump. It was dark then, I was bathed in sweat, my sweater was full of bark chips and I had forgotten to worry about the hand grenade. The future, though, was still impossible to see.

• • •

On the Friday that Sal and his "date" Mindy Meyer ate at Runway 84, Justice William C. Brennan ordered a case file from the clerk's office at Queens Criminal Court. The worker who checked out the file logged it on a card by indictment number, 3738-84, and destination, J. Brennan Chamb., and wondered why the judge wanted the file of a case that was not before him but instead before Justice Rotker.

The next day, Saturday, February 2, 1985, Brennan and his wife boarded a plane at La Guardia Airport and disembarked three hours later at Miami International Airport. FBI agents watched them on and off the plane. Brennan rented a blue Mercury Cougar from Hertz and drove to North Miami Beach, where the Brennans checked into the Pan American Hotel. That afternoon, he spoke to Bruno by phone from the hotel bar.

When Sal and Agent Meyer returned to the Runway 84 on Saturday night, Bruno pulled him outside. A steady stream of cars swooshed by on State Road 84. The restaurant's parking lot was full. From where he stood, Sal could see the Waffle House. Russo's car was out of sight.

Bruno told Sal that he had talked with Brennan, and that nothing would happen in his case for several months. "It'll take time," he said. "They got to figure out what to do." In the meantime, Sal was to sit tight. "Don't reach out no more," Bruno advised.

"Don't do nothing?" Sal asked.

"Don't go to nobody."

"Don't change lawyers?"

"You have the right attorneys."

But Bruno told Sal that his case was going to be difficult to fix. Three judges would have to be involved. "Listen," he said, "this is not going to be cheap. You know that, don't you?"

"I don't care," said Sal, "as long as I know the money is going to the judge."

While Sal and Mindy Meyer were saying their good-byes at Runway 84, Dan Russo started up his rental car and drove to a vacant auto repair shop half a mile away. He pulled between two buildings into an isolated parking area that was out of sight of the street, and waited.

Russo was torn between satisfaction and frustration. Bruno was obviously Brennan's bag man. The judge seemed to be sniffing at the bait. On the other hand, all Sal had on tape so far were Bruno's promises. Sal would have to return to New York for a court appearance the next week. Before he left, Russo wanted specifics: the amount Brennan wanted to fix Sal's case, and a plan and timetable to deliver the money. But Sal couldn't push too hard, for Brennan was cautious and his bullshit detector was very sensitive.

Headlight beams swung across the building wall and pointed up the alley. From the transmitter, Russo could hear Sal chattering away to Mindy Meyer about how his family was snowed in at the racetrack in New York. He thought of his own family in New Jersey, and hoped that his wife Mary Beth would drive safely in the snow. It hadn't been a week, and he already missed her and the children. An agent's family had to endure so many absences. All the same, he wasn't sorry to be missing the drive in and out of Manhattan in the winter weather. These were brief thoughts, for Sal and the female agent were out of the car and walking toward him.

"So he's spending all day Monday with the judge," Russo said, repeating what Bruno had told Sal.

"Is that what he said?" Sal was standing behind Russo's car with his pants down, removing the pouch and the transmitter. He pulled off his sweatshirt as he walked back and began plucking off the strips of tape that held the wires.

"Yeah. That means you've got to meet with him again before you leave. We want to try to get something pinned down here."

"I told him I'd see him Tuesday afternoon," said Sal, pulling his sweatshirt down again.

"Yeah. We'll get together beforehand. Why don't you take the rest of the weekend off? But stay in touch."

"Thanks a lot," answered Sal sarcastically. He drove away, leaving Russo and Mindy Meyer in the parking lot.

Sal spent Sunday and most of Monday walking up and down Fort Lauderdale beach, bending Limbach's ear, cruising the Holiday

Inn pool, nursing bottled Heinekens at the hotel bar. To anyone who asked, he was a businessman on a busman's holiday, a dealer in commercial real estate trying to sell some factory space in Homestead. He was walking, because each time he returned from a taping session the FBI demanded he return the keys to the rental car he'd been given to drive. Then Russo would hustle him out of his third-floor suite at The Breakers. The suite was a field headquarters for the growing cadre of agents now watching Brennan. Sal wanted to hang around and watch the operation against the judge unfold. He thought the sting's planning and complexity resembled an elaborate hijacking, and he had an insatiable curiosity about all of its details. Russo was just as determined to hand him off to John Limbach. There was little Sal needed to know about the operation beyond his role as the bait. Limbach was there, after all, to keep Sal occupied and to see that he didn't become disgruntled and difficult to handle. By Monday evening Sal was going crazy.

The phone was ringing when he walked in from the beach. Andy Bruno was on the other end. He had spent the day with Brennan at Gulfstream Park, and he wanted to meet with Sal that night. They agreed to meet at eleven-thirty at the Diplomat Hotel on Hollywood Beach, after a dinner the Brunos and the Brennans planned together at a Chinese restaurant, Christine Lee's. Sal called Russo with the news. An hour later he knocked on the door of Russo's command post at The Breakers.

Sal had gone to each meeting with a general idea of what the FBI wanted on the tape. "Here's the scenario," Russo would say. He liked that word, scenario. Russo's ideal scenario would have been Brennan on tape talking with Sal about his case.

"How did he sound? Did he sound like he had a concrete deal in mind?" Russo asked immediately.

"Hard to say," said Sal. He sensed Russo's eagerness to get him into a meeting with Brennan, but if he pushed too hard he would alert Bruno to the sting. "He just wanted to meet, was all he said."

"He spent all day with the judge. Then he wants to meet late. They must have talked about a deal."

"Let's hope. All this footsie's gettin' old," said Sal.

A room service tray of sandwiches arrived. Sal, Russo and a couple of agents from the FBI's Miami office sat down around a crowded coffee table. Russo shoved aside a stack of black-and-white photographs to make room for the tray. The top photo showed Brennan getting into Bruno's white Cadillac El Dorado. They were casually dressed, headed for the racetrack. One of the agents who had watched Bruno and Brennan at Gulfstream before turning the surveillance over to another team was in the shower. He came out of the bathroom, combing his wet hair, and said, "They bet some money today, those guys. I don't know if they won or lost, but they did some serious betting. I'm out of here. See you tomorrow, Dan."

Russo waited for the door to close. He said, "I think Bruno's going to give you the particulars tonight. That's the only reason he'd want a meeting this quick, late at night. This may be the time to tell him you want to sit down with the judge."

"Wait a minute," Sal said. "Bruno's already said the judge don't want to do that. I don't want to make him hinky."

"I don't want to make him hinky either, but we need Brennan on tape. It's direct evidence that he's involved. There must be a reason you can ask to sit down with him."

"Well, sure, I can tell Bruno there's a gimmick in my case the judge can hang his hat on, and that I have to explain it to the judge. This whole thing about my psychiatric record. But why is the judge gonna want to do that?"

"Why wouldn't he?"

"He ain't stupid, is one reason. He's got Bruno so he don't have to sit down with guys he's fixing cases for. Bruno's loose, but the judge ain't. Bruno's already said he's worried about wires. Brennan's gonna smell a rat, we push too hard."

"Don't push too hard, but push a little," Russo said.

Sal was rigged and ready to leave for his rendezvous with Bruno when Russo snapped his fingers. "Hey, I meant to remind you," he said. "Don't talk when he's talking. You've been stepping on his lines. He could say something we need and if you're talking over the top of him, it's no good."

"Well, you know me," said Sal.

"You're a great talker. Try to be a great listener," Russo said.

• • •

The Diplomat rose among the strip of condominium towers and hotels along South Ocean Drive, and though it was in Hollywood it looked more like Miami Beach. Mindy Meyer had dropped Sal off under the concrete awning that soared over the drive-through entrance. The hotel still bubbled with the waning effervescence of a balmy night. Attendants at the valet parking stand were busy with a run of Cadillacs and Lincolns. Hidden lights in the landscaping across the drive made it look as if the flora had an inner life.

Sal saw a white El Dorado turn into the hotel's drive and stop. Sal recognized Bruno at the wheel. He walked down the sloping drive and got into the car. The radio was blasting Mantovani at about a thousand decibels. Sal reached over and turned the volume down. He was relieved when Bruno made no move to turn it up again. Russo had bitched the first night about him sitting too close to the piano.

They exchanged small talk. Then Bruno said, "I've got all the information for you." He fished for the interior light and brought a rectangle of stiff paper from his pocket.

Sal leaned toward him as Bruno turned the ticket this way and that in the dim light. It was a betting slip from Gulfstream Park. Sal realized suddenly that it was filled with handwritten details of his case. "Oh, he gave you a whole rundown! Look at this shit!" he exclaimed.

Bruno read its contents, beginning with the aliases listed on Sal's arrest report. "Sal Dan Anthony . . . all your names, right? Wife's name is Rosemary . . ."

Sal ignored the mistake and leaned closer to read the betting slip. "Hundred thousand cash bail," he read aloud. He hadn't told Bruno any of this. The information could only have come from his file in the Queens Criminal Court. That meant it must have come from Brennan when he and Bruno were together at the racetrack. He concentrated on how to get the betting slip away from Bruno.

"Here's what you're facing," Bruno continued. "CS, CS, whatever that is."

"I don't know," said Sal. He didn't want to explain it meant criminal sale of a controlled substance.

"It's the first, first time fifteen to life minimum, Al."

"I know it."

"Okay. Then you got a CS, same thing, twenty-five to life minimum, Al."

"Ouff," said Sal. Bruno had the details mixed up, but they were all written down. And where'd he get this Al shit all of a sudden, anyway? Guy wasn't exactly a two-hundred-watt bulb.

"You got a second, ah, second felony, eight and three-quarters to life." Sal said he knew that, too, but Bruno continued, "That's where you got caught in the Club Diner."

"How do we get around this?" Sal asked.

"That's what I'm tellin' you. I been telling you, we're gonna get around it."

"Of course, all right." Sal realized he was muttering.

"But, they can't tell me definite at this time. They're gonna . . . you've got everything going for you. Okay?"

"Fine."

"But first of all, you've gotta give me . . . You gotta leave me some money tomorrow and I'll send it up to 'em. They want twenty-five grand sent up to 'em."

"Who?"

"The judges."

In the parking lot of the condominium across South Ocean, Russo breathed out slowly and wondered how long he had been holding his breath. His mind spun ahead to tomorrow. There was no way to get Sal the money that quickly, but the cards were on the table. The judge had named his price, or part of it, and he would wait. Whether other judges were involved was unclear. Probably not, Russo thought. Go for the meeting now.

Sal's voice came over the transmitter, intruding. "Twenty-five down now?"

"Now. Before they start anything. Before they start anything, they get twenty-five. If you're not satisfied what they do, you get your money back. You got everything going for you."

"But what is he gonna guarantee me?"

Bruno said, "They gotta read the tapes."

What tapes? Sal thought. I'm making tapes. He leaned over and tilted the betting slip to look at it. Bruno let him take it. There it was, written under Club Diner: tape recordings. They must have taped him talking to Terri on the phone before they busted him in Queens. He contained a bitter laugh at the irony of it. Bruno was saying the judges would look for a gimmick, a technicality in the tapes, before deciding if they could set him free.

"Here's what they're gonna try to get you." Bruno was pointing to a spot on the betting slip. "They're gonna try to get you one to three and maybe throw it out if they can. They don't wanna promise you this."

"I don't wanna do no time," Sal said. Bruno repeated that that was hard to guarantee with Sal's prior felony conviction.

"That's why I wanted to speak to him," Sal said, feeling dizzy with the way things were rushing past. "There's something more involved about the last motion we made."

Bruno spoke hastily in a flurry of refusals. "He'll find out everything on his own. You don't have to tell him nothing."

"I got an ace in the hole that, that he should know about."

Bruno was shaking his head violently. Sal decided not to press it. Fuck Russo. It had been stupid even to ask.

Bruno reached for the betting slip then and Sal reflexively held onto it. They were suspended for a moment like two children with a wishbone. Sal read in Bruno's heavy face the realization that Sal wanted to keep the slip. "You're not trying to set me up?" he demanded.

"No," Sal said indignantly.

"Are you . . ."

"Andy, listen to me. Andy!"

Bruno laughed at the hurt expression on Sal's face. "I'm an old man. I'm trying to do you a favor, all right?"

"I'm trying to stay out of jail."

"All right. And I'm trying to keep you out of jail."

Sal insisted Bruno relay the details of his gimmick. Bruno wrote on the front of the betting slip, "Motion to withdraw a plea," a reference to Sal's earlier case before Brennan in which he'd used his psychiatric record as an excuse to withdraw his guilty plea. Bruno made a couple more notations and put the slip into an inside pocket of his jacket. Sal watched it disappear. "I don't wanna do no time if I don't have to," he repeated.

"Let me explain to you," said Bruno. "I told him you'd be willing to give another seventy-five thousand if they got you out free."

"Yeah. The hundred, you got it," Sal said without hesitation. Too quickly, he thought in the next instant, but Bruno showed no reaction.

Sal told Bruno he had to make a court appearance in New York. He'd bring the down payment when he returned. Brennan would still be in Florida to accept the money. "I'll give it to Brennan and then he takes it up," Bruno said.

"Can I drop you off anywhere?" Bruno asked at the end of the meeting.

"Naw, I'm going to call my girl. She'll pick me up." Sal watched Bruno pull onto South Ocean and drive toward his home in Hallandale. Sal wanted to get away from the hotel. He was walking north beside the road, talking into his sleeve to give Russo his location, when he felt headlights and saw his shadow fall across the grass. The car pulled close behind him. He kept walking. The car drew even. The window descended and a dark shape leaned over from the driver's seat. Passing headlights lit up the profile of a Roman nose. "Good show," Dan Russo said.

Sal Polisi junior and his cousin Albert in a family snapshot.

*Sal and Rose Marie Polisi and
Sal junior at the wedding of
Sal's friend "Funzy" Terracone.
Sal junior was the ringbearer.
Rose Marie asked that her face
be obscured to deter
identification.*

Sal coaching a member of Sal junior's midget football team in the LynVets League in Ozone Park. The "R" on Sal's cap stands for Redskins.

The LynVet Redskins doing calesthenics at the Cross Bay Oval as Sal watches. The league practiced and played Saturday games at the field near Kennedy Airport.

The Sal Polisi family during a visit to Lewisburg Federal Penitentiary in Pennsylvania, where Sal spent fifteen months for bank robbery.

Sal and Rose Marie early in their marriage.

Sal junior and Joseph, beginning to take football to heart.

Sal junior on a pony ride at the 88th Street Playground near his house.

Sal junior as a quarterback for the LynVet Redskins.

Joseph Polisi (Number 8) ready to leave the pits at the Noto Raceway, the karting track Sal operated near Port Jervis, New York.

*Sal riding a motorbike with his nephew Albert near Sal's home in   Ozone Park,
Queens.*

N I N E

Dad came back from Florida on a Tuesday night. He called from the airport and two hours later we heard a horn tooting and tires crunching in the snow. We went outside to greet him. The air was creaky with cold, and a three-quarter moon showed the ruts of Joe's sled runs in the glittering white blanket that lay over the slopes and hollows of the racetrack.

"Madonna," he said as he stepped out of the car and broke through the crust into ankle-deep snow. He lifted his foot and started shaking it, and then the other one. "Oh, shit. This is cold. Forget-aboutit." He hopped toward the door, leaving one of us to carry his suitcase. I grabbed it from the backseat and we followed him inside. He went straight to the coal stove and started pulling off his sneakers. He wasn't wearing any socks. When he was standing barefoot in his velour sweat suit with his back to the stove and the three of us looking at him, he got a sheepish look. "I forgot it could get this cold," he said. "How're you guys doing?"

Mom gave him a hug and kissed him on the cheek. "Look at your tan," she said. "That's disgusting."

"Yeah, Pop," Joe chimed in, "I thought you were supposed to be working."

"At night they got me working. During the day I got nothing to do. Hang out. Talk to John Limbach. I got to go back."

He told us what was happening, that the judge wanted twenty-five thousand up front, and he was home for tomorrow's court appearance and supposedly to close a real-estate deal before returning with the money. The money was actually coming from Washington, or at least the approval to spend it came from there. Russo was supposed to go there in two days.

"It's time to start thinking big time about getting out of here," Dad said. "Once I pay the money, that's it. As soon as the judge gets it they'll arrest him. When they arrest him the word'll get out quick, and we're outta here."

There was something final in his voice this time. I had a sinking feeling, and a rush of resentment for the forces that were changing our lives. In this category I placed the government, the people in the mob who would want to kill my dad and last of all, my dad, for his eagerness to take us down this road to who knew what. At the same time I felt anticipation. There was a racing in the veins like when I heard my number in the huddle. At that moment I believed, actually believed for the first time, after all the talk and all the waiting, that it would happen.

In the same moment, I made up my mind to tell Linda.

It had been harder and harder to keep up the lie. We were together almost all the time, whether it was studying after school at her house or mine or out on a date or just a pep rally or something. After that Saturday before Christmas at Rockefeller Center neither of us had brought the subject up. She didn't ask, and I didn't talk about it. It was like we'd said as much as the subject required and we really didn't want to say any more because it was too painful. But for me it sat there like a snarling dog inside the junkyard fence, waiting to be dealt with.

Mom reheated a pan of baked lasagna for Dad's supper. Afterward she popped a bowl of popcorn and we sat in front of the fireplace together. It was like the nights we had come to love after we moved to Port Jervis, Dad home instead of out, he and Mom nice to each other instead of arguing. "A real American life," is what Dad called it. He was telling us about taping Andy Bruno when he fell asleep in the recliner, and Mom had to wake him up so he could go to bed.

He took us to school the next morning on his way to New York to court. He dropped Joe at the middle school. I went to get out, too, because the middle school and the high school were next door to one another, but he motioned for me to stay in the car. He drove slowly around to the high-school entrance, and we sat there with the motor idling while kids were streaming into school, huddled in their winter parkas, blowing frosty clouds in front of them.

"Look," he said, "I been thinking. There's no reason for you to stick around for the grand exit unless you really want to, is there?"

"What do you mean?" I didn't have any idea.

"Things are gonna get crazy after I deliver the money and the guy gives it to the judge. We might have to leave here all of a sudden in the middle of the night. It ain't gonna be a picnic. I thought you might want to avoid all that and leave beforehand. Go on the lam." He grinned. "I told Bruno that's what I was gonna do, I couldn't fix this case. So, you want to lam it outta here?"

"How'm I gonna do that?"

"I talked to the Prices when I was in Florida. Harold and them say you want to go out and stay with them for a while, it's okay. He was always a good influence on you. It wouldn't hurt you to spend some time with them out in California. You can hook up with us when you get back."

"Where, though?"

"We'll keep in touch. Or Russo'll know. Just get in touch with Russo, and he'll get you to where we are."

Harold Price was a guy we'd met in 1977, at the IKF Grand Nationals in Atwater, California. He was as different from my dad as you could imagine. I mean, my dad took me on kart trips where I can remember him being drunk and swinging from chandeliers in the rooms we stayed in, trashing the rooms, breaking furniture, stealing towels, just didn't care. Harold was real straight, and real sober. He was tall, with curly blond hair, a real sincere guy, and a Christian, I mean, he read the Bible all the time, but he didn't push it on you. Harold was a teenager then, like seventeen, and some kart driver. He won two classes that year. It was the first year I raced, and finished twenty-first in rookie. Anyway, Dad had made up this clutch oil, we called it The Goop, and it was about a hundred and ten degrees out there and The Goop was the only stuff that would keep your kart from bogging off the corners. That was originally what brought us together. And then we just got to be friends. It was weird how our families got along, Harold and his brother Mike and their parents and me and Joe and Mom and Dad. Dad always used to say, "What love in that family," and I think when he was around them he was sorry for the kind of person he was even though he always went back to it. Anyway, we stayed in touch and Harold had moved on into automobile racing.

"*What about school?*" *It sounded like I was going to miss a lot of school. That sounded pretty neat.*

"*Aw, your school's gonna be screwed up anyway, when we have to get outta here. You'll need two good years to impress the college scouts. Maybe you can do your junior year again when we get settled, or go to school out there, whatever. But forget about that. We'll worry about that later. The thing is, if you go you can tell Linda you're going on a trip. You don't have to just disappear. You can say good-bye to her. By the time you get back we'll be gone and it'll all be over with. It wouldn't be like you were lying to her. You'd just be going on a trip.*"

"*For how long?*"

"*Who knows? A week. A month. A few months. What's the difference?*"

He was right, in his way. It would be easier this way. I could say good-bye, at least, and that way I wouldn't be responsible for leaving without a word. Less to feel guilty about.

"*I wouldn't mind doing that,*" *I said.*

The bell rang signaling ten minutes to go until home room. I started to go and he said, "Son, I know you're going to talk to Linda. You're just going on a trip, okay? Just going to visit your friend Harold. Be gone a week or two."

I walked through the turquoise blue doors into Port Jervis High thinking how I was going to tell Linda. It wouldn't be enough to tell her I was going on a trip, even if it was technically true. Because it was a trip I probably wasn't coming back from as far as she and Port Jervis were concerned. I sat in trigonometry and wrote her a note that said I wanted to come over after school to work on homework.

I got to her house after wrestling practice. It was well dark by six o'clock, and the lights were on. I parked on the street, and walked up the driveway and around to the back. I doubt if anybody in ten years had used the front door; the Millers' was one of those informal houses where everybody went in and out the back door, and the kitchen was like the foyer to the rest of the house because it was the most comfortable way. The back door was open. I just walked in and heard Linda from the den, calling, "Sal?"

"Hi," she said when I walked into the den. She was sitting on the tweed love seat just inside the door, looking up with her blue eyes, looking cozy in tight jeans and a sweater and her legs curled up under her. Her blue slippers were on the floor beside the love seat.

"Where is everybody?" I asked.

"I don't know. Shopping, I think. They should be back in a while. Sit down." She patted the cushion beside her.

I sat down and kissed her and with that sense girls have she pulled back and said, "What's wrong?"

I didn't wait to get scared this time, or to think about the reaction she would have. I took a deep breath and said, "I'm going on a trip."

"What kind of trip?"

"To California."

"To California?" Her eyes got wide. Linda had never traveled much. "What for?"

I took both her hands. "Listen," I said, "the truth is I'm probably going to be leaving. It's . . . I can't really explain why. I mean, it's about my father and everything. Everything that's been going on. He's not going to jail, it's not that. It's just something I can't talk about. Can you understand that?" She looked like she was trying, hard. I couldn't tell what she was thinking, though. Maybe flashing back to the story in the paper that said my dad was in the Mafia, adding it all up, a little fear creeping in around the edges as she tried to make sense of it.

"For how long?"

"I don't know," I said. "I'm supposed to tell you a week or a few weeks, but it might be longer. But maybe I won't be able to come back."

Her face bunched up. "What do you mean? Not ever?"

I took a deeper breath this time. "It depends. It depends on some things that are happening. I'd never leave you forever. You know that." I didn't sound convincing, even to myself.

Linda was confused. I could see her trying to put her emotions on hold until she decided what to think, but she was doing her best to keep from crying. I wanted to make it easier on her, to lay out the whole story of how Dad was working for the government. But I couldn't. Dad had made us promise to keep it in the family. He'd told us it was dangerous information, and I didn't want her to get hurt.

"I can't tell you everything," I said. "I want to, but I can't. It's just something I have to do, going on this trip. But the way you'll know what's going on is if my parents and my brother are gone all of a sudden. Then you'll know I won't be back right away. Okay? Then I'll get in touch with you later." The idea that it was going to be completely, totally, absolutely over was just too much to think about. I didn't see how it could happen, draw a curtain on your life and never open it again.

Headlights turned up the driveway and Linda's parents' car passed underneath the window. A moment later they were coming in the back door with grocery bags. Linda's father came straight into the den while her mother and two sisters were clattering around in the kitchen, putting things away. He saw me and said, "Oh, how are you, Sal?" He didn't seem surprised to see me. I said, "Hi, Mr. Miller." He looked tired. He took off his overcoat and brown felt hat and hung them on a wall peg in the central hall. Then he came back into the den, turned on the evening news and sank into his chair near the TV.

"Oh, Sal's here," her mother said a minute later when she came in from the kitchen. Her sisters, Laurie and Lisa, came in, too, and started teasing us about sitting too close together to be studying. Just like that, the house was full, everybody treating me like a member of the family, as if I had my place in the den like everybody else, nobody paying special attention, just being friendly and nice and acting like I was going to be around forever. Linda didn't say anything. I guess she was waiting to know more.

We talked about nothing for a while, the wrestling team, the cold and snow, a competition Linda and the cheerleading squad had coming up. As soon as we could, Linda and I made an excuse to go down to the rec room and work on our homework.

Lisa was down there, watching TV. There was no place to keep talking. Linda's room was off-limits; Mrs. Miller wouldn't let us go in there alone. I tore a page out of my notebook as I did almost every day in class. Somehow writing a note was easier than talking.

"*You can't tell anybody this, okay?*" *I whispered.*

She nodded.

I wrote: "Linda,

"*Don't cry over nothing. It's hard I know because I've thought about it for weeks now. At first I was gonna go along with my father's way of telling you I was only going for a week, but it wouldn't be fair to you. You must understand this might not be what is gonna happen. If I don't go I'll be here for a long while. I don't know if it's gonna happen. If I go you must know it won't change the way I feel about you, I'll always love you and will wait 4-ever until the day we're together 4-ever. I LOVE YOU—ALWAYS. But you must be strong and have faith in God. Don't worry. We love each other too much to let a little break in our relationship hurt us. This period of time would be short compared to the rest of our life together.*"

I showed her the note and she bent over it so I couldn't see her face. I took her hand and she let it lie loosely in mine. She looked up and shook her head. "I can't believe this is happening," she said in a whisper. Then she jumped up and ran upstairs.

I felt like I'd just walked outside and turned around to find the door had closed and locked behind me. Laurie came downstairs and I pretended to be reading the note I'd just written.

"*Where'd Linda go?*" *Laurie was the oldest sister, the one with the husky voice. It wasn't the moment to remember that I thought her voice was sexy.*

"*She went upstairs. I was working on an English theme.*"

"*Is that it? Let me see.*"

I stared down at the note. "Oh. Oh, no, that's . . . this is something else," I stammered. "The theme is . . . I don't have it. Linda's got it. She went upstairs to, to look up a word in the dictionary."

"*What's the word?*" *Laurie asked.*

"*Uh, it's, it's 'judge.'*" *It was the first word that came into my mind.*

"*Judge?*" *Laurie looked at me funny.*

"*Judge, judgment. It's judgment.*"

"*Well, you know what that means.*" *Laurie had her hands on her hips and was looking at me like I was stupid.*

"Sure, I know what it means." I tried to be indignant. "I just couldn't remember how to spell it."

That satisfied her. "Oh, well," she said, and took a place in front of the TV. She was looking for a place to set her drink when Linda reappeared. Her eyes showed concern, but they looked dry, and her lips were set in a firm line. Brave. She looked brave. I prayed Laurie wouldn't ask her how to spell 'judgment.' She didn't. Linda sat down next to me and pulled her feet up under her. I looked at her anxiously. She mouthed the words, "I'm okay."

She took the note from my hand and read it again. Then she took it, wrote something at the bottom and handed it to me. I read the words, "Will you be safe?"

"Oh, yeah. Yeah," I said, "no problem."

She leaned her head against mine and I heard her say softly, "That's okay, then."

I wanted to unmake the whole thing, unmake leaving, undo the idea that I might be gone forever. I sat with my arm around her shoulder and stared toward the television glow. She took the note again and wrote on it, "Can you say you're going on a trip but just not why?"

"I guess so," I said.

"Laurie, Lisa? Sal's going on a trip to California." Just like that.

They turned around, all ears. "California?" They were as surprised as I had been when Dad talked about it just that morning. It felt like years ago.

"To visit a friend of mine out there," I said. "This family we know from karting."

"Oh, wow. When are you going?"

"I don't know. In a week or two, probably."

"For how long?"

"Just for like a week." Now that it was out in the open, it sounded like just another trip, like maybe to the deli to pick up a carton of milk.

Mrs. Miller's voice came from the top of the stairs. "Sal? Have you had anything to eat?"

"Oh, thanks, Mrs. Miller. Thanks. My mom's expecting me," I said.

"Sal's going to California," Laurie called.

"Gosh, it's late," I said, looking at my watch. "I'd better go or I'll be late for supper." Upstairs as I was saying my good-byes, there was talk of California, leaving school, how lucky I was to get out of school to go on such a journey, especially with the snow and winter weather in New York.

Linda walked me to the door and came outside onto the back steps. The night was clear, the air sharp in my lungs. "I love you, whatever happens," I said. "We'll always be together."

She put her arms around me and pressed the side of her face against my chest. I tilted her face up and in the porch light saw the beginnings of tears forming in her eyes. "I want to know why, but I don't really. I guess someday I will."

"Someday," I said. "But don't cry. Promise you won't. You have to be strong about this. We both do. We'll have time to talk to-morrow." I remembered something. "Don't keep that note. Or show it to anybody. Okay? Tear it up and throw it away. Promise you'll do that, okay?"

"Okay," she said.

She went inside. I was walking down the driveway when Linda raised the den window and called, "Be careful." From behind her I heard her sister's voice. "So how do you spell 'judgment,' anyway?"

My note from trigonometry the next morning started, "Hey, bud. What's up? How you doin' today?" I felt bruised and tentative, like not writing her but like I needed to, to make things all right. "Listen, you shouldn't worry about this so much," I wrote. "I can understand how you're feeling but not exactly. But you must be strong, like I told you last night. This is not definite, O.K. Please don't cry. I'll be yours forever. I mean it. Forever is a long, long time. Things like this are only for a while. But don't worry so much. Our love is too great to let something like this stand in our way."

The teacher was starting to go around and pick up homework assignments. The last thing I wrote before I shoved the note between the pages of a book was, "My time's up, honey." I didn't know how true that was.

That afternoon my dad said the plans were made. On Friday he came to take me out of school.

He explained to the principal that I had an opportunity to visit a friend in California for a week and that I would be sure to take along my homework. Of course the principal agreed.

Dad and Joe and I went together to see Brian Seeber. We owed him a good-bye. Coach Seeber not only had picked up that I was a better running back than a quarterback, but Joe had played for him on the freshman team and even though he played both ways, Coach had figured out that he was going to be a linebacker. Joe had the speed for it and he liked to hit, like he was angry at the runner, the quarterback, whoever. "Channel it and you'll be great," Coach Seeber told him. He coached wrestling, too, and Joe had joined the freshman wrestling team. I managed the varsity wrestlers, taking care of their uniforms and headgear and making sure the mats were mopped every day after practice, and in exchange Coach Seeber let me work out with the team's weights. Because we were close to him, Dad took him aside and kind of hinted at the story. It was okay for him to tell, but not the rest of us.

Coach Seeber was in his office in the phys. ed. department over in the middle school, sitting in his sweats behind his desk that had a nameplate carved by some kid in wood shop and a clutter of papers and little souvenir footballs and plastic helmets and little wrestling trophies. I thought of him with his flashlight that night up at football camp. He got up and closed the door when we came in, like he knew why we were there. You could still hear the phys. ed. classes outside in the gym, their shouts echoing as they played volleyball.

Dad said, "Remember the thing I told you about?"

Coach closed the grade book he'd been writing in, and nodded slowly.

"Well, it's getting ready to happen. I'm taking Sal out of school today. He's going on a trip and the rest of us are leaving soon. We wanted to come and say good-bye."

Coach leaned back and massaged the back of his neck, like he was trying to give it strength to hold up his big head. "I knew you would be, sooner or later. I kept hoping it would be later."

"So did we," Dad said. "And it hasn't happened yet. But it could be, you know, complicated. So we might not get another chance."

Coach waited. He looked like, what do you call it, a basset hound, his sadness magnified by the size of his face. I started to talk and something grabbed my throat and pushed the words back. I started again and managed, "I just wanted to say thanks, Coach. For everything." I choked it out and was embarrassed at the wetness in my eyes.

Joe rose to the occasion. He said, "I wish we were gonna still be here so you could be our coach." Then he ducked his head. He was crying, too.

Coach Seeber didn't use tough talk like a lot of other coaches. He was strict, and kids were afraid of him, but there was no bullshit about him. He said, "I'm going to miss you boys. Just keep doing what you've learned. Work as hard as you've worked for me and you'll be successful." He cleared his throat.

We all stood up at the same time. There was no sense prolonging it.

At the door I said, "What'll you tell the team?"

"I don't think I'll tell them anything. They'll find out. Somebody else can manage the equipment."

"Good luck," I said. "Tell Doug"—Douglas Keys was a wiry little kid who looked to win the state championship in the 105-pound class—"good luck."

And that was it. Coach Seeber turned his big, sad face back into his office and the door closed and we were in the hall. I went back and emptied my locker. I was just down the hall from Linda's third period English class, and I stood outside the door and tried to get her attention. We had said good-bye the night before, pretending for her parents' benefit and mine like it was really just a trip. Her mother even left us alone in her room for a few minutes. I told her I'd be back someday and not to worry. Now, when she looked up, I lifted a hand and said, "Good-bye" with my lips. She glanced at the

front of the room, and back at me, and then down at her book again.
She didn't have to mimic any words. I had seen her eyes.

. . .

Sal was back in Fort Lauderdale, at the Holiday Inn on the
beach, getting used to the sun again and the balmy evenings and,
now that he thought about it, the good food at Andy Bruno's place.
Rosario, the chef, was doing a good job. Definitely New York Italian.
Definitely Queens, New York, Italian, which the tourists on Mulberry
Street in Little Italy seldom got, paid a premium for when they did
and had to put up with strolling concertinas in the bargain. They
went to Umbertos Clam House because Joey Gallo had been shot
there, for the romance of sitting at the scene of a Mafia hit. There
were plenty of places they could have gone in Queens, and eaten
better, too.

From where he sat at the bar in Runway 84, Sal could see the
row of portholes over the dimly lighted booths, including the one in
the corner where the agents sat nursing an after-dinner round of
cognacs and comparing bogus golf scores. Bruno came in from the
dining room, complaining, "I mean all this regular food I serve, and
they wanna eat a ham and cheese?"

In the next breath he said, "Have your hearing yet? Did you
have your hearing?" He was spending less time chatting, getting right
to Sal's case. Sal liked that. But Bruno was still talking about a C-
felony, one to three years, still the best Brennan could promise
without finding a gimmick.

"Yeah, but I don't want this. You don't understand," Sal said.
If he'd been trying to fix the case for real, he would have hugged a
C-felony harder than his long-lost mother. One to three against fifteen
to life, are you kidding?

"I can't tell you nothing else until they dig into this fucking
mess," Bruno said.

"Did you talk to him?"

"Of course I talked to him." Bruno in his indignation drew
himself up and transferred some of his weight from his belly to his
chest.

"And what did he say?" Sal wanted to know.

"I told you. 'Would you tell the guy the worst he can get is a C-felony.' "

"Listen to me, Andy, did you tell him about the other case?"

"Yeah, he has a slight recollection, but he never got no money."

"What?"

"I said, 'He never got no money.' "

"He never got no money?"

"He got no money."

Sal didn't know whether to eat his Amaretto glass or hug Bruno around the neck. He couldn't believe he'd pissed away fifty thousand dollars. Fixing that case was what had brought him here, on the verge of the Witness Protection Program. And Brennan didn't get the money? Either Brennan was lying or Coiro had lied when he told Sal he'd fixed the case. On the other hand, it was the perfect opening. If you can't meet with Brennan, Russo had said, try to get him to show that he's involved.

Sal said he was worried about the same thing happening again. He said he wanted to see Brennan and Bruno together. "You going to be at the track Saturday?" he asked. "I don't have to talk to the guy. Forget that. I don't have to talk to him. I'll give it to you," he said, talking about the money, "but, I just want to make sure I see him there."

Suspicion fell over Bruno's heavy face. "You sure you're not . . . you know, wired or anything?"

"Andy, what are we dealing . . . I'm dealing with fifteen to life here, Andy. Are you going to give me a break or what? Come on."

"I'm giving you a break, but don't hurt me." He told Sal to meet him by the escalator at the Gulfstream Park clubhouse. "Then you'll see who I'm dealing with."

The FBI agents who flooded the Diplomat Hotel restaurant the next afternoon saw Brennan pull Bruno away from the table and steer him away from the other guests. The two men stood near the maître d' station, their hands moving in angry gestures as they appeared to argue. One agent overheard a snatch of conversation. "Call it off, something's wrong," Brennan said.

Sal was in his room at two o'clock when Bruno's phone call came. There was something in his voice. "Got a problem?" Sal said.

"Yeah."

"Really?"

"Maybe you created the problem, you know."

"I did?" Sal did his best to act incredulous. "I don't understand."

"Stop by and I'll tell you," Bruno invited.

"I told you we were gonna push him too far," Sal complained. "I shoulda never told him I had to see the judge. He's convinced I'm wired. I see him tonight, I'm not wearing the recorder." He said it flatly, leaving no room for argument.

"Fine," said Russo. "I agree, but the meeting's got to be recorded. Unless you're gonna remember the conversation, word for word, and be able to testify to it and produce a transcript. And we can convince a judge and jury you've got the greatest memory in the world."

Russo rolled his eyes from sheer weariness and found himself looking up through the shock of black hair that always fell across his forehead. From that angle he couldn't see the gray, but he could see it in the mirror, more of it than he remembered every time he looked. He pinched the bridge of his proud Roman nose between his fingers and massaged the inside corners of his eyes. He'd been back in Florida for a week now, since flying down from Washington with the authorization to give Sal the cash to give to Bruno if it came to that. He'd spent exactly one hour in the sun, if you counted walking across the street for lunch at Denny's, and was averaging five hours of sleep a night. Who'd have thought Bruno and Brennan would be so hard to watch? There was so much ground to cover between the Pan American in North Miami Beach and Bruno's home in Hallandale and the Runway 84, Bruno's and Brennan's lunches with their wives and trips to the racetrack. Russo's suite was more like a locker room, surveillance agents coming on and off shift, the technical teams monitoring Sal's recordings and the tap on Brennan's room phone at the Pan American, almost fifty people altogether. The Breakers' management had finally asked exactly what Mr. Russo was doing up there in his third-floor suite, with all those men coming and going at all hours. They suspected he was running a stable of male prostitutes. That was when he'd given up having the room cleaned in favor of security, instead asking maid service to knock on the door and leave the towels and sheets he needed. The maids had not complained; the spring-break college crowds were arriving in Fort Lauderdale and they had more than enough to do already.

Levin-Epstein was repeating what Russo had just told Sal. "It's got to be recorded. Everything. I told you that past history didn't matter. See, Brennan denied to Bruno that he got money from your case. Your word against his, who's going to win? This has got to be airtight." Levin-Epstein had arrived the week before. The assistant district attorney's first job had been to convince a federal judge at two in the morning to order the wiretap he sought on Brennan's room phone. He was there to keep the investigation on firm legal ground. He didn't want to prosecute a tainted case, or one he wasn't reasonably sure of winning. Sal found Levin-Epstein irritating.

"Yeah, so what are we gonna do?" Sal said. "You gotta put me someplace you can wire. Can't you stick a bug under a table in the restaurant, something like that?"

"Not and be sure it's the one you're gonna sit at," Russo answered. "Besides, you got to get a court order." He rubbed his jaw, feeling the day's stubble against the palm of his hand. Agent Vince Wincelowicz stirred himself across the room. He was coordinating surveillance for the operation, and had given everybody code names. He was "Big Daddy," Russo was "Quincy" and Levin-Epstein was "The Pope." Big Daddy said, "You know, we put that bug in Bruno's car last week," he said.

"That's right." Russo remembered. They'd done it after Bruno had met Sal at the Diplomat and they'd spent the whole time talking in the car. It had taken another application and a judge's order. "Question is, how're we gonna get him in his car if Sal's supposed to meet him at the restaurant?"

Russo got up and walked to the window and looked out, squinting at the reflection of the sun dancing off the Intracoastal Waterway. He was silent for several minutes. Suddenly he turned around, snapping his fingers. He said, "You can . . ."

Sal completed the sentence. ". . . have a flat tire."

Sal stopped two blocks from the Exxon station on State Road 84 a mile from Bruno's restaurant. He got out and walked around to the right side of the car, away from traffic. At the rear fender, he bent down, unscrewed the cap on the tire's air valve, inserted the tip of a ball-point pen into the nozzle and held it there until the tire was flat. Then he got back into the car and drove into the Exxon station with the tire flapping.

"Hey, I need my tire fixed," he called to the attendant. "It's got a nail or something."

"It will take, I don't know, thirty minutes or an hour." The guy looked like an Iranian, smoky face, black heavy beard.

"That's okay," said Sal. "I got to meet somebody. You got a phone?"

Sal made his call, hung up the phone and waited. In five minutes he saw the El Dorado's headlights coming down State Road 84. He left the pay phone and paced in front of the garage bay doors and his car with the flat tire until Bruno pulled into the station. "Fuckin' rental cars," he said when he climbed into the front seat. "I'm almost here, it just goes flat. Musta been a nail or something. What's up?"

Bruno was motioning Sal to be quiet. He steered back onto the four-lane road, busy with Friday night traffic, and handed Sal a note. Sal read, "If you can't prove you're not wired, the deal's off."

Sal went crazy. "Fucker!" he screamed. He crushed the note in his hand and flung it against the windshield. "Motherfucker!" He pulled his sweatshirt up. "Cocksucker!" He unfastened his pants, raised off the seat and started to push them down. "You want to know if I'm wired? Take a look. You want to see?" Bruno edged over closer to his door and watched Sal with alarm. He started flapping his right hand, motioning Sal to stop. A driver in the right-hand lane yelled, "Crazy son of a bitch," and gunned his car to get his wife and two kids away from the sight of Sal taking off his clothes. "What do you think I am? What the fuck?" Sal yelled from inside his sweatshirt, wrestling with it. "Am I wired? Tell me. Am I fucking wired? I almost killed a guy, called me a snitch. I oughta kill your rotten ass."

"Sal, Sal, put your clothes back on." Bruno was pressed against the door, watching Sal with sidelong glances, looking around nervously, trying to stay on the road at the same time.

"You wanted to know if I was wired." Sal pulled the sweatshirt off over his head, sailed it toward the backseat and at the same time looked around. There was the chase car, just another rental, back in the line of traffic, maneuvering to activate the transmitter the FBI had placed in Bruno's car.

Now Bruno was starting to apologize. "These guys are so fucking scared."

"What does he want me to do? Do you want me to strip down?" Sal lifted himself off the seat again, pushing at his pants. He had to save the deal, get Brennan back into the fix. He could see the Witness Protection Program going up in smoke, Levin-Epstein saying, "Did you put the money in his hands? Did you even put it into Bruno's?"

"No, I don't want nothing," Bruno said. It was Brennan. "When I kept going back to him and tellin', 'Look, he wants to see you get the money . . .' "

"I don't have to see him get the money."

Bruno shifted his glance between Sal and the road, looking confused. "There's something wrong here."

"I don't have to see him get the money. I didn't say that. I said to you, 'I just wanna make sure the guy's here.' That's all." Sal reminded Bruno that his previous bribe had never made its way to Brennan.

"All right. But you're now, you're dealing direct. Don't you understand?"

"But I don't know that," Sal said.

"Well, if you don't know it, then you don't trust the people that sent you," said Bruno, his voice heavy with frustration. But more relaxed, wanting to believe Sal. The whole thing was Sal's fault. "You made me make a wrong move," Bruno said, Sal agreeing in his mind, praying he hadn't pushed too far, Bruno quoting Brennan: " 'Why is the guy consistently insisting upon meeting me? Any deal you ever had, did anybody ask to meet me?' " But by then Sal had his sweatshirt on again, and they had all but apologized to one another.

"We don't trust each other because of all the bullshit going on," Sal confided. "All I wanted, to be assured that this guy's getting the money. You know what I mean? But you know how you make me feel? You're talking . . ."

"But you made me feel the same way."

Bruno was driving aimlessly among the Gold Coast sprawl of gas stations, fast-food restaurants, strip shopping centers, past Dania Jai Alai, the citrus stands near the Fort Lauderdale Airport, the malls that were closing for the night. In the constant flow of traffic, one rental car looked like another. As the chase car shadowed the white El Dorado, Russo waited by a bank of public phones on State Road 84 for word that the sting was on again.

Sal said, "Andy, okay, fine. My mind is clear now. My mind is clear." After a pause he said, "And what is your mind?"

"My . . . now it's clear. Now you're talking to me like this, it's clear."

"I mean, what the fuck?" Sal said. "I mean, what do I gotta do? Go get examined?"

"No, come on. You know what's goin' on in this fuckin' world today." Bruno said judges had every right to be nervous. "Let me tell you something. You give up a judge, that says you get immunity. They give you . . . lifetime parole."

"How you gonna settle this guy's mind?" Sal asked a few minutes later.

"I'll settle his mind tomorrow. I, I'll tell him I spoke with you. I spoke to somebody and there's nothin' to worry about. That's all. Okay? And it'll go from there."

They rehashed things some more and Sal said, "All right, what do you want me to do now? You want me to stick around?"

"What do you expect?" Bruno said.

"Till tomorrow?" Sal asked.

"Yeah, either tonight, give me the money. I'll give it to him."

Sal agreed to bring the money to Runway 84 the next evening after Bruno and Brennan spent their afternoon at Gulfstream Park. By now the rolling conversation had returned to State Road 84 and they were approaching the restaurant. "Maybe the car is done," Sal said.

"Let's have a drink. It won't be done yet," Bruno said.

Afterward, as they were leaving, Sal looked back at the restaurant and the tower on its roof. "What the hell you use that thing up there for?" he asked.

"Just a dummy," Bruno said distractedly. "It's supposed to represent the airport, I guess."

"This is craziness," Sal said. "I'm worried about you. You're worried about me."

Sal's car was waiting when Bruno dropped him at the Exxon station. "I found no nail," the attendant said. "Just filled it up with air."

"Hey, that's okay, pal. Probably just a slow leak. Don't worry about it. Just a rental, what the hell. Maybe somebody let the air out, just for spite." Sal paid the man, got in and drove away.

Russo was shaking his head in amazement. "I didn't know you were an actor," he told Sal, who was strutting around Russo's suite beaming with pride and reliving his encounter with Bruno. Some other agents and even Levin-Epstein were sitting there listening.

"You shoulda seen me, sitting there half naked. People going by, staring out their windows, thinking it's some crazy man." Sal was pumped. He sat down, stood up again.

"Not far wrong," Russo said.

"Heyyy. Now you know why they call me Sally Upazz'."

"Yeah, so now we've got to give twenty-five thousand dollars to a crazy man."

Levin-Epstein raised a cautionary hand. "We don't know if Brennan's gonna buy it yet. He could still say no."

"He'll buy it," Sal predicted.

Sal was in his room watching a fight on television when the phone rang the next afternoon. It was Bruno, calling from the restaurant. "Everything is okay," he said. "Drop down here when you get a chance, as soon as you can. Because tomorrow morning he's leaving, you know."

There were seven or eight agents in Russo's suite when Sal arrived to pick up the money. The curtains were drawn. Levin-Epstein was sitting on the sofa in a polo shirt and slacks, reading legal documents in the glow of the lamp on the end table. Russo sat at the dining table next to the alcove kitchenette, a small paper bag in front of him amid a clutter of paperwork and his ever-present spiral notebook. "This probably isn't much money to you, Sal, but it's a lot to the bureau," Russo said. He handed him the bag.

The money was in fifties and hundreds, a stack a couple inches thick. Sal started to reach in the bag and Russo said, "Don't touch it."

"What do you mean, don't touch it? How'm I gonna give it to him."

"Give it to him in the bag. It's got fluorescent powder all over it." And also marked, photographed and the serial numbers recorded, Sal said to himself. "We want it on Brennan, not on you," Russo said. "Besides, you might decide to go to a disco later on. You want your hands to glow? Here." He handed Sal a sheet of paper. "You've got to sign for it."

"First time I ever took money off somebody and signed for it," Sal said.

It was almost dark when Sal reached the Runway 84. FBI surveillance teams were in place, watching both Brennan and the money. Sal walked into the bar, gave Bruno the bag and left.

Bruno immediately took the bag into the men's room. On his way out, an agent passing down the narrow hallway bumped against him, and felt the bag of bills in an inner breast pocket of his jacket. Bruno emerged from the restaurant and gave the bag of money to his wife, who drove south on U.S. 1 toward Hallandale. Brennan left his hotel in North Miami Beach at almost the same time and drove north on A1A. The first FBI car following Mrs. Bruno was broadsided by a driver entering a traffic circle. Moments later, a helicopter picked her up again. As she turned east onto Hallandale Beach Boulevard, Brennan turned west on North Miami Beach Boulevard. They continued to converge on the parallel streets, both trailing convoys of surveillance vehicles. Then they were past each other. Brennan continued west toward I-95. Mrs. Bruno, with the twenty-five thousand dollars in her car, went home.

T E N

Standing outside the restaurant under the plum-colored night sky, Sal felt a sharp dissatisfaction. Handing the money to Bruno had been too easy, not nearly as much fun as everything up to that point. It was certainly no challenge for a man of his talents. It was more like he'd planned a hijacking: staked out the warehouse, laid in wait to stick up the driver, taken over the truck, done all that and then walked away before the payoff. The business was unfinished, but not Sal. Sal was finished. That was the worst part; his role in the affair was over.

It was the same helpless feeling he had feared since childhood, the insecurity creeping up in him that he would be forgotten, abandoned, as his mother had abandoned him when he was two. She was a Rockette, that's what everybody said, and when his father turned his back on the fast life, she'd turned her back on Frank Polisi and his two young children, Sal and his older sister, Rosemarie. Sal became uncontrollable. When his father remarried, a severe woman whose maiden name was Sarah Grillo, and the family moved to Long Island, Sal was punished for his outbursts by being chained, like a dog, to a pillar in the basement. Nobody had seen or heard from his mother again. There was a rumor, once, that she had moved to Florida. Sal thought of the old women nodding on the park benches here and there along the beach, or hobbling across Collins Avenue too slowly for the lights. Was she one of them? He didn't care, he told himself, and pushed the thought quickly from his mind. But he still felt lost and edgy now that he wasn't needed anymore.

Sal drove back to the Holiday Inn and rode the elevator to the floor where Kelly and Limbach were staying. He knocked on their door and entered the room talking. "Man, I'm telling you there's some gorgeous pussy on the beach tonight. We gotta get out there."

Kelly pushed an extra chair toward Sal. "Sit down and relax a minute, you deserve it," he said. Limbach got up and picked up a bottle of wine from the nightstand. He poured some wine into a plastic glass and handed it to Sal.

Sal took the wine, sat down, sipped it, stood up and walked to the window. He said, "Shit, look at 'em down there. You should see some of those girls, man." He sat down again, stared at the TV.

"How'd it go with Bruno?" Limbach asked.

"I gave him the money, then I came back here. Did you talk to Russo?"

"He's not back yet," Limbach said.

"Call him again. Maybe they arrested Brennan."

"I just called, just hung up when you were knocking on the door."

"Shit, they probably arrested him by now." Sal got up again and went to the window. After a few minutes he said, "Come on, man, let's get out of here. I got to take the car keys back to Russo, anyway. Or whoever."

Kelly stayed behind. Limbach and Sal walked across to The Breakers. Sal flipped his keys to the agent who was lounging on the sofa in Russo's suite. It looked like a cyclone had gone through. Russo was on the phone. He was in sport clothes, trying to look like a tourist in a weird Hawaiian shirt. The phone was tucked between his shoulder and his cheek and he was pacing in front of the kitchenette alcove and nodding and murmuring, "Uh-huh, uh-huh." He saw Sal and said, "Hang on a second," then motioned to the table. "Your airline ticket's there," he said. "It's for tomorrow morning. I can't talk to you now."

"Wait a minute," Sal said, "wait a minute."

"He didn't get the money," Russo said. "Bruno's wife took it home. They'll probably give it to him tomorrow. We're making plans to arrest him when he gets off the plane at La Guardia. Okay? I can't talk anymore."

"Let's go," said Limbach. They pushed through the crush of students to the Holiday Inn, bought a six-pack and perched on a wall to watch the passing throng. Looking at the kids strolling on the beach, jostling and laughing, drinking, sunburns forgotten as music blared from passing cars, Limbach felt all of his thirty-five plus years.

Sal bent forward and tried to touch his toes. "I'm gonna take this belly off," he said when he straightened, red-faced from the effort. "Now that this is over, it's gonna be a whole new life. Clean living. Wherever we end up, me, Ro and the kids, it's gonna be clean living. I coulda done this time, no problem. Or if I wanted to, I coulda fixed it, I bet anything I coulda fixed it for real. You saw how hungry Bruno was to help me out. I coulda paid the twenty-five they wanted, got one to three, been on about my business. But I'm tired of that there, John. It don't appeal to me no more. I wanna do this for the kids, get away, start a new life. Sal can make it, John, he really can. We get someplace, he has a couple of good years, he can go to college. And Joe, the little savage, he's gonna be an animal. He's not big yet, but he's gonna be, he's just thirteen. They can both start over again, go on. This is all for them, this here."

Limbach raised his bottle lazily and clinked it against Sal's. "You're right to think about your kids," he said. "What about Rose Marie?"

"Oh, man, that's a tough one. She's real close to her family, you know? But she's a mother and she knows we've gotta do this for these kids." Sal abruptly changed the subject. "You remember that Corvette I had?" he asked.

"With the fuel injection?" Limbach remembered it well. "You weren't working. I wondered how you could afford it. I was racing my 'Vette in club races out on Long Island, and I couldn't afford fuel injection. There was something bogus about that. I never had time to run it down."

"I knew you knew about that . . ."

On the beach in the night among the students just a little older than his sons, Sal told of starring in another scam and Limbach listened patiently.

Rose Marie hung up the phone and leaned back against the kitchen wall. She was tired. She called into the living room, where her younger son sat huddled in front of the TV. Or had he fallen asleep waiting? "Joe?"

The boy stirred slowly and said in dazed voice, "Yeah, Ma?"

"It won't be tonight, honey. That was your father. They think the judge will bring the money back to New York tomorrow. If he does, they want to arrest him at the airport and we'll have to leave then. But it won't be tonight, so we can go to sleep."

"Okay, Ma." Joe stood up abruptly and stumbled past her toward the stairs. He said, "Night, Ma." For an instant she couldn't remember when he had been small. A moment later she heard the springs bounce as he flopped onto his bed.

Rose Marie stared into the living room. Be ready, Sal had said. Pack the clothes we'll need for a week or two, just like a vacation. The FBI will arrange to pack the rest and seal the house. She hadn't wanted to leave things to people she didn't know. How could you trust them to come in when you weren't there and handle your good china and silver, the crystal goblets you drank from at your wedding? She had wrapped and boxed the china and the goblets, bound the silver in soft felt pouches. She had stacked the linens with extra care, and for once in her life was making sure to unload the dryer after every load. In her mind she had divided all their clothes into "going" and "staying" and had folded and hung them separately. She had cleaned out the refrigerator and was trying to use just the big frying pan, two saucepans and her favorite baking dish. And the soup pot. She had been preparing from the moment Sal had left for Florida this second time. Much had to be discarded. That was the hard part. Everything that could identify them had to go. She hadn't liked throwing out her high-school yearbook, the one from her junior year before she quit to go to work. But she'd had time to enjoy those memories. Worse had been the mementos and pictures of the boys when they were growing up, like the P.S. 60 graduation photos with the school name in the background, the pictures of the LynVets football team in their burgundy jerseys and the gold pants Sal had bought them, angering officials of the league. Finally she couldn't bear it anymore, and wherever she could she removed photos from their identifying frames or obliterated what was written on the back. She put these into a thin stationery box and packed it with her personal things.

And with all that she still really wasn't ready. She still was startled when the agent called earlier to say Sal was delivering the money and to be prepared to leave the house tonight. Frightened, she'd refused to speak to him. She knew Dan Russo's voice, and John Limbach's, but this guy with the southern accent could be anybody. "I don't know what you're talking about," she'd screamed at him. "I don't want anything to do with you. If you know Dan Russo have him call me." Then Dan had called and said the guy's name was Ron Grenier and it was okay. After which the agent Grenier called back and said we may not have to move but then again we may, and we need directions to your house. And so she and Joe had waited up, bags packed, until Sal called.

The television light still flickered in the living room. Rose Marie walked in to turn it off. As she bent to push the button, the shelf across the back wall struck her with its emptiness. She pulled a cloth from a hip pocket of her jeans and tugged up the sleeves of her sweatshirt again. She was walking along the wall, running the cloth across the shelf, when a small, gold-colored rectangle, a plaque, fell to the floor.

She picked it up, turning it to read in a shaft of light spilling in from the kitchen. Joseph Noto, it read; Noto, their karting name, 1st, Rookie Junior. Westhampton Speedway. The date was sometime in 1982.

The trophies. There had been dozens of them, from, what? seven years of racing since her husband had taken a pair of karts in payment for a shylock loan and wound up with an obsession. The trophies were small, large, simple and elaborate, and now every one of them was in the Dumpster down beside the track in a jumble of gilded pot metal and plastic. Throwing them away had been difficult for Joe. She had watched him, looking at the loving cups and little statuettes, reading the inscriptions and toting up his record against his brother's. There would have been a day in the future when his trophies outnumbered Sal junior's, but not now.

Rose Marie returned to the kitchen and tossed the plaque into the trash container underneath the sink. She took a last cup of coffee from the pot on the stove and sat down at the kitchen table. The thick, burned coffee tasted like ashes on her tongue.

As far as she could tell, everything was done. Ross Giumarra, the track employee who had driven Sal to New York the night of his arrest, had said just call and he would come and feed the dogs. Joe had begged to take Buster. The part-collie was special. He had managed to produce puppies with their Lhasa apso, Sheba. He had come with them from Ozone Park and, Joe argued, was not just a dog but part of the family. But the agents said no. No plants, no pets. Rose Marie had found a home for Sheba. Buster would simply have to stay behind. Sal had told Ross they were leaving. Ross thought he knew a guy in Pennsylvania who needed a good dog. Rose Marie lit a final cigarette, blew smoke toward the ceiling and noticed a cobweb in the corner above the window. For once she didn't care.

Almost eighteen years of marriage. She had been a good wife. Sal was not a good husband (though he had always provided, she couldn't deny that), but he was a good father. She was a good wife and a good mother, and she had the misfortune to still be in love with Sal and his crackling wit and urgent, driving energy. Still, though, she could count on one hand the times he'd kissed her, as hard as that was to comprehend. It had seemed like a perfect match at first. She hadn't known, then, about the weird, unlikely symmetry of family deaths. Sal's sister Rosemarie had died of pancreatitis the summer Sal was discharged from the Marines. In the Noto family, her brother Sal was a bad seed banished from her father's home, but it would be years before the rumor oozed up from somewhere in Florida that he was dead of an overdose. She only knew then that her husband's father and stepmother—that was another thing; both of them were raised by stepmothers—had embraced her, another Rose Marie, when they were running his little luncheonette on Atlantic Avenue near her home. She was just a working girl who had dropped out of high school to ride the A train to Manhattan and an insurance office every day. Sal returned from a trip to California and that was it for her. He was handsome, funny, charming, and she wanted to get out of the house, away from Phyllis Noto with whom, then, she didn't get along. Her father tried to talk her out of it. Each time Leonard Noto told her, "He's no good," she was more determined. That was the kind of thing you had to find out for yourself. Sal followed her on the subway to Manhattan one morning and proposed over dinner at a Mexican restaurant. They were married on April 30, 1967, Sal's twenty-second birthday. She was still nineteen.

They honeymooned at the Kentucky Derby. She should have known
then.

She had looked forward to becoming a mother, cooking big
dinners, looking after her husband and following his lead. That was
what a girl in Ozone Park did with her life. Sal could have been a
regular nine-to-five, drive-off-to-work-in-the-Chevy, Buick-if-you-
did-well kind of guy. Then, of course, she wouldn't have been sitting,
sleepless, the bitter taste of too much coffee in her mouth, the clock
striking midnight, with the last eighteen years packed into memory
or discarded.

Not that there hadn't been some moments. She'd worn diamonds
and mink, sipped French champagne, ridden in limousines. She had
caught some of the excitement of his life. They had laughed together,
now and then, although she couldn't put her finger on a time or an
event. She blessed her poor memory. It made the bright moments
soft and hazy, but the pain was just as vague. Their lives were all
about the boys now, anyway. Not about themselves. Not about each
other. Just the boys, escaping with them to some place far away and
trying not to think about the danger. I'm not afraid to die, she thought,
if they can have a good life. She tamped out her cigarette and climbed
wearily to bed.

Leonard Noto, the old man, looked up from his bed at Jamaica
Hospital and greeted his son-in-law with a weak wave of the hand.
Sheets stretched over his copious belly and pillows supported his
balding gray head. A heart attack had put him in the hospital, and
though he sorely wanted to be back behind the bar at his little
neighborhood tavern, he knew he didn't have the strength. All the
same, he hated the doctors for telling him what he could feel, and
so he was glad to see Sal in order to have somebody with whom to
curse the doctors.

"These fuckers," he said, "they want to bury me. I got tubes,
here, here"—he motioned toward the bottom of the bed—"but they
got to keep me alive till they get all my money."

"Always complaining, Pop, always complaining." Sal had gotten
off the plane at La Guardia and called the Notos' house to find Rose

Marie and Joe there visiting Phyllis, who also had been ill. With the
FBI poised to arrest Justice Brennan, each visit was potentially the
last. They had picked him up and returned to Phyllis's, but Sal had
gotten restless and decided to come see the old man. He planned to
return to the airport to watch Brennan arrive and be arrested. "Ro
was by earlier, she said."

"Yeah. And Joseph. They said Sal junior was in California.
What's in California? Some racing thing, they said. Where the fuck
were you? Where you been anyway, to get that tan? You been to
California, too?"

"Florida. I had some business to take care of there."

Leonard Noto rolled his head to one side and looked out at the
February sky. "Florida," he said. "It's nice there now, but, I don't
know, how much more time you got to see your family?"

The old man had made his peace with Sal over the years. He
knew hard work and he was practical; he'd spent three days in jail
during the Depression because it was cheaper than paying the ten-
dollar fine for some minor auto violation. He'd worked too hard on
the docks to enjoy his children when they were young. By the time
he'd bought a little leisure with his tavern, one son was dead of
heroin and another wrestling with addiction. He had one grandson
growing up without a father and two others whose father, standing
here beside his bed, had left them once to go to prison and now
seemed likely to again. Leonard Noto saw, from the perspective of
his years and his mortality, that a man could not recapture time as
it slipped by.

"Ah, well, Pop, that was kind of what I was doing down there,"
Sal said. "There are some big changes going on. I'm making some
big changes. You can believe it or not, but I'm getting away from
all this here, trying to get away from the wiseguys, and you're gonna
see a change. It's gonna be better for the family."

The old man eyed Sal narrowly for several minutes. The sheets
rose and fell with each breath, and Sal gradually became aware of
the sound of his breathing. Finally, he said, "It don't matter what you
do if it's for the good of your family. Fuck the wiseguys. Forget about
'em. You gotta do what's right for the people who're close to you."

"Thanks, Pop," Sal said. The old man sounded as if he knew what Sal was doing, and had given, in his way, his blessing. Leonard Noto had never embraced Sal with enthusiasm, but he had accepted him and dealt with him. It was more than Sal could say of his own father, from whom he was estranged. Maybe the old man would be less surprised than the rest when Rose Marie's calls stopped coming and they found the family vanished. Maybe he'd tell them Sal had done the right thing.

Sal glanced at his watch. Brennan would be landing soon. "Pop, I gotta go," he said.

"Take care of yourself," the old man said. "Take care of your family."

The Eastern concourse at La Guardia was strangely empty. Bored fliers waited with overcoats draped over their flight bags, reading newspapers or paperback thrillers. But there were no FBI agents in the arrival lounge of Brennan's flight from Miami, no television crews. Sal walked to a bank of pay phones along the wall and called Russo.

"What's happening?" he said, when Russo came on the line.

"Where are you?" Russo asked.

"I'm at the airport. I wanted to watch it happening."

"You can go home," Russo said. "There's nothing happening."

The arrest had been postponed, the agent said. The FBI had waited all night outside the Brunos' Hallandale town house. The next morning, Bruno went out followed by FBI surveillance teams who hoped to observe the transfer of the money. He drove west, into an area of farms and ranches. The agents followed him to a strawberry truck farm, and into a pick-your-own strawberry patch. Then they all, Bruno and the agents, rolled up their sleeves and picked strawberries.

Brennan and his wife boarded their return flight to New York without making contact with Bruno.

"So I don't know what's going to happen," Sal told Rose Marie and Joe as they were driving home. "It's all screwed up. We might still be here for a while. You say we're all packed. So we'll just wait. I know it's hard. I'm sorry."

Joe had arrived at a single focus. "You mean I've got to go back to school this week?" he said.

"You'll be leaving soon enough," Sal answered.

"God, but when?" Joe moaned.

By Tuesday there was still no word. Sal called Russo to learn that Bruno had taken the money, in a shoe box, to the City National Bank in Hallandale and placed it in a safe-deposit box.

On Wednesday, Brennan called Bruno and said things were fine. Bring the money up, he said. The same day Bruno's son had talked to an attendant at the gas station across from the Runway 84, who told him the FBI had been parking there. Bruno, hearing the story from his son, said it probably had something to do with drugs, the way things were going in South Florida. But he felt a little nervous, and he told Brennan he couldn't come to New York right away.

On Thursday, the twenty-first of February, Limbach and the dour ATF agent, Lettis, arrived at the Polisis' around noon. "See, what it is, we've got Doris and Cynthia making the sales," Limbach said, producing the Nagra tape recorder and its pouch and the T-4 transmitter once again. "But we didn't get a take the last time you went to talk to Julius, and we want to get something more on him."

Half an hour later, Sal was pulling into the Leonards' trailer lot again. It was rutted mud from the winter snows and snow lay about the lot in dirty patches. Sal eased his car over the heaving ruts and honked his horn.

"Where the hell you been?" the Rebel, Julius Leonard, demanded when he came outside and picked his way through the mud to the car.

"I been on the run, man. I been down in Florida."

"What, runnin' from the law?"

"No. I been movin', man. What are you up to?"

The Rebel's face twisted in a scowl. "Motherfuckers robbed my fuckin' snowmobile," he said.

"Who?" Sal asked.

"Huh? I don't know, man. I been lookin' all over the place for them cocksuckers." He looked about, as if he expected the thieves to burst into the clearing.

"Jump in," Sal said. "I want to talk to you." He told Leonard his customers were disappointed. "They weren't happy with them last two."

"Did they work?"

"Yeah, but they weren't happy. They weren't potent enough, you know what I mean? They want them bigger, something more potent, that's gonna do some, do some damage." He said his customers didn't mind paying more money. They also wanted some pipe bombs with long fuses. "You gotta stuff 'em real good, they say."

"Right," said Leonard. He wondered about the size of the time bombs. "I try to keep it down," he said.

"The size don't mean nothing. It's got to be potent."

"Oh, well, shit, then you didn't tell me that," Leonard protested. "You said you wanted something nice and compact." He looked at Sal and shook his head, rolled the window down and spat. "Ask him if an attaché case will be too big."

In the end they agreed that a bomb in a small suitcase would be just the right size. Sal said he would see Leonard the following week.

As Sal was leaving, Leonard asked him to keep an eye out for his missing snowmobile. "The same color as the hood on that Cadillac, the red-hooded one, that I had here?" he said. "If you see that motherfucker, right, don't say nothing, cause I didn't report it to the cops or nothin'. Just let me know, 'cause I'm gonna burn their ass."

"So the next one's supposed to be in a suitcase," Sal was saying. "And some pipe bombs, too, if he can get the fuses. I told him I couldn't get any more. Limbach says we'll go for some guns next, and if they don't come up with any they'll go ahead and bust them. Bust the hayseeds, is what he calls them. Julius, all he could think about today was somebody stole his snowmobile."

"I like John," Rose Marie said. "I just wish you didn't have to fool around with bombs." Limbach and Lettis had departed for New York and Rose Marie was cleaning up after a late lunch. She folded a blue-and-white dish towel in half and hung it over a cabinet door. "Just put the rest of the dishes in the sink. I told Joan Schoor I'd stop over to her house for coffee."

"Aw, whaddaya wanna go out for?" Sal complained. "It's late already, what is it, almost four o'clock?"

He was seated at the kitchen table. Joe had gathered a soup bowl, a wedge of cheese and a package of cookies and gone to his room to do homework, Buster following expectantly. They had resumed their routine since Brennan had returned to New York without the money. Sal spent most of his time on the telephone trying to drag information out of Russo. Rose Marie was working a part-time schedule at the Parkers' gift shop, Something New. Things were as they had been, except for Sal junior's absence and the worsening illness of Rose Marie's father. He had been released from the hospital, but only temporarily.

"Joan's my friend," Rose Marie said defensively. "It helps to talk to her. I'm worried about my father and you're never here or you don't have time." She paused to light a cigarette. "Oh, I almost forgot," she said, more brightly, "Sal junior called the shop this morning. He said he's having fun but he's starting to miss school. He was surprised we were still here. He said he thought we probably weren't leaving. And Linda was in, said he'd called her, too."

"He'll be back before we go, things don't start moving. Are you smoking more? It seems like it."

"I miss him," Rose Marie said, ignoring the question. "I wish he didn't have to be away. But it would be so hard for him if he were here, all this waiting with nothing ever happening."

"You're right," Sal agreed. "Joe seems to handle it a whole lot better. But he'll make it fine. Good for him, being away."

"I'll be back early," Rose Marie said. "I have to go in tomorrow morning to open up the store. The Parkers are going to the city on a buying trip, and she asked me to open up tomorrow and Saturday. I've got a regular career," she said proudly. "Substitute store manager." She put a raincoat on over her sweater—it was mild for the last week of February—and was out the door.

Joan Schoor thought Rose Marie looked drawn. Colleen, in and out of the kitchen where everybody gravitated when they came to see the Schoors, noticed how much she was smoking. Colleen was getting ready to play in a high-school basketball game, and Joan thought it would do Rose Marie good to go. It would help her forget about her father for a while, and of course everybody knew Rose Marie's husband had his problems, too.

"No. No, I just can't." Rose Marie declined Joan's invitation several times. Still, she seemed to want to stay and talk. Joan had just poured a fresh cup of tea for them both when the phone rang, interrupting their conversation. Joan held out the telephone to Rose Marie. "It's for you."

Joe said, "Ma, we're going to be leaving. You have to come home right away."

She had to ask again, to be sure she'd heard correctly. "What is it, Joe?" she said.

"Dad got a phone call. We have to leave tonight. You have to come right home."

Rose Marie nodded and murmured into the phone after Joe hung up, trying to think of what to say. She hung up the phone and looked helplessly at Joan, fighting back tears. "I have to go," she said.

Joan was sure the call had to do with Rose Marie's father. She hugged her friend and said, "I hope he'll be all right. Be careful driving."

"I will, Joan. Thank you. Thanks for . . ." It came to Rose Marie suddenly that she would not see her friend again, would probably never talk to her. "Thanks for everything," she said. She remembered to call out, "Good luck tonight, Colleen. I hope you win." She held the tears back until she reached the car, and drove toward home dabbing at her eyes. She was so frightened. She hoped she could get through the night without showing how close she was to the edge of paralyzing fear.

When she reached home, Sal said, "They said it'll be sometime tonight. We gotta pack. They'll call us later with instructions." Twilight stretched into evening and they were packed and ready. Hours passed and their anticipation ebbed, leaving them tired and hollow. Joe napped on his bed.

Sometime after eleven, with the late news on the television, the telephone rang. Sal picked it up. "Yo." He listened for a minute. Then he said, "Wait a minute. Wait a minute. Turn that off, turn that TV off, lemme hear this." He groped for the remote control.

Rose Marie said, "Oh, my God." She got up and watched Sal

talking, waiting for eye contact. When at last he looked at her, she could see excitement brimming in his gold-flecked brown eyes and she felt a new and sudden knot of fear. When he nodded, she went upstairs into the central hall and into Joe's room. The boy was sleeping on his stomach, on top of the covers in his clothes, hugging his pillow. She turned on his desk lamp and shook his shoulder until he opened his eyes sleepily. "It's time to go," she said.

He pushed up on one elbow. "What time is it?" he said.

"It's late, but we have to go."

Joe was lacing up his sneakers when Sal came into the room, fastening his jeans over a tight black T-shirt. He pulled a black turtleneck sweater down over his barrel chest. With sneakers the outfit would be complete, what he'd wear to hijack a truck or rob a warehouse. It felt like that, the adrenaline pumping now. "This is it," he said, "the grand exit. We're about to make the grand."

They carried their luggage to Rose Marie's used Monte Carlo parked outside the house. Sal had traded for the larger car in anticipation of the move. Everything but Sal's hard-sided Samsonite attaché case went into the trunk. The attaché contained a chamois bag with two hundred carats of diamonds and a zippered canvas bank bag full of Krugerrands, altogether worth close to four hundred thousand dollars. Sal had always kept something aside for a rainy day. It was peaceful and dark outside the house. A light breeze from the south rose out of the woods below the track, carrying a loamy smell and the promise of a distant spring. The brown grass underfoot had lost its frozen crunch and the frozen earth was turning, for a time at least, to mud again. Rose Marie had the crazy thought that their small sounds—talking, the clatter of the aluminum storm door against its frame, the trunk and car doors closing—would wake the neighbors, that their flight would be discovered and men with guns would appear to stop them and put Sal on trial for working for the government. Or the men with guns would be agents; they'd be shooting and laughing, saying it was all a joke. To think, with the crimes he committed, you could get away. Buster was following them in and out of the house, wagging his tail and whining hopefully.

"Can't we take Buster?" Joe said.

"Holy shit." Sal clapped a hand to his forehead. "I forgot about Buster. What are we gonna do with him?"

"Why can't we take him, Dad?" Joe pleaded. "We could change his name."

"We can't take him, we're gonna be in motels and who knows where else. But we can't just leave him here. I don't know. Jesus, I forgot about poor Buster."

"Ross is going to come take care of him," Rose Marie said. "He knows somebody in Pennsylvania who may want him. We can call him in the morning. Can't we?" She was wearing her raincoat open over jeans and a red sweater, and her hair was pulled back in a ponytail that made her look younger until you saw the tension darting on her face.

"I guess," Sal said. "Have we got everything?"

Buster, hearing his name, approached Joe sideways, feathery tail swishing back and forth. The dog bowed his neck like a horse and rose slowly on his back legs as Joe kneeled to embrace him. Buster licked Joe's ear with his front paws on Joe's shoulders, while Joe ran his fingers through the dog's thick fur. The boy looked at Sal, his eyes pleading. Sal turned away. "Say good-bye," he muttered.

Rose Marie was sending out waves of almost uncontrollable nervousness. "Let's see, what did I forget? Oh, God, oh, God, oh, God, I can't remember. Oh, God, I have to go back in. I forgot the coffee on the stove." In the kitchen, she checked the burners again, poured the coffee in a thermos, satisfied herself that there were food and water for the dog, regretted not washing last night's dishes. Outside again, carrying the thermos, she stood for a moment at the door, under the glow of the porch light. She took a deep breath and said, "Just one more trip." Joe had thrown himself into the backseat of the car and was sitting huddled in a corner. Sal had the engine running; exhaust clouds billowed out behind. Rose Marie hurried through the darkened living room to the cabinet with the glass front. She removed the Bible they'd received when she and Sal were married, the one with their names to which the children's had been added, all their wedding and birth information in neat calligraphy.

She tucked it under her arm and returned to the car. Somehow, in all the confusion of their hurried departure, Rose Marie remembered to turn off the porch light.

As he drove, Sal told them what had happened. Brennan had been leaving that morning for the courthouse when a neighbor told him that two men in a car had been sitting, just sitting, on the street near his house. It seemed suspicious. The neighbor had taken a license number. Brennan had scheduled lunch that day with his old friend Francis X. Smith, the administrative judge of the Queens Supreme Court. They were driving to a Queens Boulevard restaurant when Brennan saw another car that seemed to be following him. He shared his fears with Smith.

Smith, seeing a member of the Queens Anti-Crime Squad in the restaurant, told the cop of Brennan's concern and asked him to check out the car. Perhaps, he suggested, it was a disgruntled defendant out to get the judge.

Patrolmen questioned the agents watching Brennan, who said they were the FBI involved in an investigation. Don't mention it, the agents said. The Anti-Crime Squad officer told Smith and Brennan the car checked out; it was nothing. But Smith had the police run the license number Brennan's neighbor had given him, and learned it was the FBI. The bureau didn't know if Brennan had connected the surveillance with Sal's bribe attempt, but it wasn't taking any chances.

A dark two-lane took the Polisis through Otisville, where Sal had taken food packages to his friend and onetime partner-in-hijacking, the shambling giant Funzi Tarricone, in prison. They picked up Route 17 at Middletown, joined the New York State Thruway and then turned south into New Jersey on the Garden State Parkway. The lights of New York City loomed to the east and they passed through a series of indistinguishable suburbs. Sal left the parkway at Exit 135 and pulled to a stop just past the toll booths. The dashboard clock showed one o'clock.

"Why are we stopping?" Rose Marie fumbled for a cigarette.

"This is where he said to meet them." Sal twisted in the seat to look around. There was some kind of construction equipment, a small asphalt roller on a flatbed trailer, parked near a service shed at the end of the line of toll booths. Then he saw brake lights flash, and a blue Oldsmobile sedan backed toward them from the shadows at the edge of the pavement. The brake lights flashed again, and the car stopped in front of them. A man in a trench coat got out of the car and walked toward them.

"Who is that?" Rose Marie said. "Do you know him?"

"Never saw him," Sal replied.

Rose Marie felt panic blooming. "Ask for ID," she said. "How do we know he's with the FBI?"

"He wouldn't be here if he wasn't."

"Sal Polisi?" the man said as he leaned to look into the window. Rose Marie recognized the soft southern voice as the one she'd screamed at on the telephone, and relaxed.

"You got it."

"Follow me," the agent said. "We're just going to the Ramada Inn right over here. You'll see the sign from the bottom of the hill." He looked across the car at Rose Marie and smiled. "Mrs. Polisi, I'm Ron Grenier. I believe we've spoken on the phone. You'll be registered as the Wayne Allen family. So what you want to do," he said, nodding toward Sal, "maybe you'd just better call him 'honey.' "

As they slept at the Ramada Inn that night, Grenier and his partner Sid Casperson waited in the room next door.

• • •

California was great. It was weird not going to school, but Harold's mom let me use their car and I'd drive around during the day while Harold was working. The Prices lived in the San Joaquin Valley, and I'd drive down to Bakersfield, or up to the Sequoia National Park in the mountains. That was what I loved, the cool mountains and the big trees that made you feel like nothing you did or nothing that happened to you really mattered, it wasn't all that big a deal. You could see that you were just a little part of things.

I talked to Mom and Dad every three or four days. Dad was in Florida some of that time, and then he was home and it looked like they weren't moving.

I talked to Linda, too. I felt guilty because I was having fun, not going to school, and from talking to her I had a picture of her sitting around pining while I was meeting some pretty neat girls even if I wasn't, you know, hot for any of them. "You said you cry when you see my picture," I wrote in a letter on pink paper, which was all Harold's mom had in the house. "I don't think you do. But really if you do, you shouldn't."

I was all mixed up about our separation. I wanted Linda to be happy, which meant she should date other people, but I didn't want to give her up, which meant she shouldn't. My head said tell her to go out, but then I'd get jealous. I even tried to make her promise not to go out with anybody else, but she said no. Which made me nuts. I didn't know which way to turn.

I wrote, "Well, soon you should be bored and the time will come for you to move on with your life. Going out with other guys won't bother me because I know that you must be lonely or bored and I only want what makes you happy. If the time comes go ahead. But just make sure that you let me know what went on. If I ever go out with anyone I'll tell you. But right now nobody will come between me and you, at least not on my side. I love you—you know it. The only reason I was so upset about you not promising that you wouldn't go out with no one is that I just think about you in some other guy's arms and it hurts. I keep picturing you in these guys' arms—guys I know. It's crazy but I always see you in their arms. It makes me sick. I love you more than I ever loved anyone else by far and I know I'll never love this way again (sounds like that song). Oh, shit, guess what video is on MTV! 'You're the Inspiration!' It just came on. It makes me think of you so much. Don't ever forget me. WE WILL MARRY. Don't laugh. We will."

I closed, "I love you always, Sal" and added my old number, 23. Another memory I was having trouble giving up.

And then the shit hit the fan.

I had called Grandma Noto and Aunt Gina one day and they sounded real anxious. "Did you hear from your mom and dad?" Grandma Noto asked me.

"No," I said, "I haven't talked to them since two days ago."

"We've been calling," she said. "They weren't home last night and all day today."

I didn't think anything much about it, with Dad going to Florida and Mom working and Joe in school. Two days later, I talked to Grandma Noto and them again, and she said, "Do you know where they are? We still haven't heard from them." She was saying they were gonna call the police or something. My mom was always one to be in touch with her family, they talked all the time, even after the blowup with Gina's boyfriend Tony Capetola and my dad. And I started thinking, maybe they took off. And then they called and said they were in a motel somewhere in New Jersey, they had to take off in the middle of the night.

After all the months, it seemed as though it happened just like that.

E L E V E N

Rose Marie awoke staring at the face of a small child with exceptionally large eyes. It was a picture she had seen before, but not in her house, and then she remembered that she was in a motel in New Jersey. At the same time she felt a stab from her conscience. She was supposed to open Something New at nine-thirty and couldn't. She couldn't even let anybody know. That was the first thought of the rest of her life.

Next she remembered that her sister and stepmother would expect her to call, as she did every day, and that they would grow worried. Then she recalled in rapid succession that her father was going back into the hospital and would probably die, that she had no idea what was going to happen next, and that Buster was in the house and would be needing to go out.

There was a knocking on a door and she started, frightened by another memory, of early knocking and men with drawn pistols pounding up the stairs. Then, more unsettling, came the recollection that the FBI was in the room next door to guard their lives and that all the lies and safe presumptions of the past few months had been discarded in their eleventh-hour flight from home the night before.

Voices followed; a new shift of agents was arriving to relieve Grenier and Casperson. Then a clattering at her door and Sal came in with the morning newspapers.

"Hey, you're awake," he said. "I was over talking to the agents. They're gonna move us today."

"They just moved us last night," she said.

Sal opened the floor-length drapes, revealing sliding glass doors. Fog masked tree shapes beyond a small terrace. Neutral gray light flooded the room, making her squint. Joe stirred in the other double bed and burrowed into a pillow. "It's gonna be awhile," Sal said. "They're gonna put us in a bigger place."

"We could use it," she said, taking in the jumble of clothing and luggage in the room. "Can you call Ross?" she said. "He needs to go look after Buster. And I'd really like to call Arlene."

"I'll call Ross," Sal said, "but forget Arlene. Forget Phyllis and your sister. The fewer people know we're gone the better. They're gonna all find out eventually."

Joe's muffled voice came from inside his pillow. "Can everybody be quiet, and turn the lights off, please."

"No." Sal pulled the sheet off the boy sleeping in his underwear and tugged at the pillow covering his head. "No more sleep. Get up. It's time for breakfast. We've got to move."

When they were in the car again, following Grenier and Casperson in the same blue Oldsmobile through the suburban sprawl, Joe said, "Are we in the witness program now?"

"Not yet, son," Sal answered.

" 'Cause we didn't make up new names yet?"

"No." Sal laughed. "We gotta be thinking about that. Tell you what, you think of any good names, write 'em down and we'll try 'em on for size."

"Sure, Pa. So, uh, what are we doing now, if we're not in the witness program?" Joe leaned up and draped his arms over the back of the front seat.

"We're in what's called protective custody. The bureau . . . I mean the FBI's looking after us until we get in the witness program. That's when we'll get new names, new ID, all that. It's probably all bullshit, moving around like this, but since Brennan made the surveillance, they don't want to take no chances. So we'll have agents assigned to us for a while."

"Neat," said Joe. He sat back in the seat.

Rose Marie said, "They seem nice, the agents."

"Yeah, big surprise, isn't it?" Sal replied.

"I mean, I like John, but he's not FBI. And Dan Russo seems okay, I guess. But we know them. With the others I was expecting, I don't know, monsters or something. Because of the way you always talked." They hate Italians, Sal had always said. They live off other people's misery, the FBI. "And that time they raided the apartment and took those guns and things." In Rose Marie's circle in Ozone

Park the wives had spat venom at the FBI, how unfair it was, agents tearing up their houses with their raids, invading their privacy, breaking up their families, taking their husbands away. Now the FBI controlled her life. Agents were leading her to an unknown destination. She was finding the adjustment difficult.

"Aww, well, we gotta live with 'em now, don't we?" Sal shifted his hands on the steering wheel and jammed down the accelerator to get under a red light and stay behind the Olds. "It was just that then, they were getting in the way of business. But they were never as bad as I said. They were just doing their jobs. This is their job now, taking care of us, and we gotta trust 'em. We don't really have a choice, so the easiest thing . . ." Sal glanced up into the rearview mirror. "I'm talking to you, too, son. The easiest thing is to relax and trust 'em, and remember that we're doing something people don't hardly ever have a chance to do. And that's to start all over. Wipe the slate clean and start again. That's what we're doing here. So you gotta try to forget all that stuff I said, because that was then, and this is now, and things are different now. Everything is different."

Rose Marie lowered her window to throw out a spent cigarette. "My God, feel how warm it is," she said. "It feels just like springtime." She looked back at Sal. "I guess I'll have to learn to trust them, won't I? You're right. It would be easier."

At Westfield they turned left on Highway 28, and passed real-estate offices and furniture stores. After a mile or two the Olds pulled up in front of a white-brick building about three stories tall, with arched windows, shutters and a cupola on top in the colonial style. A discreet sign announced The Mansion Hotel. Grenier already had the room keys. He and Casperson led the Polisis through a lobby with a gas log fireplace and gilded moldings to the elevator, and pushed the button to the third floor. The room was an L-shaped efficiency with a double bed, and a fold-out couch and a pocket kitchen in the sitting area. Grenier opened the door to an adjoining room with two double beds. "Your guardian angels'll be in here," he said.

When Arlene Parker spoke to her daughter Jill that afternoon, she could hardly believe what she was hearing on the telephone.

Jill, an attractive senior cheerleader at Port Jervis High School, had come from school to spend the afternoon working at the family gift shop. The other girl told her Rose Marie hadn't been there to open up Something New that Friday morning. Jill had called, had been calling, the Polisi house, and so far there had been no answer.

"But it's not like Rose Marie to do that," Arlene said.

"I know, Mom." Jill's voice wasn't too concerned. "Maybe they just had to go somewhere all of a sudden and couldn't let us know, but she'll be in tomorrow."

"No. She would have found a way to let us know," her mother said. "Keep calling. We'll be back tomorrow night."

The Parkers had come to depend upon Rose Marie and her steadiness and good humor. She wouldn't have been absent if she could have helped it. Arlene kept asking herself, "Where is Rose Marie?" When she returned from her buying trip on Saturday night, Jill said, "I've been calling, and there's still no answer." Arlene called all day Sunday. Between calls she asked herself, "Where is Rose Marie?" The more she asked the question, the more she kept seeing scenes conjured from what she knew about the Polisi family's past. In one scene, the Polisis all were dead. In another, only Rose Marie was dead and Sal was nowhere to be found. Finally Arlene couldn't stand it anymore and called the New York State Police.

The kids at Port Jervis High and Middle School were asking questions, too. Joe Polisi was absent on Friday and again on Monday and Tuesday. On Wednesday afternoon, Joe's best friend Tony Digiantommaso asked his sister Gina to ask her friend Linda Miller if she had heard from any of the Polisis. Later, at cheerleading practice, Jill Parker told Linda that Rose Marie hadn't shown up for work. They decided to go investigate.

When practice was over, Linda and a couple of the other cheerleaders piled into Jill's infamous baby blue Dodge Dart, and they drove up 209 to Cuddebackville. They reached the racetrack a little after seven.

It was warm for the end of February. The evening was pitch-black, without moon or stars. The girls got out of Jill's car, but hesitated at the enveloping darkness. There was not a sound, and nothing stirred. They could just make out a car parked next to the tractor shed to the right of the house. It was eerie, as if somebody had been there just a minute ago. There wasn't anybody here now, though; they could feel it.

Linda remembered Sal, sitting in her den. He'd said, ". . . if my parents and my brother are gone all of a sudden. Then you'll know I won't be back right away."

She said, "I don't think anybody's home."

Jill, with Linda following, picked her way along a row of flag-stones to the corner of the house. She opened the storm door, took a breath and knocked. They looked at each other as they waited, half expecting the porch light to come on. The other girls were on their tiptoes trying to see in the front windows set four across in the house's thick stone foundation wall. Drawn shades blocked the view except for a sliver at the corner of the first window from the door, the one above a cedar bench that shared the patio with the Adirondack chairs. Jill backed up her car and shone the headlights toward the house. Standing on the bench and peering through the window then, they could see furniture, but no signs of life. Linda had a glimpse of her reflection in the glass and told herself to try and act surprised.

"Wow," she said, "this is really weird."

The girls drove back toward town, and they all agreed with Linda that the Polisis' disappearance was indeed really, really weird.

Sal Polisi's problems were well-known in Port Jervis. Specu-lation over the disappearance of the family became a favorite subject. Most people assumed it had something to do with his unsavory past.

Phyllis Noto was used to talking with her stepdaughter every day. When she didn't hear from Rose Marie, she got on the phone and started calling. She learned Rose Marie hadn't been to work and Joe hadn't been to school. She talked to people who should have known what had happened, but couldn't learn a thing. She, too, got somebody to have a look around the Polisi house at the racetrack in Cuddebackville. The word came back, "They're gone."

Phyllis stewed in fury and bitterness. Sal obviously had taken it on the lam and disappeared with his family. With Rose Marie's father dying of his heart condition. With Ralph the shylock holding a fifty-thousand-dollar mortgage on their property for Sal's bail. The man never had a thought for anybody but himself. He should have stayed and taken his punishment. All that fancy talk about moving from Ozone Park because it was no good, he takes his family away upstate and he gets back in the same thing again. So he got caught. If he took his punishment like a man, Rose Marie and the kids, her grandkids, would be home in Ozone Park again, so what was wrong with that? It never occurred to her Sal and the family were in protective custody. Forget about it. Never happen.

Dan Russo sat in his suite at The Breakers in Fort Lauderdale and chewed his knuckles in frustration. After Andy Bruno had wound up in the strawberry patch instead of handing the money to Brennan, Russo had been so depressed that Ethan Levin-Epstein, out buying T-shirts to take back to his kids in New Rochelle, had had one made for Russo that said, I DON'T GIVE A SHIT in five-inch letters. The twenty-five thousand was still sitting in Bruno's safety-deposit box at the City National Bank in Hallandale. Now Brennan knew the FBI was watching him. Maybe he'd connected the surveillance to Sal's bribe attempt, and maybe not.

Sal's drug case remained active in Queens Criminal Court, or so it was made to appear by the secret agreement between Queens District Attorney Santucci's office and Dearie, the U.S. attorney in Brooklyn. Sal kept appearing in court to maintain the facade. Carloads of FBI agents accompanied him to court in case word had gotten out that Sal was trying to approach Brennan and wasn't it an interesting coincidence that the FBI was watching the judge at the same time. Somebody might decide to go rat hunting. The agents made Sal lie down in the car as they approached the satellite courthouse in Long Island City, and ringed the courtroom while he received yet another postponement. The case against Brennan was wispy at best. It wouldn't improve with the death of a key witness. But if Brennan hadn't linked Polisi to the FBI surveillance, maybe the sting could be revived. Russo wanted to find out.

On March 1, a Friday, Sal was back in Fort Lauderdale, to press Andy Bruno about what was happening with his case.

While Sal ate sautéed escarole with Agent Mindy Meyer, Andy

told him it was still okay, for Sal to continue to expect postponements. He said he still was awaiting word from Brennan to take the money to New York.

On Sunday, the third, Sal had a long dinner at the Runway 84. He ordered a steak and a salad, and asked Bruno enthusiastically if he had seen the story in the papers: John Gotti, with boss Paul Castellano facing two federal indictments, was now acting boss of the Gambino family in New York. "My friend, Johnny Gotti. They made a big splash with John," Sal said. He talked about Jackie Donnelly, how the feds had found millions in cash and diamonds hidden in his house inside stuffed teddy bears. Bruno said nothing had changed. He expected a call from Brennan any day now, telling him to fly up with the money.

Bruno called Sal the next day with an urgent message: get in touch. Sal walked into the Runway 84 at twenty-five minutes after seven. The dinner trade was just beginning.

Bruno came out of the kitchen wiping his hands with a towel. He looked worried. They walked outside together, and Sal said, "What's going on?"

"I don't know what's going on," Bruno said. "They called me at the house today and told me that they can't do nothing. You know, they used this terminology, forget the apartments, we can't do anything with apartments, give back your deposit."

"What?" Sal was incredulous.

"That's all. I don't know."

Sal walked a few steps to gather himself, turned on his heel and approached Bruno again. "I don't believe this," he moaned.

"I can't question it," said Bruno.

"I don't believe this," Sal repeated.

"Let me tell you something else," Bruno offered. "Don't let no fucking laywers use you, because they can't do nothing there."

"Oh, my God," said Sal. "Who called you?" he asked. "Brennan himself?"

"Yes."

"And he said he can't do nothing?"

"Can't do nothing with the apartments." Bruno said. "When I heard his voice, I said, 'All right, this is it, they must want me up there.' " But Brennan surprised him by telling him to return the deposit. Bruno handed the brown paper bag with the twenty-five thousand to Sal.

Sal opened the bag and looked inside. "I thought you gave him this money," he said.

"No, he was leaving Sunday, you gave it to me late Saturday night, so when I spoke to him he says, 'Hold it, you come up, you bring it.' He had planned to do that until Brennan called to say the deal was off. "I feel so fucking bad for you," Bruno said. "This is the first time that I know that he ever told me that nothing could be done."

"Nothing could be done." Sal stared at the twilight sky above the restaurant. He noticed for the first time that the fake control tower that rose from the roof resembled a prison guard tower. He put on a stricken look, as if contemplating many years in prison.

"This is the first fucking time," Bruno said. "Now, I don't know what it is, but something is wrong. Whether it's all this shit that's going on or whether it's something with you, I don't know."

"Bad timing," muttered Sal. "Bad timing." If only he'd gotten there earlier to deliver the money.

"I think it's the timing, myself," Bruno agreed.

Sal reached into the bag of money and offered Bruno a tip. "I'll leave you five hundred," he said.

Bruno at first declined the money. "I don't care," he said. "I feel very bad for you. Honest to God. I really wanted to do this for you."

Sal begged to know what had gone wrong. Maybe Bruno could come to New York and talk to Brennan. He'd need plane fare. Sal offered the money again, flapping it to try and spread the fluorescent powder. "Here, take the nickel, take the nickel and that way you got, uh, you know what I'm saying?" Bruno took the money. "All right. I'm going to go," Sal said. "God, what a mess this is." He shook Bruno's hand in parting.

Bruno left the restaurant and went straight to the Hallandale dog track, where he gambled away the five hundred dollars. The agents who watched him were struck by how badly he seemed to want to get rid of the money.

The mood was glum in Russo's command center at The Breakers when Sal returned with the bag of money. Russo took the paper bag and tossed it onto the littered coffee table. "You could have tipped him a hundred," he said sourly. "You didn't have to tip him five."

"Give me a break, I was giving him air fare," Sal replied. "What is it, anyway? Your money?"

Russo had envisioned a high-profile arrest, the judge caught with the dirty money in his hands. His best hope now was to find the pari-mutuel ticket Bruno had showed Sal the night they talked in his Cadillac outside the Diplomat. The scribbled information on the ticket showed Brennan's interest in Sal's drug case; so far it was the one clear link between them. Agents had gone through the garbage bin in Bruno's town-house complex every day, searching vainly for the ticket.

"Forget it, it's gone. We're never going to find it," Levin-Epstein told Russo. "We're just going to have to do without it."

Russo had Sal make one last phone call to Bruno on March 6.

Bruno said there was nothing that the judge could do to help him. "You know the best thing for you to do," he said. "Get everything together."

New York State Trooper Tom Scileppi went to the racetrack in Cuddebackville at six forty-five on the morning of March 6 and broke the lock on the front door of the house. It was a legal break-in: Scileppi had been there the day before and seen a long-haired dog when he looked through the kitchen window. When no one responded within twelve hours to the note he left on the door, he was empowered to come back and free the dog.

Scileppi was assigned to the Middletown barracks of the New York State Police, and he'd long harbored suspicions about the racetrack's owner. They began when he'd received a tip about a stolen road grader in use at the track. That hadn't panned out, but then he'd read about Polisi's drug arrest, and was more convinced than ever the guy wasn't one hundred percent. He was just the kind of guy, Scileppi thought, who'd take off and leave a dog inside the house to starve, but when he broke in he found the dog had been fed and watered, so he went room to room looking for bodies.

The light inside the house was dim. Shades covered every window but the one in the kitchen through which he'd spied the dog. Scileppi went around raising the shades, letting light into the house. He found clothes in the closets and drawers, dishes in the sink, unmade beds as if people had jumped up and left suddenly in the middle of the night. It was like one of those abandoned ships sailing along with food still steaming on the galley table. But a shelf in the living room was strangely bare, and some boxes were stacked in a corner of the kitchen.

Scileppi canvassed the track's neighbors. No one had seen the owner or his family for several days. Finally, the trooper put the dog in his blue-and-gold patrol car, dropped it at the pound and returned to the Middletown barracks to report what he had found to Investigator George Elston.

Elston had gone to high school in Port Jervis with Arlene Parker. He called to give her the news personally even though there wasn't much news to give. Trooper Tom Scileppi had found the house deserted except for a long-haired dog that appeared to be part-collie. The dog seemed to have been cared for, and was taken to the Orange County Humane Society. There were no signs of violence.

"Well, thank God for that, at least," said Arlene.

Scileppi tried to find out more about the racetrack's owner. He was checking telephone records when an FBI agent visited the Middletown barracks and told him to forget it.

Joan Schoor was another person who repeatedly called Rose Marie and then began to worry. She recalled that afternoon in her kitchen, Rose Marie's drawn face, her heavy smoking, her distraction, and then the phone call and Rose Marie's sudden departure. She decided there must have been more to all this than her friend's father's illness. She found Gina Noto's phone number, and learned Rose Marie's family was mystified as well about her whereabouts. One afternoon Joan got in the car with her husband Harold and Colleen and they drove to the racetrack to see for themselves.

Peeking through a front window, Joan exclaimed, "Look at this. All the furniture's still here and everything. It looks like they've just gone to the store or something." It looked, she thought, as if the occupants had fallen off the face of the earth.

It was then that her husband, who knew Sal well, said, "Maybe this is one of those witness things. Maybe he cut a deal."

Joan said, "I hope he cut a good one."

• • •

California was starting to get boring. Then one day the Prices' phone rang and it was somebody wanting Harold to come to England for a race. It was like, the next day or something and he said, come on, let's go. Dad was back in Florida, and Mom and Joe were still at some motel with the FBI, but I got in touch with them and they agreed. They thought it would be good for me to see another country.

We went out and bought some clothes for the trip, sweats, jeans, like that, which just helped add to the excitement. We got on a plane at Los Angeles and flew all night, over the North Pole, and arrived in England on March 6.

Everything looked so green when our plane broke through the clouds to land at Heathrow Airport. But on the ground everything seemed gray, the airport, the long empty corridors with rubber moving sidewalks like flat escalators, the view through the raindrops on the windows. The parade of rock stars I expected, Boy George and Duran Duran and Elton John, was nowhere in sight, not even posters of them, only long lines of sleepy people.

We rode a van to a rental car place, and Harold rented a funny little car, a Vauxhall, and we started driving in the pouring rain.

We got on what they call a motorway and drove. I kept messing with the radio but there wasn't anything on but people talking, BBC this or BBC that, and some pretty basic music, like your basic Top 40. I wasn't too impressed. The rain kept coming down and I kept looking for a bright spot on the dial. Harold was wringing the Vauxhall out pretty good, but no way would it go over eighty. And driving on the left was weird.

The four-lane motorway went to a two-lane. We went through the place where Shakespeare lived. Then the road went to something smaller. Harold wanted to go fast, but the rain and the slow-moving trucks and buses caused backed-up lines of traffic. The diesel exhaust was so thick it was almost solid. You could hear their gears groaning. I started getting a headache, and Harold was getting pretty frosted.

He got a break near the end of a straight piece of road and pulled out to pass. We made two cars and had the truck in front of them to go when another truck came at us out of the bend. It was just there, like a fear you forget and then it steps out in front of you as you're walking down the street, a high square grille and two evil lights shining through the rain, on top of us. There was no way we could miss it. I flashed on Joe tumbling out of his kart the day we raced. Harold put us into a four-wheel skid that took us off the road and into a grove of trees.

It was quiet in the woods. The rain didn't come in sheets but in big drops down from the treetops. You could smell burned rubber. A little steam came up from around the hood. Sounds returned gradually, like switches clicking on; all of a sudden on the radio people burst out laughing, like they were laughing at us there in the woods, but I guess it was a comedy show or something. Harold and I got out of the car at the same time to inspect for damage. He waved off a driver who had stopped and was peering into the grove at us. There was nothing wrong with my side of the car, and I said, "It's okay over here."

"Over here, too," he said.

We met at the front of the car and surveyed the grille. Not a scratch. We looked up from the car and at each other, and we saw the relief in each other's eyes. He started laughing first, a little chuckle like, and I couldn't help it, I started laughing, too. Our gratitude for being alive flooded out in gasping whoops that left me feeling weak.

Harold caught his breath and said, "That's what I get for driving on the right side of the road."

I said, "You mean the wrong side."

He said, "The right side is the wrong side."

It took me a minute. Then I got it. I said, "You're not very funny, Harold, but you drive good."

Sometime later the road started rising and falling through some hills and then we were in the little town of Bridgnorth. It had a main street with parking and a row of shops, almost like Port Jervis. But off the main street, everything was old and brick, and the rain gave the whole town a dull gleam like blued metal on a gun. Harold pulled up in front of a place at the foot of a bridge. It looked like an old mill or something. A sign said it was the Severn Arms. Harold said it was our hotel.

It was like a boardinghouse, this place. It didn't have a TV, or a radio, which sucked, and you had to go down the hall to go to the bathroom. Which sucked, too. The room we were in had two double beds and old windows with cracked frames where you could feel the air coming through. There was a table with one lamp between the beds. There was like a big cupboard where you hung your clothes, instead of a closet. It was like no place I'd ever been before.

For the next week we'd get up in the morning and eat breakfast there at the Severn Arms in a dining room with a low ceiling and old crooked beams. The girl who served breakfast was real pretty, and she gave me looks that made me miss Linda. After that we'd run two miles up a mountain to an industrial district and this car factory Harold was supposed to drive for. The run was our workout. The first three or four days it either rained or snowed. Once we got to the factory, there wasn't anything to do. Anson Cars made chassis for Formula Three race cars, what they call Super V's, with air-cooled Volkswagen engines. Harold had a partner who was going to import them, and he was going to be the factory driver, like. There wasn't much more to it than that, and so we'd get up there and sit around and drink hot chocolate. That was our big drink.

There was nothing much to do in the town either. A lot of the time we just lay there on our beds and looked at the ceiling and talked. Harold knew about the witness program, so we could talk about important things. About Linda. About my dad. About what was going to happen.

• • •

Rose Marie started cooking on the little stove in the efficiency at the Mansion. There was a park nearby, and the agents ran with Joe and took him to play basketball and racquetball. They came and went in eight- and sometimes twelve-hour shifts and sat up at night when the family was sleeping. Rose Marie prepared her specialties and fed the agents, too. When she accumulated a washload of dirty clothes, she asked one of the female agents to take her to a Laundromat. The agent took her to her home instead, and Rose Marie used her washer and dryer. When Sal was still in Florida, Ron Grenier and another agent took Rose Marie and Joe to a movie. Harrison Ford was playing in *Witness*. His character, John Book, goes into hiding to protect a young Amish murder witness who is the key to uncovering police corruption, and in a phone call Book's partner asks, "What are we gonna do? FBI?" At that line Rose Marie and Joe and the agents all looked at each other and laughed and laughed.

Rose Marie longed to call Arlene Parker and explain why she hadn't been able to open up the store. It reflected on her character not to have done it. She wanted badly to talk to Phyllis and to her sister and most of all to her father, to explain things. She thought of it each time she was near a telephone. It can't hurt, she would tell herself one minute. Then she would worry that even one call might be too dangerous. Fears would awaken and stir: she might say something revealing, the call could be traced, someone was waiting in Phyllis's kitchen for just such a call to threaten her unless Rose Marie gave them information. She would put the thought aside.

Andy Bruno was still in bed when Dan Russo knocked on his door on the morning of March 7 with a warrant for his arrest for promoting bribery. Ann Bruno let Russo and a search team in reluctantly, complaining that it was an invasion of privacy. Bruno got dressed and went with Russo and Vince Wincelowicz to the FBI resident agency offices at the federal building in Fort Lauderdale. The other agents stayed behind to search his house and car.

Bruno was denying everything when Russo excused himself to take a phone call. When Russo returned, he leaned against the closed door of the interrogation room and said, a little smugly, "Guess what we just found?"

The February 4 betting ticket from Gulfstream Park—an across-the-board bet on the number 11 horse in the third race—had been in the bathroom wastebasket. Bruno must have just thrown it away. Water stains did not obscure the notes Bruno had scribbled about Sal and his case the day he talked to Brennan at the park. Russo watched Bruno's chin drop toward the tabletop. Then he directed Bruno to a phone, because he had asked to call his lawyer.

On March 11, the FBI confronted Brennan at his home. By then

the judge had received a letter from New York Telephone informing
him his phone records had been subpoenaed by the U.S. attorney
for the Eastern District. He knew the FBI was watching him. The
agents who went to his door told him Bruno had been arrested.

Brennan said he had never heard of Sal Polisi.

Vince Wincelowicz searched through thousands of records in
the Queens Criminal Court clerk's office. He breathed the dust of a
thousand cases before he found what he was looking for. It was the
charge-out card listing the release of the record in Sal's drug case
to Justice Brennan's chambers.

• • •

We got back to the Severn Arms one night about a week after
we got to Bridgnorth, and Harold had a message to call home. His
mom said I was supposed to fly home right away. He drove me to
Heathrow Airport the next day.

We'd just gotten on the motorway when Harold spotted a Jaguar
and swung the Vauxhall behind it. He said, "The only way to get
this sucker over eighty is to draft somebody. This guy's gonna beat
it when he gets the room, you watch."

He was right. Traffic opened up and the guy went past eighty
with us on his tail. He kept looking in the rearview mirror and pulling
us along, past ninety, toward a hundred. The Vauxhall was barely
on the road. It was tumbling in the wind behind the Jaguar, vibrating
like a loose guitar string. Harold had this wild grin. With his curly
hair he looked like that guy, Marjoe something. It was a weird time
to have a conversation. "Where are you supposed to be going,
anyway?" he said.

"I don't know. All's I know is what your mom said to tell me,
that I'm supposed to pick up a ticket to Kennedy Airport."

"Oh, yeah," he said, "I forgot you been here with me the whole
time." His voice sounded like somebody was strumming it, we were
shaking so hard. "Where do you think you're going?"

"I don't know." I'd give Harold these short sideways glances to
let him know I was listening, but I couldn't stop watching the back
of that Jaguar about six inches in front of our bumper. "I hope we
go back to Port Jervis."

"That'd be nice, but you better not count on that."

All of a sudden I realized I might not see Harold again. First Linda and now Harold. He'd been like a big brother to me for a lot of years. I mean, we'd been really close and I hadn't thought until just then that when I got on that plane, I wouldn't know where I was going except that I was going to disappear from another person that I knew. Grandma Noto and the rest of my mom's family, my little cousin Albert who called me L'al because he couldn't say Little Sal, Ross, Coach Seeber, Charlie, the guys on the team, I was thinking of all those people in a strange country, going down the wrong side of the road at a hundred miles an hour, to take a plane to a home I didn't have. *"Why do I have to go at all?"* I said.

At that moment the Jaguar's tail dropped in a little boil of smoke and he threw us off his draft. Our speed fell to eighty and Harold let it slide from there to something the Vauxhall could stand a little better.

He looked over, serious now. *"I know what you're thinking. You're thinking, 'Why do I have to give up my life?' And you're right, you've got a lot of friends, and Linda, and people who care about you. But when they're all gone to other things what's left is your family."*

"But why do I have to give up everything I've worked for?"

"Not only you. Your brother and your mother. Don't feel sorry just for yourself."

"Well, okay, all of us. Why do we? What did we do?"

Harold looked at his digital runner's watch. Our hundred-mile-an-hour run behind the Jaguar had brought us to the outskirts of London. He turned right onto another motorway. When we'd gone through the interchange and started picking up the signs to Heathrow, he said, *"Sal, sometimes you've got to give up something in order to get something even better. You're giving up the good things in your life, but your dad's life was real different and to get beyond all that it takes all of you to move. You should ask him. I don't know what all he's done, but you should. You're gonna have to, anyway. 'Cause if you don't you're gonna hate him for all this without knowing why he did it."*

I was watching the signs anxiously, looking for the TWA terminal. "He said he did it to keep us together. I can understand that."

We passed a row of square black taxis. Harold said, "Yeah, but you don't understand why you have to go away to stay together, and why things can't be like they were. Ask him. He'll tell you. I'm telling you, you need to know. I'll tell you this, too. He's doing it because he loves you and your brother. It's not easy for him either."

I said, "He makes it sound easy. The whole time he's been saying how great it was going to be."

"C'mon, Sal, he's trying to make you believe it. Do you ever remember a time when your dad wasn't a cheerleader?"

I didn't. From the first LynVets football practices at the Cross Bay Oval, he'd pushed and urged and encouraged belief against all odds. I'd always assumed that he knew something I didn't. The idea that it was all sleight of hand, that we could go forward simply if we believed we could, fired by nothing more than his imagination, that was new to me.

Harold turned under an overhang into a parking area. We parked and went inside. There was a line at the counter. The clerk had my reservation and handed me a ticket and took my suitcase. Harold walked with me as far as the security gate. "Well, sport, this is it," he said. He stuck out his hand but we couldn't let it go like that. We hugged each other. People were walking all around us.

"I'll call you if I can," I said.

"If you can't," he said, "I'll understand. Good luck, Sal."

He stood there after I went through the metal check. I could still see him from the end of the corridor, his hand cocked in a half-wave, and then I had to turn right toward my gate. My flight was boarding when I got there and I didn't have time to go back and see if Harold was still there.

An agent met me at Kennedy Airport and put me on a plane to Buffalo.

TWELVE

I had time while I was flying to think about what I knew about my father.

I remembered him taking me to a McDonald's near a duck pond, and feeding French fries to the ducks. I was so small then I could only hold his finger as we walked together, and the ducks' rushing for the food was scary. I remembered him not being home a lot, and him and my mother fighting, like yelling at each other, when we lived in Ozone Park. When I was four or five I saw him beat a man, much bigger than himself, outside Grandpa Noto's bar; he banged the man's head against the sidewalk until people had to drag him off, and he stood there cursing at the man who limped away. I remembered the trips to Pennsylvania when Mom said he was in the hospital. Joe and I used to play cops and robbers with the cars behind us. We were always the cops, never the robbers. We'd pop up over the backseat and point our fingers at the cars behind us, "Pow, pow, pow." Sometimes they'd shoot back and I'd go down and say, "I'm hit, I'm hit." Then Joe would pull the imaginary bullet out of me with his fingers and I'd say, "Thanks," and we'd be best buddies forever. If he said he was hit, though, I'd just say, "No you're not," and go on shooting. When we got there Dad would be wearing, like a uniform, faded prison-issue khakis, and we would sit in lawn chairs in a yard with brick walls all around.

When he came home, he didn't get up in the morning and go to work in a factory or an office. He had the car shop, and we always had nice cars, and money. People came to the back door sometimes at night. He would hand them packages and they'd be gone. One night—he wasn't there—Joe and I were doing our homework at the kitchen table when there was a pounding and this kid we knew, who sold weed in the park across the street, came flying in. He screamed, "Rosie, Rosie, the bulls, the bulls are after me." She said go down to the basement but he said no, I'll try the bathroom. He was hiding behind the shower curtain in the bathtub when they found him. As the police were leading him away he rattled his handcuffs and yelled, "See, you kids, see? You saw it all. Police brutality. This is what they do." Thinking of my dad, and memories like that, they were all tied up together.

When I thought about him coaching midget football, I remembered him always going to the bar afterward, across the street, to have his Heinekens with all the other dads, on game days, and the time he left there with me and Joe and drove crazy under the Liberty Avenue el. He was weaving, missing the el supports by inches, and laughing, and I was laughing, screaming like we were out at Coney Island on the Cyclone, but Joe was scared and crying in the backseat. And a time when we were older, racing on our bicycles, when Joe got hit by a brown car that never stopped. We were near the house and Dad came out and picked him up and a cop car was coming by and he just stepped into the street and the cop took them to Jamaica Hospital.

Dad was always there, two afternoons a week, to help coach our team, the Redskins, and he was always there on Saturdays for games. Sometimes, I'd be calling signals and looking from side to side to see what I could figure out about the defense, and my gaze would jump over to the sidelines where he'd be huddled with Dominic Cataldo, who supplied the heroin he sold, or somebody he hijacked with. (I didn't know that then, of course.) One time Frankie Gotti, John Gotti's son, who was a big kid and a good blocker, missed the weight limit and the head coach, Don Murphy, had to cut him from the team. Dad said John Gotti came to the field in his big Lincoln saying, "Where's that coach? I'm gonna kill that fuckin' coach." Dad said, "You can't kill the coach for that, John." Later, Frankie Gotti was killed when a car hit him, and then later, the driver disappeared. It was in all the papers. Dad said he thought it was Funzi Tarricone who made the driver disappear. Funzi was a big, huge guy. I carried the ring to the altar in his daughter's wedding.

My dad wanted me to be a star at football, and Joe, too. He worked real hard with us. It was like something he never got to do. He tried to play in high school, but his life was too full of other shit,

I guess. Then he dropped out and went into the Marines. I figured out after a while that I was living his dream for himself, the life that he had missed, and also that football represented something that the rest of his life didn't.

Whenever Dad talked about the witness program, he talked in the same breath of my making it in football. Staying out of prison was part of it, I knew, but that seemed to diminish in the bargain. His hope for me, and later for my brother, to succeed at football seemed by itself strong enough to tear him from his entire past. I don't know what he would have done if we had been piano players. Who cares? But what was in his past that required such a final break for all of us? He'd said he'd done enough stuff that it took all of us to pay for it. I started to wonder how much I didn't know.

Mom and Joe were waiting at the gate when I got off the plane in Buffalo. I saw them first. They stood off to one side as the swirl of travelers passed, causing a little bulge in the flow like a rock jutting out from a riverbank. I called out, "Mom, Joe." She beamed when she saw me in a way that emphasized the creases in her face, and I realized with a start how hard it must have been for her while I was gone. My butt was numb and I was dazed from so much flying, and when she hugged me I lost my balance and we reeled into a man who stepped back and muttered, "Fucking drunks."

"Oh, Sal, look at you," she said. "I haven't seen you in a month. You look good, honey, but you look so tired. You must have been on that plane forever."

"One plane or another."

Joe stepped up then and said, "How you been, bro? Did you see Boy George?"

"Nah, he wasn't where I was." I threw an arm around his shoulders. He had really gotten bigger in the month since I had seen him. We joined the stream of people walking toward the baggage claim. "Where's Dad?" I asked.

Mom said, "He's with Dan Russo. They're moving some things into our apartment."

"We have an apartment? Is this where we're going to live?" Through the windows along the concourse I could see workers scurrying in heavy padded parkas as if they were being blown by the

wind. As we landed I had seen a white fringe of snow around the airport. England seemed attractive now.

"No," she said, "this is just until the witness program takes us in. We'll move into the apartment in a day or two. We're in a hotel for tonight."

Joe added, "We've been in hotels for about a month." He leaned close and said, "It sucks."

"Why'd I have to come back?" I asked.

"It didn't matter to the FBI," Mom said, "but the U.S. marshals—they're the ones who run the program—wanted everybody together. In case they have to move us fast, I guess. I'm just glad we're all together."

The Sheraton Inn in downtown Buffalo was a lot better than the Severn Arms. While I was unpacking, looking for a toothbrush, I heard Dad's voice saying, "Look who's here." He came over and gave me a big Italian hug. Right behind him, another voice said, "The traveler. Welcome home."

Dan Russo stuck out his hand and I had to force myself to shake it. Whenever I wanted to blame somebody for the turn my life had taken, I thought about the government. Which meant Dan Russo. The FBI, the ATF, the U.S. marshals, who cared? Russo was the one who was always telling my dad where to go and what to do, like making him turn against his family by taping little Albert's birthday party. Dad had done his thing with the judge, I'd figured that out, and now we were in some kind of twilight zone and Russo was still here pulling the strings. Plus I hadn't seen my family in a month. What the hell was Russo doing there?

"Why is he here?" I asked Dad when Russo was gone. I felt prickly all over, like there was a fight around the corner.

"Helping us get settled. See, it's complicated. There's paperwork before we can get in the witness program, so we're still the FBI's responsibility." He sat down on the edge of the bed and unzipped the jacket of his sweat suit. He was starting to lose his gut a little bit.

"Why Buffalo?" I walked to the window and looked out over the bleak city.

"Oh, that's interesting." Dad could get interested in anything.

"Dan used to be a coroner up here somewhere. Niagara County, I think it was. Or maybe Chautauqua. Yeah, it was Chautauqua. Anyway, he was a coroner. He had a code name, Quincy, when we were down in Florida doing Brennan."

"He handled stiffs?" The picture made me shudder. I thought of shaking hands with him. It seemed cold near the window, and I went back and sat at the desk opposite the beds. I could hear Joe in the next room, switching television channels.

"Sure. Before he joined the FBI. So what? So we're here while they assess us for the witness program. It's more complicated than I thought. You have to have a bunch of tests, and interviews and stuff. Anyway, you and your brother need to be back in school."

"Why do you have to have tests? What do they want to know?"

"If we're suitable." His face cracked into a big wide grin. He leaned back onto the bed and then rolled off it onto the floor and started doing push-ups. He did ten or twelve and then said, puffing, "You got to be suitable, you know."

"Are you suitable?" I don't know what I meant. It just popped out.

"Am I suitable?" He was talking into the carpet. "Well, if I'm suitable enough to go undercover on the judge, I'd better be suitable for the witness program."

I said, "Dad, if it's just the judge, you know, why do we have to go through all this? I mean, what can a judge do?"

He did a few more push-ups, the veins standing out on his straining arms like gopher burrows in the yard. Then he rolled over on his back, red-faced, chest and belly heaving. After a minute he said, "The judge could do plenty. He's been hanging out with the wiseguys for years. Shit, he used to sit and drink with Jackie Donnelly at Bruno's place in Queens, the Pan Am. Did I ever take you there, the Steak Pub? No? Well, the wiseguys all hung out there, and there wasn't no bigger wiseguy than Jackie Donnelly. But it's not just what the judge could do." He sat up, crossed his legs and swung around to face me.

"It's that once you go over you can't go back, you know. I mean, I knew all those guys back there, remember back there around the Bergin? I used to take you there. You think I could hang around close to New York, when those guys find out I worked undercover with the FBI? Those guys I hijacked with, and gambled with, and sold drugs with? Forget about it. Plus I had to tell the FBI about all that, and sooner or later they're gonna try somebody I told 'em about, and I'm gonna have to testify. Like I'm gonna have to testify against the judge, if they ever arrest him. You know what that'll mean to the wiseguys, to have a judge they could get to taken off the bench? That's serious."

Now he unfolded his legs, stood up and walked over to the window. He stood looking out for what seemed like a long time. I didn't know whether I was more tired, or hungry. Tired, I guess, because I started to nod. He woke me up when he said, "But we would go through all this anyway. It's good." He turned around and his face, backlighted against the window, was full of trouble. "You and Joe, you're good kids. I never wanted you to live the life I lived. I never endorsed myself to you. My father, even after he went straight, was still fascinated with crime. Or maybe he was just trying to entertain me. He used to tell me bedtime stories about Willie Sutton, how he robbed banks, so I went out and robbed banks when I grew up. But I don't want you and Joe to rob no banks. And I say I'm doing this for you, so you'll have a chance not to have to live my life, but I'm doing it for me, too. I was tired of that life. I had to get away. You kids, I don't know, maybe you were the excuse. But see, if you do good, like if you keep doing good at football, and if you go to college, well, that will mean that . . ." He made a funny helpless motion with one arm, like he was curling a ball onto the carpet at his feet. He looked at me, suddenly defiant. "You think this is easy, this here?" he said. "It would've been easier to do the time."

I don't remember getting undressed and into bed. When I woke up early the next morning, still on England time, I heard Dad in the adjoining room already up and rustling the morning papers. I peeked in and said, "Yo, Sal."

"Yo, L'Al," he said, using little Albert's name for me. "Happy birthday, son."

Sometime in the night he and Mom had wrapped a present for me. It was sitting on the low dresser in the room, a medium-sized box with red paper, I guessed a sweater or a sweatshirt. I was close; it was a Buffalo Bills jersey with my old number, 23. I opened it after Mom and Joe were up, before we went down to breakfast. Russo wasn't there, and I learned we would be in the Sheraton another night before moving into the apartment. Mom said everything was in, but it wasn't settled and she hadn't shopped for groceries and she didn't want to have to spend my birthday putting things away in drawers.

We were back in the motel restaurant that night, and this time Russo was there. He ate dinner with us. I could see he wanted to be friendly, asking me about England, and wishing me happy birthday and all that.

"Don't mention it," I said. "Just don't let them sing me happy birthday. The FBI could tell them not to do that, couldn't they?" People having birthdays should never go in restaurants, because the waiters always end up bringing a cake and singing and everybody looks at you. It's embarrassing.

"Too late," he said.

I looked in the direction of the kitchen and saw the waiters gathering. The swinging door opened and a telltale blaze of light appeared and I heard a little murmur at the next table and here they came, all singing. I felt my face go hot. Then Mom and Dad and Joe joined in. I kicked at Joe to stop him, and he kicked back and giggled. The people at the next table started singing, and this chorus of waiters was standing all around and this cake was right in front with all these candles burning. It was easier to blow them out and get it over with. When I did, everybody said, "Happy birthday," and started clapping, even the people at the next table. It takes a lot of nerve to say happy birthday to somebody you've never met. But people do it all the time.

Somebody handed me a knife. "Isn't that nice?" Mom said. "Dan ordered it."

I thought maybe I should cut him, but I cut the cake instead, and said, "Thanks, Dan." Mom would have made me anyway.

He didn't even know I was embarrassed. He had this smile, like he'd done something really nice. "That's okay," he said. "Happy birthday, Sal."

*As I cut the cake on my seventeenth birthday, I wondered where
I would be when I was eighteen, and what my name would be.*

• • •

Tom Goddard parked around behind the pizza-and-chicken-
wing joint and followed the two kids to the small apartment building.
They entered at one end, climbed to the second floor, chose a door
and knocked.

Sal put his eye to the peephole and saw the distorted faces
against a circular rendition of the hallway. He pulled open the door.
"Hey, Coach, how ya doin'? Come on in. What say, you guys?"

The two boys went straight into the kitchen. Goddard stepped
into the small apartment and looked around. There were no pictures
on the walls, no personal mementos that he could see. It confirmed
everything he'd heard about this family that had arrived suddenly
and mysteriously in the Buffalo suburb of Cheektowaga, dropping a
surpassing football prospect upon his doorstep at Cheektowaga Central High.

The kid had showed up in his gym class one Monday in the
middle of March. He wasn't tall, but he was well-muscled and quick
on his feet. And quiet. Very quiet. He'd flushed beet red when
Goddard welcomed him and introduced him to the class. "This is
Sal Polisi. He's a transfer." Goddard didn't know from where, and
at first he didn't think to ask.

He had thought of it later, though. Once he'd timed the kid in
the forty-yard dash. He stood there looking at his stopwatch, looking
at the kid coming back to put on his sweats after the run, looking
down at the stopwatch again. "You ever play much football, Sal?"
he asked.

"Just a little."

"Where?"

"Just a little place downstate."

Later he'd taken the kid to the weight room. Again the kid had
been embarrassed. He'd looked around and said, "I haven't done a
lot of lifting, Coach. Where we were, the wrestling team had some
equipment and I worked out with that. But that was on my own."
He put Sal on the bench press, and with no technique at all he'd

lifted two fifty-five. With technique he'd probably have done three hundred. For the first time Goddard dared to think about the fall. At the same time he thought of the college recruiters. They came each spring asking the coaches who they should look at in the coming football season, and by now Coach Goddard thought he had a prospect on his hands. Goddard called the school office and asked for the kid's transcript. When it didn't arrive, he called again. After another week went by, he went to the office during his free period. There was an odd sort of stir when he said he was looking for the transcript, like the secretaries had been waiting for something like this to happen. As soon as he said the name he had the feeling everyone was listening. The next thing he knew someone was showing him in to see the principal.

"Yeah, hi," Goddard had said to principal Leslie Lewis. "I wanted to get a transcript for the Polisi kid. The one who just came here with his brother? The recruiters are going to want to know about him."

Lewis rubbed the bridge of his nose where his glasses pinched him and looked at some papers on his desk. "I can't tell you anything about that boy," he said uncomfortably. "About either boy," he added.

"What do you mean?" Goddard said.

"I just can't tell you anything."

They began a game designed to preserve the principal's integrity. He would volunteer no information. So Goddard asked questions, speculated, really, and Lewis would confirm only what Goddard guessed correctly. Like a game of read my lips, thought Goddard.

He said, "Nobody's supposed to know where these people are, right?"

Lewis said, "That's right."

"It's some kind of deal with the government, like the FBI, right?"

The principal said, "That's right."

"Are you telling me they're on a deal like the Witness Protection Program?"

The principal nodded his head. Relaxing now that Goddard had guessed the Polisis' situation without his telling him, Lewis said, "We have no records of where they came from." Then he threw the bomb. "They could be gone any day," he said. "They haven't changed their names. Maybe they'll still be here in the fall and maybe not."

Goddard had left still determined to tell the recruiters that he had a prospect. He'd talked Sal junior into going out for track, and soon noticed his father was there every afternoon. He had dark curly hair and a round face, about Goddard's height, five-nine, but heavier than his one sixty, and he'd sit in the stadium bleachers bundled in a heavy coat, watching the kids run around the cinder track with the dirty snow pushed off around the edges. He took his son home after every practice. Finally Goddard said, "Look, Mr. Polisi, I'm going to need some information on your son, some statistics and stuff, for the college recruiters. I mean, he may be a prospect." Besides, I'm curious as hell, he thought.

The guy had said, very confidently, "Why don't you come down to the apartment? I'll show you some film on him and you can judge for yourself."

And so here was Goddard, standing inside the Polisis' door wondering what he'd gotten himself into.

Sal introduced his wife. Rose Marie greeted Goddard with a nervous smile, waving her cigarette smoke away with her left hand. She had been attractive once, Goddard thought, still was, even, but whatever they had gone through had been rough on her. Sal called the two boys back in from the kitchen and handed them some money. "Why don't you go out and get a milk shake or something, so the coach and I can talk?"

When they had gone, Sal turned on the television and put a videotape into the machine. The tape rolled and Goddard learned for the first time that Sal junior had played for Port Jervis High School. Then he could hardly believe what he was seeing, the kid just ripping people apart, scoring left and right and running over and through and around people. Try as he did to stem it, the stream of Goddard's imagination filled and overflowed; he saw a district championship.

Sal said, "Now you know what my son can do, but I can't allow you to give any information out to any colleges. Just tell 'em to come back in the fall and see for themselves. The thing is, see, I'm working for the government and I can't let my identity get out."

Sure, thought Goddard. He was wondering if he dared ask what the chances were the family would still be there in the fall. He was clearing his throat when a knock sounded on the door.

Rose Marie called, "Who is it?"

A rough voice came back, "Laundry man."

Goddard thought of every story he had read about the Witness Protection Program and the Mafia. The Polisis hadn't changed their names. That meant, oh shit. Goddard looked toward the windows, wondering which one to leap through and how far it was to the ground.

Rose Marie looked through the peephole and opened the door. A man entered wearing a gray jumpsuit with a name patch, carrying a load of laundry. Goddard relaxed, grateful he hadn't tried the windows.

After that meeting, he asked Sal junior to stop and see him every day before home room, just so he could assure himself the kid still was there.

The first track meet of the 1985 season was in April, at home on the sorry cinder track at Cheektowaga Central. It was a cold day, the wind kicking off Lake Erie in a mockery of spring. Goddard had his hands shoved deep inside the pockets of his parka and was wishing he had worn a hat when Kenny Maciejewski, equally bundled, came and stood beside him. Goddard had envied Maciejewski until the Polisis came along, because Depew Central, where Maciejewski coached, had the fastest kid in the district, a kid named Rick Gorzynski.

"You got anybody in the hundred?" Maciejewski asked. He sounded to Goddard like a guy on his way into a posh restaurant, asking a street bum if maybe he weren't just a little hungry.

"I got this new kid who came in, who's gonna be a tailback for me. He's pretty quick."

"Well, we'll see how fast he is."

The runners were doffing their sweat suits and lining up for the hundred-meter dash, jumping and stretching in the cold in their tunics and shorts. They knelt and then leaned forward in the starting blocks. The gun sounded. Goddard tried to focus on both Sal and Gorzynski but his eyes followed the one runner who leaped in front and finished a good five meters in the lead.

"Way to go, Sal," Goddard called as Sal wheeled and ran back toward the starting line to put his sweat clothes on again. He felt Maciejewski staring at him and smiled. "He's gonna fit right into my backfield," Goddard said. He saw a division championship *and* an undefeated season.

Andy Bruno had a change of heart in April.

At first, when he was arrested, the restaurateur did everything he knew to protect his old friend Bill Brennan. He told the FBI that fixing cases was his scam and not the judge's. He tried to warn Brennan by contacting a Queens attorney, Melvin Lebetkin. He went before a federal grand jury in Brooklyn in March and told, he later estimated, eighty percent of the truth, again trying to protect Brennan because of his position. All the while, he was trying to reach out to the judge to find out where he stood.

In April, rebuffed in his attempts to contact Brennan and persuaded by the government's threat to charge his wife as an accessory to bribery for carrying the money Sal had given him, Bruno returned to the grand jury and told the truth. He recounted a fifteen-year history of accepting bribes from mobsters and delivering them to Brennan.

All this was going on in secret while another case was in the news. Sal's old friends John Gotti, his brother Gene, John Carneglia and seven other Gambino family figures had been indicted on federal racketeering charges at the end of March. The criminal enterprise in which they were accused of participating was, in essence, the Gambino family. Among the acts that made up the enterprise were three instances of murder. Prosecutors began to pencil in the names of witnesses who knew about Gotti's life of crime.

Dan Russo was still sorry he hadn't been able to arrest Brennan with the money in his hands, but even with the judge still unindicted he was beginning to consider the investigation a success. His two main witnesses were safely squirreled away, Bruno in Lexington, Kentucky, and the Polisis in Cheektowaga, outside of Buffalo, New York, where they were safe for the time being. He was interviewing other witnesses.

Early on the warm spring morning of May 6, John Limbach and

Joe Kelly led a team of agents from the Bureau of Alcohol, Tobacco and Firearms and New York State troopers to the Leonards' trailer on the dirt road in Godeffroy, New York. They arrested Doris, Cynthia and Danny Leonard, a son, on charges of conspiracy to deal in unregistered firearms—the bombs the Leonards sold Sal. The Rebel, Julius, was down at Tenke's auto parts. He was coming out of the junkyard when he was confronted by Limbach and the other agents in their bulletproof vests and windbreakers marked with ATF in twelve-inch letters, and urinated in his pants.

Tom Goddard was grateful each morning that Sal junior greeted him before home room. He was telling the college recruiters, "Look, I've got this kid, it's a touchy situation, but just see me, or call me, in the fall, because this kid is definitely the best football player I've encountered, and definitely Division One material."

Rose Marie went to work in a cafeteria-style steak house. Russo had gotten her the job to give her something to do, but her mind wasn't on it and she stayed for only a few weeks. Sal played pool, a reprise of the summer before he married Rose Marie when he drove to California and back hustling pool and gambling. His two-piece Frank Paradise cue, inlaid with diamond-shaped mother-of-pearl and carried in a padded case, was the only really personal thing Sal had brought with him when he left Port Jervis. He chalked it up almost every day at a pool hall on Walden, somewhere near the indistinct line between Buffalo and Cheektowaga, but he always stopped his game in time to appear at the high-school stadium for track practice.

Russo reappeared in Cheektowaga in the middle of May. He would show up like that, when the Polisis needed money, to ease their introductions to the U.S. marshals. This trip he rented a room at the Sheraton East and brought Sal and Rose Marie there to meet with a psychologist from the Bureau of Prisons.

Dr. Al Smith's hair was thin and cut extremely short; that was predictable enough. Sal, who had seen his share of mind doctors and head shrinkers, didn't find his hair unusual. It was his left arm, obviously muscular under his shirt sleeve, and his empty right sleeve, pinned at the shoulder. He offered his left hand and Sal shook it with his left when Russo introduced them. Sal looked beyond Smith into the room, where an array of materials was spread out on a round table. He saw sheaves of paper, some with indistinct pictures, test booklets, wooden blocks with pegs.

Sal said, "What's this?" There was an edge in his voice that caused the psychologist to study him.

"Just some tests," he said.

"This some kind of entrance exam we gotta take?"

"No, not exactly," said Dr. Smith. His eyes were alert and very pale, seeming to match the thinness of his hair. "It's routine. Just some questions for a profile. A psychological profile. They do it with everybody entering the program."

Sal gave a harsh, impatient laugh that Rose Marie tried to soften. She said, "Yes, Dan told us we'd be taking tests today. It's nice to be able to do it here." She looked around at the atrium of the hotel, which enclosed a pool, a jungle of large potted plants and, scattered among them, café tables and chairs.

Rose Marie remained with Dr. Smith while Russo took Sal into the atrium with a booklet of multiple-choice questions. "First you guys with the lie detectors and now this," Sal complained. The FBI had tested Sal on the polygraph at the beginning of his cooperation. He bent over the booklet and started marking answers.

After a time, Rose Marie emerged from the room and found Sal and Russo in the atrium. "Your turn," she said.

"What is it?"

"Just a lot of questions. What does this picture remind you of? What word do you think of when you hear another word? Like that. Oh, and you have to put pegs in the right hole. Knowing you, you'll put the round peg in the square hole." She laughed gaily. The tests were fine with her; anything to move them to an end to waiting.

Sal didn't laugh. He went to the room and knocked on the door. The psychologist was rearranging the papers and the wooden blocks on the round table. Sal watched him with a darkening mood. The interviews were all alike, he told himself, the chumps poking and pushing and trying to paint a picture of you from your answers. Sal had figured out from the beginning you could make the picture turn out a certain way, from the moment more than twenty years before when he'd decided he preferred a Marine Corps hospital to marching and digging foxholes and saluting. The inspiration had come to him with a blow on the head, when the flagpole he was helping raise fell and caught him squarely. He malingered, complaining of headaches and sudden blackouts, until he fell genuinely sick aboard a troop ship on the way to Spain for military games. When the pericarditis— an inflammation of the heart-encasing membrane—had subsided, Sal was back in Queens at the St. Albans Naval Hospital.

Over the years Sal had given himself all the credit for fooling the psychiatrists, for making himself into Sally Upazz', Crazy Sally. But there was an uncontrollable anger inside him and its eruption, there at St. Albans, was what put him into the psych ward in the first place. Sal thought he was only being flamboyant, and besides, the corpsman was an asshole. The corpsman wanted Sal to stay in bed—those were the orders on his chart—and Sal preferred to wander and kibitz. So one day, when the corpsman asserted his authority, Sal started a fight it took six ward attendants and a sedative to end. He came to wearing a straitjacket, in a padded cell. Six months later, he was out of the Marines with "mentally unstable" written on his record.

The psycho rap was convenient after that. Oh, he was angry; who wouldn't be, he thought, with his sister Rosemarie dying that summer of pancreatitis, his full sister and his link with the mother who had left them, suddenly gone, then his half-brother Eddie, at age fifteen, drowning barely six weeks later in the Great South Bay, found washed up on Fire Island after going out to dig for clams? Sal's anger had come out in different ways. Once he'd gone into a trance, beating the floor with his fists and crying as his young half-sister Nancy watched in fear. More often he robbed and fought, and if his uncle Tony couldn't fix his case and keep him out of jail, he'd check into a Veterans Administration hospital and complain that he was hearing voices. He'd done it first for greed, actually, after a VA contact officer told him, "If you act a little crazy, you can collect money. Once in a while, check into a hospital and tell them you're depressed." The guy's name was Dulaney, and come to think of it, he had one arm, too. Sal had followed Dulaney's advice and wound up with the full pension that was like a gift every month from the government.

That first trip to the Franklin Delano Roosevelt VA Hospital upstate in Montrose had been enlightening. Nassau County detectives were after him for forging checks he stole from a car he'd broken into to steal the radio—that was his main business then—and so Sal was very depressed. At Montrose he was placed among lunatics. You didn't have to be too bright to look around at the damaged war veterans and imitate what they were doing. Sal talked to himself, screamed occasionally and would say that he heard voices. He tried to hide his tranquilizers until he could spit them out. He was apparently convincing, for the VA doctors classified him as paranoid and schizophrenic, with sociopathic tendencies. When he tired of their authority and sitting in bed painting pictures on black velvet, he escaped.

He chuckled involuntarily to think of it, causing the psychologist to study him again.

Yes, I know your kind, Sal thought again, I can fool you if I want to. The escape had been so clever. He had asked to call home from the pay phone near the door, then burst out and dashed for the woods in his blue hospital pajamas, eluding his pursuers by jumping an electric fence and hitching a ride back to Long Island. Frank and Sarah had returned him to the hospital; if only his father had treated the escapade for what it was, more of a caper, look at me, Dad. But no. Frank Polisi was tired then, and out of patience. Then the forgery charges were dropped and Sal saw it paid him to be crazy. Crazy Sally. Sally Upazz'.

It was a game, pretending to be crazy. You had to take some shit, like from the prison shrink at Lewisburg who wrote that he was fragile and weak, and would rather be a baby than a man. (Wrote that from a safe distance after the interviews were over, the cocksucker.) Said he should learn a trade. What a joke, and then the appeals court had sprung him and he was laughing. It was all a joke and a game. A game like the rest of his life, so crazy he didn't always know where the game ended and the real Sal began, with his combustible nervous energy and his murderous temper and his need to show them all, to take the suckers for a ride, to fuck the world. So many crazy things, all games, until the wheel had spun too fast and he'd had to get off. It made him dizzy to think of it, but exhilarated, too.

The psychologist finished arranging his materials. He shook a cigarette from a pack he took from his shirt pocket. Holding the cigarette between his lips he reached into his pocket and brought out a matchbook, which he held against his side with what was left of his right arm. He reached across his body, tore out a match and lit it, touched it to the cigarette, inhaled and let the smoke out slowly. "Now," he said.

First it was the blocks, putting the square peg into the square hole and so on, ridiculous. Then the pictures and what Sal saw in them. Then word association. When the psychologist asked Sal to count off ten, twenty and thirty seconds without looking at his watch, Sal stood up and started pacing.

"I want to just ask you a few questions now," Dr. Smith said when he'd finished making his notes about Sal's time perception. He put the matchbook underneath his arm while he lit another cigarette. He asked Sal what he thought about his mother.

"I don't know. I never saw her face. She left me."

About his father.

"Forget about it. We don't talk. After he remarried, I was like a stepchild." Sal fidgeted, stretched his arms in front of him palms out and flexed his triceps.

Dr. Smith asked more questions, made more notes. He tapped the butt of his pen against his notepad and said, "As you know . . ."

Humor me, Sal thought. Patronize me.

"As you know, the Witness Protection Program places people like you in communities as ordinary citizens. Ordinary, average citizens. I'm wondering whether you think you can conform to society and be an average person like your neighbors, a nine-to-five Joe?"

A nine-to-five Joe? Sal almost laughed. Instead he growled, "You got a better chance of seeing God."

Dr. Smith made some quick notes on his pad, then looked up, his eyebrows arching quizzically over his pale eyes.

"Okay, that's enough," Sal said angrily. "No more questions. I'm through with questions. I mean, this here is a joke." He bounced once or twice on the balls of his feet. "I'm not talking about you, but it's a joke. The government's testing me to see if they're gonna let me in a program they're gonna let me into anyway because the

mob would like to kill me? Give me a break here. You don't know
this, maybe, but I've taken a thousand tests like this. I'm a guy who
manipulated the government for twenty years. I been telling you the
truth, but enough's enough. All this is stupid. I quit, okay? I quit
the test. Write that in your notebook." He stalked out of the room.

Dr. Smith tamped out his cigarette. He made some more notes
on his pad.

Rose Marie had finished marking her answers. She looked up
to see her husband coming across the atrium, walking intently, with
his face drawn in an angry frown. Russo followed her eyes and said,
"Here he comes. How was it?"

"It was stupid," Sal said, pushing a chair out of his way. The
sound of it scraping on the floor echoed in the atrium. "I've answered
questions. I've done interviews. I'm up to here. I wouldn't finish it.
I'm not gonna finish it. That's what I told him."

Rose Marie glanced at Russo with alarm. She said, "But what
about the program?"

"What about it?" Sal replied. He stared at Russo, challenging
him.

"Well, wait a minute," Russo said, "I don't think this has
anything to do with getting in. I don't think you have to answer every
question. I think they just want to find out what your chances are
for survival in the program. I don't mean if you're going to get
whacked. I mean for blending into a community, not committing
crimes, that kind of thing."

"But they could decide they don't want you, couldn't they?"
Rose Marie interjected. "If they thought, I don't know, if they thought
you'd get in trouble?" She wanted Russo to deny her fears.

Sal dragged a third chair to the table and sat. "It's just bullshit,"
he said. "We'll get in because we need to be protected. It don't
matter whether this guy likes me. I don't care what he says about
me. It don't matter anyway, see, because I know what I'm gonna do.
I know I'm not gonna go out and commit no crimes. Who cares what
this guy thinks?"

Russo rolled his eyes and hurried off to the room where he'd
installed Dr. Smith, carrying Rose Marie's test booklet. When he
returned he said, "Dr. Smith is very disappointed in you, Sal."

Rose Marie stood up. She said, "I want to tell him that my husband is just impatient. That we're all impatient and it's hard because we don't know where we're going, and, and . . ." She stopped talking, because she felt suddenly about to cry. She marched toward the psychologist's room.

Dr. Smith had returned his materials to his briefcase and had risen to leave. Rose Marie knocked and entered the room without waiting for an answer. She blurted, "My husband . . . It's just very hard. We just want to be where we're going and for it to be over."

Dr. Smith appraised her. "I understand," he said. "It is difficult. If you feel you need any help, any counseling once you're in the program, that's one of the things the government provides. Good luck." His voice did not sound optimistic.

"Oh, thank you." Rose Marie offered him her hand. The psychologist put his briefcase down and held out his left hand. The gesture embarrassed Rose Marie, and she blushed and said, "I'm sorry."

"Not at all," said Dr. Smith. "I'm used to it."

. . .

It was beginning to be clear to me that this move was real. We began talking at home about the new names that we wanted for ourselves. It was fun at first, like trying on new clothes. It was cool to think you could have any name you wanted, like maybe you wished from the time you were a little kid that your name could be something else because the other kids teased you. Like the Jewish kid, Manny Segal, we all called Seagull. Or the Underhill kid on one of the other LynVets teams, I forget which, we called him Underwear until the day he caught one of our second-string linemen alone out by the cyclone fence and put the linking pattern of the fence next to his ear.

Anyway, we tried on some outrageous names. Mom was going to be Roseanna Danna and Joe and I were going to be Danny and Donny Danna and Dad would be the Don. We discarded those names after we couldn't stop laughing about them. Dad acted serious for the better part of one night about our becoming the Balboas. We looked at names of jockeys (Arcaro) and race-car drivers (Andretti)

and football coaches (Lombardi) and movie stars (De Niro, Pacino).
The problem was none of them sounded right once we had them on.
Finally we picked names the marshals would approve, names that
wouldn't draw attention.

The marshals also told us to make up a family tree, in case
anybody asked us our grandmother's name, or what my mom's name
was before she was married. One night sitting around the kitchen
table, we drew it out like a real tree with fruit hanging from the
branches. We put the basic characters in, going back two generations,
and gave them the new names.

June 10 began like any other school day. Mom served me and
Joe breakfast and Dad paced around, looking at the local papers and
USA Today, waiting to drive us to school. He was never able to keep
still, and now the waiting made him more nervous and on edge than
usual. He had already been up for two hours. There was a pile of
papers at the kitchen table, was how I could tell.

There was a year-end feeling in the air when we got to school
that day. Summer was right around the corner. I went by Coach
Goddard's office, just checking in like he wanted me to do, and he
said, "Hey, Sal, how're you doing? Starting to feel like summer, isn't
it?"

I was leaving when he said, "Sal, ask your brother to stop by
to see me, will you? I'm planning to use him in the jayvee backfield
next year, and I'm going to want him to work out over the summer."

Summer was on everybody's mind. In home room and all through
the morning, kids were staring out the windows, not paying any
attention to the teachers. The teachers weren't even paying attention.
It was nice to slip outside between classes and feel the sun on your
face and walk through the grass without ice crunching under your
shoes. Every time I heard a locker slam I thought about housecleaning, clearing out, leaving things behind and moving on. Something
was stirring. Something surely was about to happen.

The bell finally rang for the end of morning classes. I met Joe
outside the double doors leading to the cafeteria and told him what
Coach Goddard said. Joe said, "That's a goof. Be nice if we were
staying." We got in line, and moved slowly toward our luncheon date

with mystery meat; school cafeterias are all the same. We saw three guys we knew, and sat down at a table with them. They, too, were talking about summer.

"What are you guys doing when school's out?" somebody asked me.

"Working out, I guess," I said. "Getting ready for football." That was true, as far as it went.

"Yeah? That's great," the other kid said. "Maybe we can work out together. Have you got a job this summer? Going on vacation?"

"We're going somewhere. I'm not sure where." That was also true.

Joe started rattling about going out for jayvee football and I was about to shut him up when I noticed Mr. Radka, the assistant principal, standing in the cafeteria doors, craning his neck. He was looking for us, I just knew it. But I waited for him to find us. He did. He came walking over to the table. He said, "Sal, Joe, Mr. Lewis wants to see you in his office."

This was heavy. I tried to be cool. "We're almost finished," I said, "we'll be there in a minute."

"You'd better come now."

The other kids around the table took the weight of this, the assistant principal coming to get us in the cafeteria. But Mr. Radka was a pretty neat guy, so they started carrying on. "Oh, man, sounds like trouble. I bet you're flunking out. Seeee youuu later." My heart gave me a little nervous double time.

I looked at Joe and he looked back. He was a smart kid for just fourteen, and he gave me a little nod. So he knew, too. We got up at the same time, across the table from each other, giving each other this secret look. I said, "No, we'll be right back," and we walked out of the cafeteria together.

My dad was waiting in the office. Not waiting. Pacing back and forth in front of the principal's desk. When we came in Dad didn't say a word, just turned and showed us this newspaper he was carrying. It was the New York Post. Big black letters filled the page: JUSTICE TOOK BRIBES FROM MOBSTERS: FEDS. Dad said, "My name's in the story. We gotta go." It was in there, all right, all spelled out how

*he was a "Gambino crime family associate working with the feds."
Now they knew, and they would want to kill him. Mr. Radka looked
nervous, like he expected a bomb to go off any second.*

*We didn't waste time talking. Joe and I went to our lockers and
got our stuff out. We left our books with Mr. Radka, and he said
he'd see that my track uniform was handed in. He shook hands with
all of us before we left. When he got to me he said, "Good luck,
Sal." It was the last time anybody called me that outside our family.*

*It would have been nice to go back to the cafeteria to tell those
guys good-bye, but there was no way. We just had to disappear.
Still, you like to give people a chance to remember you, to fix you.
We never got a chance to know we'd be remembered. My brother
will tell you, "We never saw those boys in the cafeteria again." And
of course they never saw us either. I could see them sitting there
around our empty trays, maybe eating our desserts, while in their
minds our faces were dissolving. I wondered if Linda would be able
to remember what I looked like if she lost my pictures. Joe was right.
We never saw those boys again.*

T H I R T E E N

We never went back to our apartment behind the place that sold pizza and Buffalo wings either. Dad drove us straight downtown to a Holiday Inn where Mom was waiting. Russo flew up that same night and prepared to hand us over to the marshals for good.

We were pretty nervous that first night. I mean, there didn't seem to be any way anybody could have found us. Mom hadn't called her family once, even though you knew it killed her. Still . . .

Dad laughed off our nervousness. He liked the idea that people were talking about him. He said, "The phone lines must be buzzin'. I'd love to hear what they're sayin'. They're probably sayin', 'That scumbag Polisi, that lowlife, that rat.' Ro, can you imagine? What do you think Phyllis is saying right now?"

"Something like that." She kept going to the window to look out over the parking lot of the hotel, and insisted on ordering from room service instead of eating in the restaurant. I was conscious all through the night of footsteps in the hallway and doors being unlocked and closed.

The next night we put together all of our identification, every-thing that said who we were, to turn over to the marshals. It was sad, doing that. I hadn't had my driver's license even a year. Man, did I hate to give it up. I took it out of my wallet and looked at it a long time before I put it in the pile we were making on one of the double beds in Mom and Dad's room. Joe didn't have much, just his Social Security card and school ID and some notebooks with his name in them. Something seemed to be missing. I said, "Joe, that's it? You haven't got anything else?"

He said, "I had the karting trophies, just like you did."

I had forgotten all about the trophies that had dominated our living room at the racetrack. I just figured they were packed away somewhere waiting for us to find a home and bring them out again. It hadn't occurred to me they were a form of identification, that we would have to turn them over to the marshals. "Oh, yeah," I said. "Where are they, anyway?"

Joe got this disgusted look. He said, "Gone," with a bitter voice.

"What do you mean, 'gone'?"

"Gone. We threw 'em away back at the racetrack, one afternoon when we thought we were gonna have to leave that night. Me and Ma, we took them all and threw 'em in the Dumpster."

"Even the Grand National ones?" I pictured the pile of trophies glimmering at the bottom of the Dumpster, like the gold that Spanish shipwreck spilled all over the bottom of the ocean somewhere near Key West. There was a story about it on TV.

"All of them," Joe said. He was sitting on the edge of the bed. His opened wallet lay beside him on the flowered bed cover. He said, "I counted them. You had more than I did, Sal, but some of mine were bigger."

Mom broke in. "We thought of taking all the nameplates off and keeping them, but it just seemed silly to do that."

Dad was sitting in a chair with his feet on the bed. "That's part of the old life, son," he said. "We had to get rid of all of that. We're looking forward now. We're not looking back no more."

I snorted. "Too bad you never had a driver's license you had to give away."

"I had one once," he said. "It got suspended."

Mom had brought from the apartment, wherever she kept these things, a department store shirt box full of items she added to the pile on the bed. She went through them one by one, handling them carefully as if they were fragile, first some old yellowed newspaper clippings, a story from a local paper about the Polisi-Noto wedding and some from Kentucky papers, all about the Kentucky Derby and the winning horse, Proud Clarion. "What's this?" I asked her.

"Oh," she blushed, "when your father and I were married, we honeymooned at the Kentucky Derby. And I bet the winner," she said, holding up some tattered betting tickets.

"I couldn't believe it," Dad chimed in from across the bed. "She bet this horse five or six times and he paid sixty-two sixty on

a two-dollar bet. We paid for the whole honeymoon. The horse I bet
was Horse of the Year, Damascus, but it was raining that day and
he finished third. We were drinking mint juleps."

"And Bob Hope was sitting about four seats away. Remember
that?"

"Yeah, I paid big money for those seats."

Mom said, "We started out with a bang, didn't we?" She had
a soft smile as she remembered.

She laid the clippings on the pile and on top of them, tied in
a white ribbon, their wedding invitation and announcement. There
were some official-looking papers with fancy borders: their marriage
license and both their birth certificates. She handed the next two
papers to me and Joe. I looked down at my name drawn in calligraphy,
Salvatore Daniel Polisi, Jr. A separate sheet was attached bearing a
pair of tiny footprints. It was my birth certificate from Jamaica Hospital. I didn't remember ever seeing it before. "Look at those creases
in your feet," Mom said. "Your feet were so fat."

Joe was bent over the document Mom had given him. He was
measuring his baby footprint, laying his index finger alongside it;
they were the same length.

I leaned over next to Joe and pretended to study over his shoulder. "Joseph James Polisi, Southside Hospital, Bay Shore," I read
from the page, which was marked with the round imprint of a notary's
seal. "No, this one's wrong."

Joe looked at me. "What do you mean, it's wrong?"

"It can't be right," I said.

"Why not?"

" 'Cause you never had feet that small. You were born with size
thirteens."

He pushed me and we rolled on the pile laughing, scattering
the papers that traced us back to our beginnings.

There were some things we kept. Mom scratched the name off
the cover of the family Bible. She said she couldn't bear to give it
up, that she had carried it when she and Dad and Joe left the racetrack
in the middle of the night. She used a laundry marker to obliterate
all the names on the presentation page inside the cover, where their
marriage and our births were written down. She kept a little thin box

of pictures, too, with the identifying names marked out. Dad said we had to keep the videotapes of my Port Jervis games to show the coaches wherever we were going; he already had erased the parts where it said Port Jervis. We'd put my clippings on the pile, the stories from the sports pages of the Tri-State Gazette and the Middletown Record, but I couldn't let my high-school letters go. I just couldn't do it. I had earned them, and I didn't even tell anybody I was going to keep them. I just did it. That night, late, I took them all, including the new track letter from Cheektowaga, and wrote over my name on the back of them, adding lines and flourishes to make a different name, the new one that I had chosen.

The next morning, New York papers carried the news that Judge Brennan had taken a leave of absence because of the stories getting out about the bribery and the undercover sting. Dad came back from turning everything over to the marshals. He walked into the room and said, "Now there's no more Polisis."

Russo came to say good-bye. "It's going to be the marshals from here on," he said, looking us over as he stood inside the door of Mom and Dad's room with his suit bag slung over his shoulder.

Mom especially had come to depend on Russo. She hated having to learn to trust new people, and more than the rest of us she found the waiting unnerving. I guess she was smoking about three packs a day. Dad's relaxation was the pool hall. Joe and I could run or swim. Mom was happiest when she was cooking, and without a kitchen to relax in she spent her time walking back and forth and filling the room with cigarette smoke. That morning, when Russo told her we'd be here for a few more days, she'd screamed, "I can't stand it," and burst out crying until he told her he was only kidding. "Tomorrow," he said, "you're going to Washington tomorrow."

Then he congratulated my dad on what he'd done to make the Brennan case. "That case had been kicking around for years at a dead end," he said. "If you hadn't gotten in touch with Limbach it would still be dead."

Dad shot a quick look at us. I wondered why he looked like that, like Russo had just said something he didn't want us to hear. If he hadn't looked I never would have paid attention. Then the clutch popped and it was clear to me. "If you hadn't gotten in touch with Limbach . . . ," Russo had said. Dad had told me and Joe that day in the woods that the government had him up the creek, they had come to him and told him he'd never see the outside of a jail again if he didn't help them. But Russo was saying something different.

I looked to see if anybody else had noticed. Mom had the same dawning look I could feel on my face. Joe had a curious frown and he was listening hard. I could see him working it over. Then he snapped his fingers and said, "Yeah. Yeah." He didn't even wait to see what anybody else was thinking. He said, "Dad, you told us they made you."

Dad acted surprised. "Did I say that?" he said.

Joe said, "Yeah, that day out by that phone booth. You said you were working undercover 'cause they forced you."

Russo looked confused. He said, "Did I let something out?"

But Dad maybe had thought about this for a while, because he didn't try to deny what we had heard. He said, "Aw, that was my ego talking, son. I wasn't ready to admit it, what I did, that I went over on my own. It helped me to tell you what I was doing, and what was gonna happen. So I lied a little. But I don't mind saying now, nobody forced me. It was the only way out, so I called Limbach. What difference does it make?" He stopped abruptly, daring us to challenge him.

It made no difference, really. Forced or voluntarily, we were at our jumping-off place. It changed nothing except my understanding. Of course he was enthusiastic; the whole thing was his idea. I suppose it meant he cared more about himself and his family, and less about his friends. Loyalty goes to blood when it comes down to it. Who could argue if he'd put that spin on the ball? We were his family, not some gang with a name that sounded like a circus troupe. I didn't argue, and neither did Joe, and Mom was just eager to get on to the next phase where she could make her life generous again, where she could make friends and bake pies and sit my teammates down to dinner. We were here, and it did nothing to change that.

Russo was relieved when the disturbance on our family waters calmed. Mom hugged him—hugged an FBI agent!—and he shook hands with me and Joe and wished us luck. Dad followed him out into the hall. Then he was gone. I didn't hate Russo anymore. I liked him, actually. He was just doing what he had to do, just like Dad was and we all were, and he'd turned out to be a decent guy in spite of ordering me the birthday cake back then.

The next day we flew to Washington. Two marshals met us at National Airport. I don't know how they knew us, but they came up to Mom and Dad when we got off the plane and said, "Mr. and Mrs. Edwards?"

Dad said, "Bingo."

They took us to a Days Inn, across the Potomac River in Arlington, Virginia. We waited there, in the summer heat of the Potomac, for the government to reinvent us. The marshals gave us money to spend, and we rode the Washington Metro to Crystal City to go shopping. We joined crowds of tourists wandering the Washington Monument and the Lincoln Memorial and the Smithsonian Institution and all the museums. We went to the Pentagon, and one day, Dad made us go with him to the Justice Department and take his picture standing by the sign. We had no ID at all, and the first time we went out Mom said, "What happens if somebody gets hit by a car, if we have to go to the hospital or something?" Having no ID was worse than not having clean underwear.

I can't say we felt much danger. Not then, not after we left Buffalo. You tried to be aware of the people around you, but it was more like we were at camp and couldn't leave. It was just boring after a while. We spent so much time in museums it was like being in school. Plus the frustration of not knowing where we were going, or how soon. The heat in Washington made the waiting worse.

I still could not decide how to approach the sticky question I had to ask my dad. Which basically was, What brought us here, to this? Okay, he had jumped and not been pushed. But what were the secrets I didn't know? What had he done with the men who hung around the Bergin Hunt and Fish Club, where he took me sometimes after LynVets football games, and who came around our house in Ozone Park on Sunday afternoons in summer to drink beer while he grilled steaks and we kids played in the backyard pool? I knew vaguely, but I wanted sharp, clear pictures, because wherever we

were going and whatever my brother and I were going to become,
we had his stamp on us. I wanted stories, like an immigrant's child
wants stories from the old country. I wanted to know who he was. I
needn't have worried. One afternoon, when a morning rain had left
a steamy haze in the heavy, drenching air and Joe had gone with
Mom to buy new Nikes, and Dad and I were alone sitting by the
swimming pool, he said, "It was a day like this we robbed the fur
truck."

"What fur truck?" I raised myself on one elbow to take a swig
from the bottle of Gatorade we were sharing between our two lounge
chairs. I didn't want to seem too interested.

He was lying back in his chair, a white visor tilted down over
his face and a Sports Illustrated open, facedown, covering his lap.
His shoulders were pink from the sun. He'd announced that morning
that he was going to quit drinking, because our new circumstances
required him to stay alert, and he was thinking of going into training.
That was why I had to share the Gatorade. He raised himself and
adjusted the chair so he was sitting up. He said, "It's kind of why
we're here, that robbery. Because that's when I found out the mob
will screw you. It was back in my hijacking days. . . ."

• • •

Sal had spoken impulsively. It had been such a day, but why
he spoke of it he wasn't sure. It was as if, now that the past was
safely behind him—he thought—he had to preserve it. Now that
there were no more Polisis, he suddenly wanted himself back. He
meant it, he told himself, to be a lesson in contrast: this is what I
did; don't you do it. Like the time he had slapped Sal junior for lying
after he'd come home late and said he was helping another kid, Joey
Stabile, and his father, when Rosario Stabile had been found shot
dead in the trunk of a burned car at Prospect Park in Brooklyn back
in April of '72 and the truth was they'd been out to Coney Island on
the subway. It was the only time he'd ever hit the kid. Don't ever
lie, he'd said. And how many lies had he told? Too many to count.
Ah, well, they were away from all that. He could talk about it now
without falling back into the muck.

The information had come to the Bergin from Tuttie Lauget.

Tuttie was a fur man. That is, he once had worked for a private carter
who picked up garbage in the fur district of Manhattan, and he had
arranged thefts with men inside who pilfered mink coats and set them
out in garbage cans. Information about furs still came to Tuttie, and
in the summer of 1972 he came out of the sunshine into the club on
101 Avenue in Ozone Park blinking and looking for Angelo Ruggiero.
Somebody called, "Hey, Quack," Ruggiero's nickname for his open-
toed stance and waddling walk. Soon Quack and John Gotti were
talking to Sal and Foxy Jerothe, Sal's best friend and partner in
crimes, including hijacking and selling drugs.

"It was Foxy and me and this guy Tuttie, and a guy named Red
Collins from Paulie Vario's Lucchese family crew, and we were laying
up there in the Bronx watching that fur truck come and go."

"I remember Foxy," Sal junior said, "he was always with a
different girl."

"That's right. He was deadly with the women. That's what got
him killed. Probably that's what it was. Anyway, we watched that
truck for a couple of weeks and then, on a hot summer day that
started out raining, just like today, we were gonna do the robbery."

Sal remembered the traffic hissing by on the Bruckner Expressway as he and Foxy watched through the rain the red truck being
loaded with furs at the Rapid Fur Dressing plant below the bridge
where they stood. The truck pulling out, turning onto the bridge
toward the Bruckner. Collins and Tuttie cutting it off, Collins driving
an old bomb of an Olds, a hotski Tuttie had gotten from somewhere,
swearing it ran, swearing the radiator had been fixed.

"Foxy and I nailed it from both sides," he said. "We opened
the doors. There were three Italian guys in there, older guys. They
didn't even have a gun, but the truck had an alarm, which went off,
a siren-type alarm, like an ambulance. So we had a problem there."

Sal junior broke in. "Did you have guns, you and Foxy?"

Sal studied him. "What do you think? Of course we had guns.
You're not gonna hijack no truck without no guns. Me and Foxy both
used thirty-eight Smith and Wessons. And we liked to keep a little
snubnose either in our back pockets or taped to our legs."

Sal junior shook his head and looked off into the sun, squinting.

"What's the matter? You didn't think we'd carry guns?"

"Nothing," Sal junior said. "Go ahead. What happened?"

"Anyway," Sal continued, "I was trying to get the alarm turned off—it had these buttons under the dash you pushed, one-two-three—and all of a sudden I hear Foxy say, 'That fucking Tuttie,' I look up and Tuttie is running away. Running away across the bridge. He looks like he's paddling with his hands trying to go faster. Red is standing there yelling after him, and looking at us, like, 'What am I supposed to do with this?' And Foxy screams at me, 'Go get that sonofabitch.'

"So I go running after him. When I do that, one of the guys in the truck runs away, and Foxy had to go get him.

"This is in the middle of the street in broad daylight. I catch Tuttie and he's gasping and gulping, hyperventilating, like. Finally, I get him back there, and we get the three guys from the truck and throw them in the Oldsmobile. In the meantime, the alarm is still going. It rang a few minutes, but we got it off.

"Foxy and Red took the truck. I'm driving the Olds, with Tuttie covering the hostages in the backseat. The plan was to get lost in Manhattan traffic. So we're going down Second Avenue headed for the Midtown Tunnel and we're crawling, the traffic's for shit. By now it's stopped raining and it's getting hot. The guys in the backseat, all three of them, are praying in Italian. They're crossing themselves, and one of them is crying. We get into the sixties, and the car stalls. It won't start. There's steam coming from around the hood. We're in the middle of Second Avenue and these hostages are praying, 'Don't kill me. Don't kill me.' You can picture it, right?"

Sal paused to glance at his son watching him from under a hand shading his brow.

"So I say to Tuttie, 'We gotta get some water.' I look around and there's a vegetable market. So I say, 'Go over there and get some water from that guy.' Tuttie gets out of the car, goes, comes back, no water. He says the guy didn't have a bucket.

"Now I see a police car passing about two traffic lanes away. The guys in the back are praying harder than ever. I tell 'em to shut up, because now I've got Tuttie's gun. Then I see a grocery store. I say to Tuttie, 'Go over there and buy club soda.'

"Tuttie's gone about ten minutes. Then I see him, struggling with this bag. He's got this big bag with six big bottles of club soda. White Rock, no less. I get out and dump it in the radiator while he goes back with the hostages. And what do you know? The car starts."

"You put club soda in the radiator?" Sal junior said. He was in the same position he had been in minutes earlier, looking at Sal, shading his eyes with his hand. "And it started? That's wild."

Sal had driven the hostages to Queens. Before he dropped them off he took their addresses from their wallets and threatened to kill them if they talked. He left them by the roadside somewhere in Fresh Meadows, wearing handcuffs. He remembered how they looked to him in the rearview mirror, staring after the car as if they'd just been released by aliens.

"That's another thing," he said. "We always used to use Smith and Wesson handcuffs. Know why? 'Cause that's what the police used and they could unlock 'em right away. You didn't want your hostages to get pissed off, 'cause the madder they were the more likely they would be to talk. Most of the time I'd give 'em fifty-dollar bills before I'd leave 'em."

Sal junior said, "So how did you get screwed?"

"Oh, yeah, I almost forgot." Sal looked at his son from under his tilted-down visor. He took a drink of Gatorade. "We got any more of this? God, it's hot." He mopped his face and chest with a room towel. "Because when we went to get paid they wouldn't give us what the load was worth. See, the thing about the mob, everybody had to wet his beak. There were all sorts of people in the middle, loaders, unloaders, the guy who owned the drop. I was supposed to give them a piece of my hard work I put my balls up for?"

There must have been six or seven thousand pelts there, mostly mink. Sal had figured they were worth two hundred thousand, although he might have been a little high. Even so, hijackers expected a third of wholesale for the merchandise they stole. Carmine and Danny Fatico at the Bergin had fenced the load and Gotti came back to Sal and Foxy with a twenty-five-thousand-dollar offer. Sal had complained. It had even come to a sit-down between Joseph Broncado of the Colombo family, since Sal was with a Colombo crew, and the Faticos in the Gambino family. The result was the same.

"They told us we could find another buyer, but the storage fee would be five thousand a day," Sal said. "What could we do? We took the twenty-five. John put the money in Foxy's jacket and patted him on the cheek like he was a good boy.

"So that's when I decided I didn't want to work for them guys, because I saw how you got screwed. I figured I was better off working for myself. John came to me about that time and asked me to line up with the Gambino crew at the Bergin. He said, 'You're here every day with us. You eat with us, you drink with us, you gamble with us. You should be with us.' I said, 'No, I'll do business with you but I don't want to be obligated. I just want to be your friend.' So I stayed on my own, more or less, and I didn't have loyalty to any of them."

Sal junior swung around on the lounge chair to face his father. He leaned forward for a moment with his elbows on his knees, hands clasped, looking at the space between his feet. When he looked up again, he said, "If you didn't want to be with those guys, why'd you do that stuff?"

"Aw, God." Sal looked around, wiped his face again. "I wish we had something to drink here." He paused. "Because I got excitement from it. It was my jones, my habit. I liked planning the jobs, doing 'em. I didn't want no status from it. A lot of those guys dreamed of the day they'd get their buttons, get made into the families. Foxy was like that. Of course, he never would have made it, because he was only half Italian. For me, though, it was just the excitement. Every day was an adventure, and I didn't care, you know. I . . . until you and Joe got older, I just didn't care what happened. Now I get excitement thinking about you guys, and how you're gonna do in life. But then . . . Ah, shit, I never should have told you, but that's how I was then. And that's why we're here and not going back."

• • •

I dove into the pool to clear my head. Drifting through the clear water to the bottom, I tried to imagine myself wearing cement shoes, drifting to the bottom of the Hudson. Not the kind of thing you want to dwell on. When my feet touched the blue bottom of the pool, I kicked upward and broke through the surface into the sweet, heavy air.

I had been four years old in the summer of 1972. Later, my brother and I had played not only youth football in the LynVet league but the other usual whacky games of city children. We lit fires in the street just to watch the fire engines come. We stole bread from behind the Wonder Bread outlet on Atlantic Avenue. We snuck into the abandoned factories farther along Atlantic Avenue and prowled among the debris and the shadows and thought of lighting fires there, but that was too big for us. Then it was. But the story I'd just heard sounded like just another prank, something kids would do, not the holding people up with guns part, but the adventure of it and how much fun it was to talk and laugh about it after. Except the guys they kidnapped never laughed about it probably. Aside from that it was like anything that's scary and dangerous that you get away with that you're not supposed to do. It was like you could go from one thing to the other really easy, and I thought, well, I guess it's a good thing Dad took us out of Ozone Park.

Dad's confession, if you could call it that, opened some kind of floodgate. As we waited there in Washington, he began to tell us other stories from his past. Like once he'd started he had to get them off his chest. "It's time to face up to this," he'd say. Or maybe he was bragging, or maybe it was a little bit of both, confessions that he liked the sound of himself telling.

He directed his stories at me and Joe, but he didn't mind if Mom was around even though she wasn't thrilled to hear them. There was no sequence to his memories. Sometimes they'd be triggered by something he saw, or heard. Sometimes he'd just start talking, about this hijacking, or that robbery or some other scam or scheme or episode. The sight of a jewelry store window got him started about a hijacking he did with Foxy and Funzi Tarricone and Tommy DiSimone of a coin and silver shipment coming from Kennedy Airport, when he learned he could sell a bag of silver coins to a Manhattan dealer for four thousand when Gotti and the Bergin wiseguys were paying less than three thousand. Looking at his watch, a cheap Casio, one day reminded him of robbing a warehouse at Kennedy Airport of fifty-eight thousand watches. Each job was done with guns and threats; each story had a punch line. One bag from the silver robbery wound up buried in the Notos' basement, where it was for-

gotten until Grandpa Noto found it four years later and thought it was a miracle. Sal and Foxy and a third guy stayed up late to count the watches so they could divide them, and when somebody asked what time it was, nobody had a watch set to the right time.

It took only the sight of a small man in a bright shirt one day as we were leaving the Air and Space Museum to set him off about Eddie Provato and how they got caught for bank robbery.

"Look at that guy," he yelled, pointing at a fireplug of a guy wearing a shirt the color of orange Jell-O. He was walking with an equally short woman, and a kid carrying a balloon. Eddie Provato was short, he said, and he was wearing a shirt like that the day in 1971 Dad first became acquainted with the FBI. They and a third guy had robbed the Franklin National Bank on Horace Harding Boulevard in Queens in May, a spur-of-the-moment thing, and Eddie's handkerchief mask had slipped down around his neck as he was rifling the cash drawers. Eddie was an old-time bank robber, in his fifties with gray hair, and soon the surveillance photos matched up with FBI files.

"So one day late that summer," Dad said, "I was at this candy store on Woodhaven, making a phone call, and I look down the street and see Eddie coming out of his front door. He's wearing this gaudy shirt, a pair of pants with big huge checks, and big sunglasses. He looks like a tropical drink. And he's got this dog on a leash, a short, squatty dog that looks just like him. They're going down the street toward Atlantic, and the dog is doing his business, and all of a sudden I notice a bunch of other people on the street, and I see they're following him. They're in cars, moving real slow.

"Eddie gets to the end of the street and goes into the bar on the corner, Club Ninety-three. The cars all go down there, too."

Dad said he knew right away it was the FBI, because it was August and they were wearing suits. As he talked, we were sort of following these other people, the short couple with the kid. They bought some ice cream from a vendor and sat on a bench. We bought ice cream, too, and sat on a bench in sight of them.

"So I call up the bar and get Eddie on the phone," he continued. "I tell him, 'Hey, agents are watching you.' "

He said Eddie was actually surprised. Maybe he figured the bank camera had run out of film, or forgot that his mask slipped. "He says, 'What're you talking about?'

"And I say, 'I'm telling you, there's agents crawling all over the neighborhood. Eight or ten of them, right there on the block outside the bar. Look, here's what you do. You've got to make the grand (exit). Go out the side door, and I'll pick you up.'

"So he says, 'What about Petey?' "

"Who was Petey?" Joe and I said in unison, with Mom only a beat behind.

"Petey was the dog," Dad said. "Agents are getting ready to arrest him, and he's wondering what to do with Petey. I tell him 'screw Petey. You got to get out of there.'

"So Eddie walks out the side door, and I pick him up on Atlantic near where the pizza store used to be. And I drive around the block to show him the agents. Then he remembers he's supposed to meet a guy at the bar to plan another bank robbery. So I say, 'Listen, I'll go back there and tell the guy what happened.' "

I looked at Mom, then at Joe. Nobody said anything.

Dad continued with his story. "I was driving Dominic Cataldo's car, a brand-new Cadillac. So I pull up and park and go into the place, and the agents are already inside, moving around looking for Eddie and asking questions. The bartender's name was Fat Mike. He doesn't know a thing. Then Petey comes out of the kitchen, whining and sniffing around. And Fat Mike's memory suddenly returns. 'Oh, yeah,' he says, 'the guy came in and went out the side door, left his dog. He lives down the street. I don't know nothing about no bank robbery.' "

"So how did you get caught?" Joe wanted to know. He waved a wasp away from his ice cream.

"Well, the agents took the names of the people in the place, and my uncle Tony had a kid also named Sal, who had a record for bank robbery. So they look up Salvatore Polisi, and they find this record. And one of the agents thinks I look like the guy in the bank pictures. I was wearing a wig and a mustache in the bank, but they notice a resemblance. Plus they traced the Caddy's registration to Cataldo, and he had a record. Anyway, by the time I left there they had me as a suspect. The FBI started watching our house after that, and following me places."

"Well, why'd you even go in there?" Joe asked in an angry voice. "It just sounds kind of stupid."

Mom said, "That's your father. He was, it was like he wanted to dare them. He was always like that."

Dad said, "I don't know, son. What can I tell you? Your mother's right. I just had to be close to the edge. It was like if I could do that, and they didn't catch me, then I would know I pulled it off. But a worse thing happened at the trial." He looked at his watch. The sun was lowering and we moved to keep the shade. The other family had disappeared; I thought I saw the kid's balloon away across the mall, but I saw two or three other balloons, too.

"The trial was really funny," he said. "They had the tellers and all in there to testify, and they talked about me and Eddie running into each other, which we did. I vaulted over the counter, and he came after me, and that was when he lost his mask. One teller said he reminded her of Johnny Puleo in the Harmonica Rascals, which was a group on TV. 'That little guy who used to clown around a lot,' she said.

"But I had worn this wig and mustache. And sunglasses. You remember that raid, Sal, when you were about four? They took guns and one of your mother's wigs, but that wasn't what I wore. Anyway, the prosecutor, this guy Kaplan, wasn't sure he could identify me. We kept staring at each other, macholike. And he accused me of flirting with this woman on the jury, which I was doing."

He glanced at Mom. She tapped her foot impatiently.

"My lawyer, it was Mike Coiro, kept talking about a lack of positive identification. And I think the jury was convinced until the last day, when this guy Kaplan is making his summation. And he walks over to me and points, and he screams that I'm wearing the same white turtleneck I was wearing in the robbery. He held up the surveillance picture. I couldn't believe it. I looked down and you know what? He was right. One of my favorite Damon knits. I didn't even know it. The jury took about twenty minutes to convict us.

"And that was how I ended up in Lewisburg. Okay, what now?"

He looked at his watch again and this time was reminded only that it was late and hot, and we returned to the Days Inn.

It wasn't altogether fair that he could talk about the old life that we had to leave behind. We were cut off from the good parts of the old life, and he threw the bad parts in our faces, but his stories reminded us of why we had to be here. He answered that question in my mind over and over, and as long as we viewed his life from a safe distance, it seemed impossible for it to overtake us.

While Dad told his stories, we busied ourselves with the future, too. We sat in the room at night, practicing our new names over Trivial Pursuit and studying our made-up family tree.

One day at a bookstore at a mall, Dad bought a Rand McNally road atlas and we took it back to the Days Inn and opened it to the national map and imagined where we would be. The marshals had had us list three states that were our first, second and third choices, but there weren't, like, any guarantees. We stuck pins in the map where we knew the best high-school football programs were: Valdosta, Georgia, was one place; the high school there was always ranked in USA Today. We stuck pins in Banning, California, Massillon, Ohio, Midland, Texas, and South Bend, Indiana. Then we did it blind-folded. Joe came in somewhere close to Fort Smith, Arkansas. Dad hit near Socorro, New Mexico, which turned out to be near Truth or Consequences. Mom stuck her pin in at Crookston, Minnesota, where she said she couldn't go because she had bursitis and couldn't stand the cold. I wanted to go to California, and stuck my pin into the Pacific Ocean southwest of Tijuana.

Sometimes, joking around, we called each other the numbers the marshals had assigned to us: Dad was No. 4664, Mom was 4665, I was 4666 and Joe was 4667. The names we'd chosen sounded like the names of distant cousins you saw maybe once a year and had to think to remember.

• • •

On the morning of her birthday, June 21, Rose Marie got on a plane at National Airport and flew to Buffalo. She was met there by the marshal, named John, who had put them on the plane to

Washington. They drove to the apartment she had left suddenly eleven days before.

Even such a temporary home evoked a slight feeling of nostalgia. Rose Marie felt it as she packed her dishes and the kitchen pots and pans, the framed pictures of her sons she kept on the bureau in the bedroom where she and Sal had slept, the boys' sports equipment that lay in a clutter on the floor of the closet in what had been their room. Their time in Cheektowaga had been a stopping point, a way station between the life she had known and the one that waited for her. The dust she traced her finger through on the glass top of the coffee table was like that old life, she thought, as she idly wrote the name, Polisi. She had not called, or heard about, her father's family since the night she and Sal and Joe had left the racetrack at Cuddebackville and driven south into New Jersey. She wondered how her father was. They knew by now, everyone knew by now, what had happened, surely. Arlene would have understood her not opening up the store and Joan, her distraction on that final day. She'd made no friends like that in Cheektowaga, but having been there, she'd come to understand more clearly the importance of the break they'd made. The coach (who had seen his district championship fly away the afternoon he picked up the phone to hear the principal say, "They're gone.") had been so enthusiastic about Sal junior's chances.

She was babbling about that as she packed. She must have been, talking about how Sal junior could win a football scholarship. Maybe she was really on a flight of fancy, talking about him being a star at a major university, when John broke her train of thought. "Aren't you afraid?" he asked.

"Afraid?" she said.

"Yes. You know, that somebody would see him on TV and recognize him."

My God, I don't know, she thought. Am I afraid? For who? For myself? For my husband? And then in an instant, without thinking anymore, she decided.

She said, "John, if your son had a dream, of running track in the Olympics, say, and had worked already, hard, for four or five years, how could you take a dream away from him? We can't turn around and say to them, 'Okay, Sal and Joe, we're in the program now, so you can forget about playing football, or basketball, or running track, because you might be noticed. Because you're too good.' We don't have the right to do that to these guys. So no, John, I'm not afraid."

She finished the packing, and was back in Washington in time for supper. The waiters at the motel restaurant brought no cake and sang no song for her thirty-eighth birthday, and Rose Marie was both relieved and slightly disappointed.

· · ·

The week after Mom went back to Cheektowaga, the marshals told us to be ready. Dad hung up the room phone, turned to us and said, "Tomorrow."

Mom said, "Oh, my God."

That night was not a good night for sleeping.

We spent the first part of it with the atlas, looking at the whole wide country, wondering. In between packing, trying to get all our new clothes into our suitcases and finally having to stuff shopping bags, we sat on the edge of Mom's bed and passed the map around. Mostly we just stared at it.

Dad tried to get us started. He'd push the map from one to the other of us and say, "Where do you think it's going to be?" But all any of us could say was, "I don't know." And when Joe pushed it on around to him and said, "Where do you think?" all Dad could say was the same thing. "I don't know. For once in my life I don't know."

Where before we had stuck pins in the map and speculated, now we only wondered. It was too late for fantasy, and we couldn't see reality. We were excited, and suddenly afraid. Not that something was going to happen, but that they'd send us to some awful place, some desert or some swamp or some place with a bunch of rednecks who would hate us because they didn't like our accents.

Most people when they move know where they're going. Like when we moved to Port Jervis, we knew. And you can figure things out that way, figure whether people drive pickups or convertibles, and what kind of clothes they wear and what the weather's going to be, and if there are delis and can you get a good pizza and Boar's

Head cold cuts. So you can adjust beforehand, and kind of get used
to things. It even helps to know if it's a big place or a little place,
so you can figure out, you know, if the kids are going to be cool or
not. We kind of figured we wouldn't be going to a little place, because
they want you to blend in. Aside from that it was a mystery.

Dad was easiest about it, naturally. Things were finally out of
his control, and he could sit back and enjoy the ride. Joe went along
with him. It was an adventure to Joe. He was just getting started in
life. I had my football career at stake. It was more than an adventure
to me. I wanted to be at a place where there were good schools so
I could play, where colleges came to do recruiting. And Mom was
wondering if she could make new friends, but was mostly eager to
have a house around her again.

When we finally got into our separate rooms and went to bed,
as soon as the light was out, Joe said, "Where do you think we're
going, ———?" He used my new name and said, "God, that sounds
so weird. It doesn't sound like you."

"I know. ——— doesn't sound like you either."

"Where do you think we're going?" he asked.

"I don't know. I wish I did."

"You know what's going to be hard?" I heard him push up on
one elbow, and knew he was lying there looking at me in the dark.

"What?"

"It's gonna be hard to hide from the karting world."

"What do you mean?"

"Well," he said, "we went all over with the karts, and met
people from all over the country, racing in the Grand Nationals and
all. Plus Dad gave that award, you know."

Yes. There had been a picture of him in karting magazines, Sal
Noto giving the Charlie West Memorial award to the best family effort
in national competition. Charlie was just a little guy who tried hard,
was why Dad named it after him. He said he wanted to recognize
guys like that, who weren't supported by professional speed shops.
We were racing on drug money, but some folks were really hand to
mouth. Joe was right. Everybody in karting circles knew him, knew
us, and it just meant more people we would have to hide from. More
people still pushed into the past with Linda, and Charlie Wilkerson,

and Harold, and Mom's family. I said, "I guess we'll have to stay away from karting." It wouldn't be that hard for me to do.

Joe said, "I was just getting good."

"You're getting too big," I said. "You'll be better at football. Maybe we'll be someplace football's really big. That's what I hope."

"I wish we knew," he said.

Our suitcases were packed and we'd eaten breakfast the next morning when the marshal came to pick us up. It was early, with a cool edge still in the air. Dad had read each of his morning papers for about two minutes, and he kept picking the papers up and opening them and putting them down. He wasn't even looking at the pages.

The marshal's name was Al Roberts. We were helping load our bags into the back of his brown station wagon when Joe asked him where we were going.

"Can't say yet," he said, hefting a bag over the tailgate.

Once we got on the road, though, he reached into the inside pocket of his sport coat and handed Dad some airline tickets. He made like a presentation of it. Dad opened them. We held our breath. He turned to us, sitting in the backseat, and said, "You're not going to believe this. You guys wanted to play football. . . ."

F O U R T E E N

We flew for an hour, or it might have been two, or three, or four, or even five. It seemed like days, that's how eager and curious we were, and on the other hand it seemed like minutes because we were so relieved to be going someplace finally. The plane edged down over a landscape that might have had mountains, or water, or forests, or the kind of slight roll dotted with trees that you associate with nearly everyplace. The airport certainly was like that, long concourse spikes sticking out of a terminal, messages of welcome on signs and posters on the wall showing local attractions. I think there were new cars, set in roped-off displays sponsored by dealers. All around us were people in suits, people in jeans, people in uniforms of one kind or another. We were somewhere in the middle of America, between the Hudson River and the setting sun.

A toothpick-chewing marshal met us at the gate. He said his name was Jack. He was wearing a brown suit and he must have weighed two fifty. We followed him to the baggage claim, and waited. The first bag hadn't trundled into view when Dad said, "What's the best high-school football team around here?"

Jack sawed the toothpick around between his teeth and considered it. "There's quite a few of 'em," he said.

Dad turned to me and Joe. "Hear that, you guys?" he said. He had to ask again, because the two of us were trying to get the feel of the place. Joe had wandered through one of the electric doors to the curb where arriving passengers were waiting with their luggage while cars went by in a steady parade. He came back in and said, "It's hot."

"As hot as Washington?" I said.

"Hotter."

Dad made Jack repeat the news about the football, that there

were a lot of schools we might consider. "That's right," Jack said,
real abrupt, like he didn't much like being ordered around by this
pastrami accent from New York. He shifted the toothpick from one
side of his mouth to the other with his tongue. Something attracted
his attention over by the Avis counter and he stared that way for a
long time. Jack didn't look as if he liked his work a lot. Or maybe
he just didn't like us.

The heat was such that by the time we got our luggage in Jack's
car, all of us were sweating. Outside the airport, our new home was
a place of concrete and on-ramps and off-ramps. The sky was higher
and wider than I remembered it back home. We rode along an eight-
lane interstate past shopping centers, banks and auto dealers. Beyond
them in some places you could see the rooftops of houses and apartment buildings. I saw plenty of pickups, but when I saw my first
convertible there were two girls in it, blond girls with great tans,
laughing, and I caught a snatch of sound from their stereo as they
went by us. Joe punched me, grinning, and I said, "Yeah." Then
we turned onto a cloverleaf that went under itself, and pulled into
another motel and unloaded.

Motels were getting old. Mom looked over the luggage stacked
up in our adjoining rooms, just like it had been stacked up that
morning before we left Washington, and asked Jack in this kind of
weary, dead-end voice, "How long do you think we'll be here? How
long will it take to get our papers and get settled?"

Jack rolled his toothpick around. He said, "Well, I just paid
for your rooms for thirty days in advance." I thought she was going
to cry. He gave us some money, like our allowance, and left.

By the following Monday we had explored the neighborhood
around the motel. There wasn't much to it. We found the cafeteria
across the highway Jack had told us about, and a few other eating
places scattered among the shopping centers and parking lots. Dad
found a pool hall, and there were a six-screen movie theater and a
bowling alley near enough for walking, but this was not a walking
town. There were no sidewalks, so we had to walk along the roadsides
and scamper across the multilanes.

We decided on Monday that we wanted to range farther. The
motel had a van that people could take to the airport, or downtown.

*We asked them to take us into the city. As we got close, the downtown
had that kind of anonymous look of glass and steel and concrete that
I guess every city in the country has. The driver dropped us at the
main downtown tourist attraction, which I guess every city also has,
and we said we'd be ready to go back at five o'clock.*

*It didn't take that long. Outside the fancy restaurants, hotels
and apartments of the tourist area and the big office buildings that
turned a blank face on the streets, the downtown was a bleached-
out place of hopelessness and poverty. The men and women we saw
looked abandoned, like the buildings, and angry, like they were out
of place. Empty half-pint wine and vodka bottles littered out-of-the-
way windowsills and corners. We turned up one block and down
another, and finally wandered into a dusty-looking sporting goods
store for relief. MEL'S SPORTS EQPT., said the sign on the door.*

*"Man, this sucks," said Joe, picking among a row of aluminum
baseball bats.*

"It sure does," I said.

*"I don't think I want to stay here," he said. He hauled back on
the bat he was holding and struck a batting stance. He cocked the
bat and brought it around, slowly and dead level, and skimmed a
row of baseball caps off a glass shelf. It looked like that was the
gentlest thing he planned to do. I stepped away from him and said,
"Jesus, Joe." He swung the bat again, flipping the sleeves on a rack
of satin baseball jackets, but then he dropped the bat back in its
slot in the display and leaned down to scoop up the caps he'd knocked
onto the floor. He looked at me and made a face. I said, "Maybe
it'll get better."*

*"I'm tired of living in motels," he said. "This is the hottest
place in the world. It's gotta be. And did you see those people on
the street? I just don't think we belong here."*

*I didn't have much argument. It was like we'd walked into this
nightmare of unfamiliarity, where you couldn't leave and you couldn't
wake up. You'd go around a corner expecting your next sight to be
one you'd recognize, something from home, but you never saw anything you knew and people just kept looking at you like a stranger.
Across the store, Dad was asking a tall guy with gray hair and a
beard what he knew about the high schools, and Mom was standing*

with him. I wandered, and came upon a display of free weights, with a bench press bench set up with a rack at one end. The bar was loaded with weights; I counted 275 pounds. Nobody was watching. I lay down on the bench, scooted up under the bar and tested it. I got it up easily enough and brought it down to my chest, feeling the strain and enjoying it, how the effort of it made you zero in and concentrate on nothing else. I lifted it, brought it down, lifted and down and up, forgetting everything, willing my muscles to raise the bar and drop it slowly.

The last time I couldn't raise it. I lay there with 275 pounds across my chest, with no way to move it. I rested a minute, and strained. The bar moved about four inches before my arms gave up from the pain. "Joe," I called, forgetting he had another name.

"Yeah. Where are you?" He heard the strain in my voice.

My face was red from exertion, keeping the bar off my chest, when he followed my voice to the weight display where I was trapped. He helped me get the bar up and into the rack and when I let it go my arms, quivering, almost raised themselves over my head. Joe looked amused. "How'd you do that?" he said.

"I did six reps, creep," I told him.

"You shoulda done five."

"I was just into the lifting. I forgot where I was." I was rubbing my arms to stop the muscles jerking.

"You forgot my new name, too," he said in a low voice.

"Oh, God, I did." I was forgetting everything. We looked around but nobody had noticed. This place that was supposed to be our home already had a feel to it of clumsiness and failure. The streaked store windows showed a scene of the exhausted streets. A man in a torn white shirt stumbled past the window. I said, "Let's go tell Dad we want to leave here."

We went from the sporting goods store to a Woolworth's and Dad called Dan Russo on the telephone.

• • •

The call to Russo brought the marshal, Jack, to the Polisis' lodgings the next day. He loaded them into his car and, with his toothpick pointing the direction, took them around to look at schools.

The day after that, a football coach knocked on the door of their rooms. He had a drawl that, when he spoke at all, sounded like rich earth, a cheek that surrounded a cud of tobacco and a pair of eyes that gave a weight to everything he saw. He had a team that had won ten games the previous year before losing in the play-offs. The coach looked at Sal junior and Joe and saw a pair of bodies that he liked.

One by one, problems were resolved. Sal returned to the motel one afternoon in a frustrated rage. He had tried to buy a car, offering cash. He was perfectly willing to drive without a license; he had been doing it that way all his adult life. The dealer was not used to Sal's way of doing things, and refused to sell unless he could produce a license. Rose Marie's were the first papers to arrive. The week following the Fourth of July, Jack drove her to a state license testing office. He led her into a private room, and presented a paper from the government, a sort of internal memo that said she had been licensed in New York. Rose Marie put her new name on an application. An officer deliberately smudged her thumbprint on the form. She took the test, and left with a temporary license. That afternoon, Sal paid cash for a used white four-door Ford, as inconspicuous a car as it could be.

New Social Security cards arrived, allowing them to open a bank account. Sal and Sal junior got their licenses on the same day, when a license examiner assumed Sal junior's letter applied to both of them. They walked out laughing together. "You're legal, Dad," Sal junior shouted. It was the first time since he was twenty-one that he had had a license.

A week later Sal made a rental deposit on a four-bedroom ranch house on a curving street of similar houses.

They moved out of the motel with six days remaining on their tab, and moved into the house before their furniture, taken from Port Jervis and stored, arrived from Washington. Sal junior and Joe were so eager to sleep in a house again that they spread blankets and pillows on the floor.

Sal awoke the next morning to the reassuring noises of suburbia, the normal sounds of barking dogs and shouting children, music playing, garage doors opening, automobiles passing, the distant hum of highway traffic and, one by one, air conditioners clicking on as the summer heat rose with the sun. He put on a pair of swimming trunks and walked barefoot into the backyard. The dew in the spongy grass was cool on his feet, making him shiver before he emerged from the shadow of the eaves. He walked to the back fence. Beyond it was a mirror of the yard where he was standing. A German shepherd raised its head and looked at him, pricking up its ears.

Legitimate slob, thought Sal happily. I'm a legitimate slob. Who would've thought?

The legitimate slobs were the ones they laughed at around the Bergin, and the prison yard at Lewisburg, the ones who existed to be plucked and fleeced. Of course Sal wasn't really a legitimate slob. He knew that in his heart, because he was here with his freedom, and it hadn't cost him a thing. Freedom always cost something in Sal's experience: a bribe, a stretch of time; everything had cost in his world, a choice cell, a telephone call, but now he was free for free, standing in the backyard of a house he was renting with money the government had given him and the only cost the past, wiped out and done with.

Turning to take the sun on his face, he saw movement in the kitchen. Rose Marie was up and making coffee among the odds and ends of kitchenware the coach's wife had lent them. Sal walked inside, stretched himself expansively and hugged her. "We made it," he said. She looked startled at his impulsive embrace.

It was the idea of freedom that made Sal think of prison. His bank robbery conviction had been so depressing that he'd fled to the Veterans Administration Hospital on First Avenue in Manhattan before his sentencing. A pair of U.S. marshals had had to drag him out in chains. Judge Edward R. Neaher had sent him to Lewisburg for psychiatric tests. When Sal came back, the judge looked at his case with its thirty-month record of delays. Doubtless reasoning that enough was enough, he denied the competency hearing Sal had asked for and handed him eight years at Lewisburg.

At the federal prison in Pennsylvania, Sal saw old friends and made new contacts. Eddie Provato had gotten there ahead of him. So had Joseph Vitale, the third man in the Franklin National robbery who had pleaded guilty to a string of bank jobs he pulled to feed his heroin addiction. Part of the Gotti crew from the Bergin was there: Angelo Ruggiero, in for hijacking, as was a future business partner, John Carneglia. Sal met the Lucchese family capo, Paulie Vario, in for income tax evasion, and Johnny Dio, the old-time labor racketeer who ran the airport unions and had helped Jimmy Hoffa gain control of the Teamsters by setting up bogus locals. Everybody said he'd been behind the acid blinding of labor columnist Victor Riesel in 1956, but all the witnesses got scared and wouldn't talk. The feds finally had put him in Lewisburg for stock fraud.

Sal fit in well with the Italian oligarchy at the prison. His connections got him an individual cell. Johnny Dio got him switched from the plumbing shop to yard detail. When he got word two months after he arrived that the Court of Appeals had overturned his sentence because he'd been denied a competency hearing, he called again on Johnny Dio.

Sal had wanted to phone Rose Marie with the good news. You had to wait days to make a call, so he went to the priest's office to beg a favor. The priest said no, but Dioguardi was there, and he'd said, Yeah, sure, let this kid make a call. He'd smiled at Sal, a perfect row of white, capped teeth shining in a face as gaunt as a skull. Sal had talked to Rose Marie and thanked Johnny Dio profusely for the favor. When I get out, he said, anything you need, just let me know. Johnny Dio had smiled around his perfect teeth and said, It's good to return favors.

There was no cool, dew-soaked grass underfoot now. Sal was standing in his kitchen with his first cup of coffee of the morning, free. But everything cost, and he shivered again as he thought of Johnny Dio and the price of that one phone call.

He was out of Lewisburg a few weeks after that, headed back for New York and a new round of court appearances. He had learned as he went into prison that Foxy had been killed, and as he left, Angelo Ruggiero told him Tommy DiSimone had done it. Sal was stunned. Foxy and Tommy had hijacked together; they had even streaked together during the height of that craze, running naked down Lefferts Boulevard when they were high on cocaine before coming back to Sal's and roaring around the neighborhood in a pair of his karts. But Tommy had gotten jealous of Foxy over a woman. "Well, then, I will kill Tommy," Sal had vowed. Angelo said no, he and John had plans for Tommy, but the death of his friend had hardened Sal.

The boys emerged from their rooms, moving stiffly from sleeping on the floor. "Yo," Sal greeted them, "how does it feel, sleeping in a house again?"

"Great," Sal junior said. "Hard," said Joe.

"C'mon, it feels great, doesn't it?" Sal was almost prancing. "We got a car, we got a house . . ."

"All we need is furniture," Rose Marie said. She was starting to cook breakfast in her borrowed pots and pans. "It would be nice to have a place to eat."

"Aaah, what do we need furniture for? We'll have a picnic." Sal brought a blanket from the bedroom and took it out into the yard. "Come on, we'll have a breakfast picnic."

They ate sitting on the blanket, and when Sal was finished eating he said, "You guys remember that night I got out of the MCC?" The Metropolitan Correctional Center on Park Row in Lower Manhattan was the federal jail where prisoners were held during trial and other court appearances. It was Sal's last stop before he was released on bail. Rose Marie and Phyllis and Sal junior and Joe had been there to pick him up on that September evening.

"Yeah, we went to San Gennaro, right?" Sal junior said.

"That's right. Your mother wanted to go home, but I wanted to celebrate."

The annual Feast of San Gennaro brought thousands of revelers to Mulberry Street in the heart of Little Italy. Game booths and food stalls lined the street. Sal had wandered with his family among the jostling crowds, taking in the smells of sweet sausages and onions and sweet peppers frying, listening to the barkers luring players to their games.

"I was so happy to be out," Sal said. "I just wanted to be out there on the street, but then I saw this game. I don't think you guys saw it, this game with the rat? It was like roulette, a big wood wheel painted in different colors, like a pie, with holes around the edge, and people were betting on the colors. The guy had this cow bell, and he started rattling it over this hole in the middle of the wheel.

He's yelling, 'Heeeeerrrre's Johnny,' like Ed McMahon, you know, and in a minute this rat pops up his head. A white rat. Poor rat, he's looking for a way to get away from this cow bell, so he runs to the edge of the wheel and jumped in one of the holes. Where he ends up in a coffee can, and in a minute the guy dumps him in the middle hole and they do the whole thing again. It was awful."

"So what's the point?" Rose Marie said.

"I don't know." Sal was lying back, hands behind his head, staring at the pure blue sky. "Just that I didn't want to ever be that rat. Trapped and running from one hole to another. Just coming out like that, you know, it made an impression on me."

But that's what I did, he thought. In some warped way the scene, like Foxy's death, had fed his detachment and his anger and he'd started running then, really running, with the heroin business, and the car shop that was really just a front for it, and the cold-blooded violence that protected it. He'd learned in that part of his life that he was capable of worse than hijacking and robbery and assault. He'd learned he was capable of almost anything, and again he thought of Johnny Dio.

"Well, look at this." Jack appeared around the corner of the house. "I been ringing the doorbell," he complained, his toothpick waggling up and down, his suit coat over one arm and dark sweat patches extending from his armpits. "Came to tell you the truck's on its way. It looks like you could use some furniture."

That night they slept in their own beds for the first time in almost two months.

When their phone was installed at the end of the week, Sal called Russo to learn that Brennan had been indicted the day before, July 25. Bruno had told everything. The judge, who had been on the bench for sixteen years, was charged with taking forty-seven thousand dollars to fix four cases between 1973 and 1985. It added up to twenty-six counts of racketeering, conspiracy and extortion. Brennan's lawyer said the case was nothing but "the wild charges of Salvatore Polisi."

The *New York Post*'s story noted that Sal was living under a new identity as part of the federal Witness Protection Program.

· · ·

Before football practice started the second week of August, Coach brought me around to school to meet some of the other kids on the team and show me the facilities. It was like the pros compared to Port. The practice field was better than any stadium field I'd seen. They had a weight room like you wouldn't believe, about a dozen separate racks and benches, Universal gyms, leg machines, knee machines. There were a bunch of boxes for what they called plie-metrics, where you'd jump up and jump down; it was to improve your vertical leap. There was something for every part of you.

"You're not gonna have to work out with the wrestling team here," Coach said. "Come on, let me introduce you to one of our good players."

There was this kid on one of the bench presses, lifting what I guessed was two sixty or two seventy. He did a final rep and his partner guided the bar back into the rack and headed off in the direction of the showers. The kid was sitting on the bench resting when we walked up to him. The coach called his name and said, "Let me introduce a transfer. Another running back."

He was taller than me, skinnier. He had straight brown hair and he spoke in the accent of the region as he offered his hand. "How you doin'? Where you from?" he said.

"Just a little place back East, northern New Jersey," I said.

"Say you played some football there?" he asked.

"A little bit. It wasn't, you know . . . They didn't play much football there. Not like here." I looked around at all the equipment. "I had to work out with the wrestling team so I could use their weights."

"Welcome to ———," he said, grinning proudly. "Say you're a running back?"

I said I was.

"Me, too," he said. "I was a backup last year when we went to the play-offs. I'm a senior this year and I'll be starting. Did Coach say you were a junior?" I nodded; I was enrolled as a junior because of all the school I'd missed. "You might have to be backup for a year," he said. He had a sort of cowboy cool about him, easy, not threatened, just a little cocky but not enough, you know, to be an *asshole. Just a friendly guy who was the preseason's designated starter. "Say, where you living?" he asked.*

I told him the street and his look was a mixture of pride this time mixed with curious amazement. "That's my street, too," he said. When I told him the number, he said, "Oh, yeah, I saw the moving truck. I'll be. We're just about across the street from each other. That y'all's Z-28 I've been seeing in the driveway there?" It was, a new Camaro Dad bought as soon as he and I both had our driver's licenses. He got the money from somewhere. One day he just had it. You didn't ask. Jack looked suspicious, but I guess there was nothing he could do. Anyway, we needed more than one car to get around and it was like a reward for getting settled and getting our new start. Then he went out and bought an old Volkswagen Rabbit for himself.

My new friend asked more questions the marshals had told us to expect, like did your dad get transferred here or what. No, I said. He just got tired of the weather there and we moved here for the climate. Oh, well, what's he do? he asked. He's in the jewelry business, the kind of thing where you can live wherever. Well, that's great, he said. We agreed to ride to practices together and he said, "Okay, ———. See you tomorrow, then."

After that we started our two-a-days, twice-a-day workouts without pads. We did drills and calisthenics and ran through the plays on offense. I had to forget all the numbers I knew from Port Jervis and learn a new playbook. Both schools played the I formation, but this one had a playbook which was twice as thick. I was having enough trouble just remembering my name. We spent a few minutes of each day in the weight room. The trainer adjusted my technique, and right off I went to two eighty in the bench press.

One day I saw my neighbor studying the strength chart that was posted outside the locker room, and updated day to day. He looked unhappy, and when he saw me he frowned and said, "You're lifting two eighty. That's pretty good. It's hard to believe they didn't play much football where you were."

Riding home that evening, I felt that he was starting to distrust me, and ask himself questions about who I really was, like maybe all the easy answers I'd given earlier didn't quite hold together. Dad was hanging out at practices, for one thing, which right away made people think, *Who is this guy and why isn't he somewhere working like everybody else?*

At the end of that week, we put the pads on.

It always felt good to settle into the equipment. It was like putting your armor on again, and you could look forward to those moments then when everything would work just right and you got the right block and made the right cut and then it was just a matter of outrunning the guys who thought they had the angles or running over them. Nobody asked then where you were from or what your dad did. Or what you did last year or whether you were a senior. They just wanted to see what you could do.

Then we played a couple of scrimmages against other schools. I alternated at fullback with my neighbor, and a pair of brothers shared the tailback spot. During my time on the field, I made some good blocks, and I found a lot of holes and broke a lot of tackles.

The week before school started and the season opened, the coach called me into his office one day after practice. He was hunkered down over his desk like he was protecting something on the top of it. There was a spit cup on the corner of the desk and he reached over and pulled it to him and got rid of some brown juice and pushed the cup back out to the corner of the desk.

Then he leaned back and said, "I'm gonna start you, ————. I told you when you came here I didn't care how fast you were, or how big, or what you did before, you were going to have to earn a starting spot. And you've proved to me you deserve it. You've proved it to the coaching staff." He drew the cup back and got rid of some more tobacco juice. "Now you've got to earn that respect from the players. You're new, and you're taking a starting spot from a boy's been here three years. I'm going to move him over to defense. He'll do all right there, so it ain't a big thing and he'll get over it. But don't look for everybody to be happy when I post the starting lineups. Just hang in there and do what you've been doing, and things'll be just fine." He spit again, and smiled in a way that crinkled up the skin around his eyes.

I said, "Thanks, Coach."

"You earned it. Now earn it from the team," he said. "Good luck."

My neighbor was waiting outside when I left the coach's office. I guess the coach was going to tell him about me starting, and moving him to defense. He walked in without speaking to me and I thought it might be a long season.

• • •

The supper plates were in the dishwasher. Rose Marie's men, her family, were in the living room with the television tuned to an exhibition football game. That's how she would remember it was a Monday night, August 26. Sal junior had his playbook in his lap, and Joe, who would play on the freshman team, was seated on the floor with his back against the couch, studying his own book of play diagrams. How quickly time passed; they were on the verge of a new season. But of course the family's new season already had begun. Rose Marie was beginning to feel comfortable, even though people looked at her strangely almost every time she spoke. The words she had heard most frequently were, "You're not from here, right?" Rose Marie hated profanity, but sometimes she wanted to say, "No shit," just blurt it out for the shock of it with every Ozone Park inflection she could think of. She didn't, though. She wouldn't. Nobody had been unfriendly. It was just that she wanted them to fit in and be seen as just another family. Nice and safe. Anonymous.

The laundry room was beside the kitchen, and she unloaded the dryer and started folding laundry. It was amazing how between the heat and two athletic sons, the washer was going almost all the time. It was something you never got ahead of, not even for a day, but she couldn't complain about the football. It was the football, the incredible focus on it here, that had brought them quickly into the community. Already they were friends with the family across the street, and even though her son had beaten out theirs, she felt the friendship would survive.

The phone rang and Sal called, "I've got it." The silence that followed made her skin prickle. Sal appeared, stretching the cord from the wall set, catching her eye and nodding somberly. "Just a minute, she's right here," he said.

She took the phone, knowing what it was, but not wanting to hear it from a stranger. Holding the palm of her hand over the mouthpiece, she said, "Tell me."

Sal nodded. "Yeah, it's your father. He died today. That's Jack on the phone. He wants to tell you to call Russo."

"Thank you," she said firmly. She spoke to the marshal and hung up the phone. She sank into a chair across the kitchen table from her husband and said, "My father died."

"I know." Sal looked at her strangely.

"My father died," she said, and added in the same mechanical voice, "I have to call Dan Russo."

"I'm sorry," Sal said. "I liked the old man."

Joe wandered in and opened the refrigerator. Reflexively, Rose Marie said, "You just ate supper." Her voice trembled, and Joe looked at her. "What's wrong, Ma?" he asked. "Who called?"

Sal called into the living room to their other son. "Come in here a minute. We've got something to tell both of you."

When they were all together, Sal said, "Your grandpa Noto died."

They went to their mother, the two boys, and surrounded her, one on each side, just to be close, like bodyguards. They leaned down and embraced her, Sal junior with his face buried against her shoulder, Joe with his cheek awkwardly against her cheek, while she sat and bit her quivering lip and brushed at the tears with fluttering hands. "What'll we do?" Sal junior said.

"What do you mean, what'll we do?" Joe said, straightening and looking at his brother.

"Are we going to the funeral?"

"I don't think we can do that, son," Sal said. "Maybe your mother can go back, I don't know. We'll have to talk to Russo."

Rose Marie learned the next day she had the option of returning to New York, not to attend her father's funeral, though. The marshals would take her to the funeral home at night, when no other visitors were there. She would be allowed to spend some time alone with her father, alone with his casket, while the marshals stood guard outside.

Her grief would be hers and hers alone, and when she had grieved long enough, the marshals would return her to the airport and put her on a plane back to her new home. It wasn't the way she wanted to mourn her father, or remember him.

"I just don't think it would be a good idea, Mom," she said to Phyllis Noto on the telephone. It was the first time she had talked to her stepmother since before they'd left Port Jervis.

"It's a terrible thing you can't come," Phyllis said darkly.

"They say I can come, but I can't see anybody. I could just go to the funeral home. I couldn't see you or Gina or Lenny."

"It's terrible you went away with him," said Phyllis.

"Mom, please don't tell me that," said Rose Marie. "The boys are fine. They're happy. They're playing football. They miss you, but they like it here. They . . . they're good boys. They're going to be fine here."

"They'd have been fine here, too," said Phyllis bitterly. "Now they're away from the people that they know. People who love them. And all because of him." She made a sound of disgust that carried easily across twenty thousand miles of space from New York to a satellite dish and back to earth across the country.

"Don't be bitter with him, Mom," Rose Marie begged. "He wanted to do what's right for the boys."

"He wanted to do what's right for himself. He wanted to save himself. He should have done his time," said Phyllis. "You should be here for your father's funeral."

"I can't, Mom," Rose Marie said between her tears. "We're trying to work it out where we are now. It just wouldn't be a good idea. Please don't make it any harder. Say good-bye to my father for me. Please? Please do that, okay?"

"I'll say a prayer for you," said Phyllis, "and a curse your husband goes to hell. It's terrible you can't be here with your family."

• • •

My brother and I, we weren't, like, the smartest kids in our school, but when it came to smarts, like street smarts, we were the smartest. We knew about stuff these kids had never heard of. And they'd be asking, you know, when we told them we were from New

Jersey and around New York City, they'd ask questions like, "Is it like you see on TV, people with guns, killing each other?" They thought everybody who walked around New York at night got mugged.

We'd say, "Get outta here. You've been watching too much TV. That stuff don't happen in real life."

We'd just blow off questions about our past, like it wasn't no big thing. We trained ourselves to get off the subject and go on to something else, like the marshals had told us, but we were lucky, because we developed a history pretty quickly there, because of football.

It was intense. I had never seen so many fans when we ran out onto the field for the first game of the season. Like, ten times as many as came to a Port Jervis game, all going crazy cheering.

On the opening kickoff, the other back and I were deep just like Charlie and I used to be, and he was a black kid, too. He took the kick and I moved out to block for him. A path opened up down the left side and we took it. I could feel him behind me, sense him— it's one of those things, you know he's there but you don't remember looking for him, it's like you're a unit, tied together, like, or maybe the crowd lets you know because there was this swelling sound that crowded out the field sounds I could hear inside my helmet—and then I was looking at a clear field except for one kid who had an angle and I took him out and the roar just washed over everything. A runback for a touchdown.

He and I hugged and I might have called him Charlie, because he looked at me strange, but it might just have been the block I threw because it was a good one.

I gained 120 yards that game. I scored two touchdowns. I started to spin the ball in the end zone after the first one, the way I used to in Port Jervis, but I remembered somebody could recognize me that way, maybe.

The postgame clamor in the locker room was like I'd never heard. The air was close with shower steam and perspiration when the trainer came up to me and said, "We're gonna name you, 'the Beast from the East.' "

I laughed. "Get outta here," I said.

My neighbor from across the street had started at linebacker.

He'd made his share of tackles. He approached me from across the locker room and he had the same loose grin I remembered from the first time. "I really wanted to hate your ass," he said. "Can't after tonight, though. You played a real good game." We shook hands and I felt grateful we were friends again.

It was starting to feel like we belonged here after all.

The second game I gained 110 yards, and we won that one, too. On the last play of the game, with just a few seconds left, this big lineman on the other team, he must have weighed three hundred pounds, fell on my legs. I felt something in my right knee give, but I got up and no problem, so I blew it off. The important thing was we were two and nothing for the season.

The trainer iced me down after the game to keep the swelling down. Dad put ice on it when I got home and then I went to bed. When I woke up Saturday morning the knee was swelled up like a balloon. I hobbled in to breakfast and Dad took one look and made me lie down on the sofa with my leg up on the back. He started putting ice on. It went like that all day. When my leg was numb from cold I said, "It's not helping. And it's cold. Why not just let it go?"

"The first forty-eight hours is the most important time. We've got to keep it iced," he said. He was, like, preaching. He kept talking about the first forty-eight hours, and bringing the ice. When his hands got blue and wrinkled from the cold and wet, he got a pair of gardening gloves from the garage and put them on. From my spot, on my back on the sofa, watching him hold the ice on each side of my knee with his gloved hands, concentrating on keeping it in place, he looked softer than I'd ever seen him, but not any less determined. It was like he'd brought us this far, gotten us away from the effects of his life and he wasn't going to be beaten by my knee. He was determined that I was going to play college football, and this was just one more obstacle to overcome.

Night came. We ate, I on one elbow. We watched all the television we could stand and Mom and Joe went to bed, but Dad stayed up and kept on with the ice packs, every twenty minutes, as the night slid on toward morning. He was like some robot nurse.

He started talking at first just to stay awake. That early morning energy that got him popping at daybreak usually was gone by the middle of the evening. I watched him a lot of times nod out in the living room just after supper. He'd stumble off to bed by nine o'clock, and by the time the rest of us got up in the morning he'd be up, restless, going through the papers. Today I had napped off and on all day long, each time waking up to the sharp feel of a fresh ice pack on my knee. Sometime after midnight he dropped the ice pack and it landed in my crotch. I jumped and yelled, and found him with his head lolled on the back of the sofa next to my foot. He woke up and blinked. He looked rough. His round face looked like the moon under a ragged cloud. He said, "How does it feel, son?"

"Cold. Better, I think. The swelling's gone down a little, maybe." I couldn't see it, but I wanted to go to sleep and him to go to bed.

He probed it gently with his blunt fingers. I noticed, or at least it registered for the first time, that he wasn't wearing a pinky ring, where once he was knuckle to knuckle with diamonds on his little finger. He pushed on all sides and up and down to where the swelling tapered back into my leg. Even the light pressure made me wince. He raised his head wearily and said, "I don't think so." Then he pressed his face against the ice bag for a minute.

When he looked up again he said, "How do you like it here now, son?"

"I like it fine, Dad. I, you said we'd like it. I didn't think we would. But I think it's pretty cool."

"What about your mother? She was upset she couldn't go home when Grandpa Noto died. I mean, she could have gone, but . . ."

"I think she's into the football, the boosters and all. Dad, you know how we got the kids over here the night before the game?" It was something the parents did, have team meetings, talk about the game. We'd just had our first, and Dad gave a little talk, like he used to do with LynVets. He was a good motivator, and the kids thought he was funny. "I heard some people talking about how good the food was, and how nice Mom was. Like how nice we were fitting in. That's what makes her happy, to feel like we fit in. Oh!"

"What's the matter? Is it hurting?"

"No. I heard one mom telling her, like real embarrassed, after *you talked, she said, 'I don't want to insult you, but when your husband talks it reminds me of The Godfather.' "*

"No. You're joking." *His eyes got a little life in them hearing that, rising from a dull coffee-grounds color to their normal gold-flecked brown, as he smiled.* "What about your brother?" *he asked.* "You think he's adjusting?"

"Well," *I said,* "it doesn't help that we can hear the karts." *There was a kart track maybe a quarter mile away. We could hear the high buzz from our house on weekend nights. We for sure knew somebody over there, and it drove Joe crazy he couldn't go over and do a little racing.*

"Yeah, we shoulda checked that out. But otherwise?"

"He's doing good at freshman ball. The kids at school all like him. They like us both. They think we talk funny. But I think he likes it fine."

"That's good." *Dad rose to resupply the ice pack. When he returned he said,* "So you understand better now, about all this?"

I said, "I guess."

He went on, like he needed to keep talking. "You remember asking me about why we had to move? You said you and Joe didn't make any mistakes, or your mother . . ."

"And you said you'd made enough for all of us. I remember that," *I said.* "You told us about some things. You told us about some hijackings, and the bank robbery and the trial. I remember going to Pennsylvania. Mom told us you were in the hospital, but I knew it was a prison. I remember you had the car shop and the jewelry business. And you sold drugs. I knew about that. What else?" *For some reason my heart started pounding, like a door was about to open and something ugly was inside.*

"I hurt some people, son."

I asked another question I didn't want the answer to. I didn't know how to stop. It was like a song you couldn't dance to, but the music went on and on. "How bad? Did you . . ."

"I'm not gonna talk about that, son. About killing people. I had the opportunities, I'll tell you that. They asked me to dig a grave one time. Cataldo did. But then they took care of it another way. And I woulda killed Tommy DiSimone, 'cause he killed Foxy. But

John and Angelo took care of that. I beat up one guy, had a tail, a drug dealer named Carmine, ran me over with a Buick and I beat him with a tire iron. And I woulda killed him, too, but when I went home to get my pistol, he hit a cop with a crowbar and they shot him. Beat me to it, and the autopsy showed he had a little tail. His tailbone curved out instead of under."

He was riffing, dreaming. He didn't need me to ask the questions but I couldn't help it. I felt like I was on the edge of something, that it was going to fly out of there if I didn't take another step, and another after that. I said, "What, then?"

His eyes were closed, his face had a serene expression. He said, "I cut a man's balls off one time."

I stiffened, and the first thing I felt was the blood pounding in my temples. "You did what?" I said.

He opened his eyes, but didn't move. "Cut a guy's balls off. Castrated him. With a Sheffield carving knife."

The taste of metal on my tongue made me swallow. I stared at him. In a flash of intuition I understood why we'd had to flee his past, and why it would always be with us. He kept talking, lazily.

"After I came out of prison, I guess a year later or maybe even two, I got a call from this guy who said he was calling for this guy I knew in prison. A guy I owed a favor. Named Johnny Dio. He wanted me to go to Florida. I go down there, see a guy, he says we got a problem. The problem is they got a guy in prison, he's got a young wife, the wife is cheating on him with a kid, who to make it worse is the son of one of their captains. They want to make an example of this kid."

He looked off for a moment at something in the air, remembering. His body was slumped to one side against the sofa back; there was no resistance in him. He took a breath and continued. "I said, 'Wait a minute, this is serious.' The guy says, 'Johnny says you'd do him a favor, anytime he asked, anything.' I said, 'Yes, but.' I even went home to think about it. But I went back. I had to even my account."

I was wide awake now, listening. Water from the ice bag was trailing up my leg but I didn't feel it. The wall clock chimed an hour, I think three. It was like I was watching this scene the two of us were in, hearing the story with a comprehension once removed from mine.

Dad said, in that same slow cadence of a voice, talking not to me but just into the air, the atmosphere, the heavens, "I went to the house. The kid's white Cadillac was there every day, just like they said. I got a guy to steal a UPS truck, and a uniform, and I went and got a set of carving knives, Sheffield carving knives with mother-of-pearl handles, wrapped them up, drove over to the house and rang the bell. She answered, a good-looking blonde, and I said, 'UPS. I have this package. Have you got a pen?'

"She went to get the pen, which was stupid because every UPS man has a pen. I shut the door and took my gun out. She said, 'Oh, my God, I don't have any money.' I said, 'Darlin', you don't need no money. Just get your boyfriend in here.'

"He was out by the pool. I brought him in, this Italian stud type, into a room with a big pool table, and tied him up to it. She was screaming, carrying on. I said, 'Listen, don't make this difficult. This is the price you gotta pay.' 'For what?' she said. I said, 'It's nothing personal. It's what's gotta be done.' And I gagged him and I sliced his balls off.

"He was screaming. She was screaming. I had to knock her out to shut her up. And I walked out, drove back to the parking lot where I had a car, drove to the airport and flew home. I left his balls right there on the pool table.

"I never heard a word, never heard nothing from Johnny Dio, not a thank you. It was a sick fucking thing to do."

He blinked his eyes as if he was waking from a dream. I said, "What was his name?"

"I never knew his name," he said. "I never knew hers either."

I asked, heard myself ask, "What was the favor?"

"What favor?" he said. "Oh, the favor. A phone call. I had just gotten word the Court of Appeals had overturned my sentence, and I wanted to call and tell your mom. Johnny Dio told the priest to let me use the phone. The favor was a phone call." He shifted the ice bag on my knee, touched the tender swelling gently. "More ice," he said, and shuffled to the kitchen.

I dozed, and when I woke Mom was sitting with the ice pack

on my knee and the early sun was showing on the tops of shrubs in
the backyard. She said, "Your father must have been up all night.
He just came in and woke me up and then fell into bed. How does
your knee feel?" It felt swollen and sore and wet and cold, but it
looked and felt better than it had and I wondered if the night had
been a dream.

But the horror of that story crept in and sat in me, like a dog
hunkered over something it had killed. I knew without being told it
was a secret, released only to me, only in that time and circumstance.
I knew it was true from the slack, unresisting way he told it, as if
he'd gotten tired keeping it in and just relaxed a muscle to let it
come floating up from somewhere. I couldn't rationalize it as an act
of temper, or just making a living, or like drugs, that alcohol was a
drug, tobacco, so cocaine and heroin, what's the difference. It was
sick, it was part of the haunted, troubling past he seemed so eager
to forget. It made me glad at last that we had left the past behind,
but I didn't realize how much a part of him it was.

It was two weeks before my knee was well. I sat out those two
games and we lost them both. The fifth game of the season was
against an undefeated, state-ranked team. Our opponents hadn't
lost in our division since 1983. Their defense was fearsome. They
hadn't given up a hundred yards to a running back in five years.
They hadn't given up a hundred yards to a team. We were heavy
underdogs.

The beauty of football distilled in the forty-eight minutes we
played that night before ten thousand screaming fans. When we took
the field I felt the need to run, to block and to hit but most of all to
run. Out of the past and into whatever lay ahead, like if I ran hard
enough I could break through to a different plane of memory.

Our line blocked so good. The holes were there just so, flickering
open just long enough. They were there, and if they closed I never
knew it. I was tackled, but I never felt it. The defense started keying
on me in the second half, but everything kept working. It was one
magic night. I don't think I even knew when the game was over,
except the crowd rose up and our team all fell into a happy pile.
They told me later in the locker room I gained 145 yards and scored
two touchdowns. We won 21 to 17.

I didn't count on the attention. When I came out of it, I heard Coach telling a reporter I was "just a transfer from back East." I tried to tell the reporter the offensive line had done it. "Who ever asks their names?" I asked him. It scared me, all the questions. Somebody named me their Player of the Week, and my picture was in the paper the next day.

FIFTEEN

Rose Marie sat in her bathrobe at the kitchen table, studying the picture of Sal junior that by now was in kitchens and living rooms all over town, at diners and fast-food breakfast spots and in the restaurants and lobbies of hotels. She had been excited at the postgame supper after the big win. After a night's sleep she was feeling paranoid.

"Did he look like this when we left Ozone Park?" she asked.

"Nah, he looked like a kid. He looks older now. His hair's a lot different." Sal tried to brush off her concern. They were talking over morning coffee while the boys were still asleep.

"I don't know," she said doubtfully. She had brought her collection of photographs out from their stationery box, and now held one up next to the picture in the paper. "This one doesn't look like him, but . . ."

"Alice the Alarmist," Sal said. She looked up sharply and he laughed. He and the boys chided Rose Marie for worrying that they would be discovered, just as she worried when he was wired up and working undercover. Sal tried to be alert outside the house, shying from tourists with cameras and keeping one eye on the rearview mirror when he drove. "But you can't go to sleep every night worrying that they're gonna find us," he said.

She compared another photo with the picture in the paper and said, "I'm not Alice the Alarmist. I just think we should be careful, that's all. Look at all the questions reporters have been asking. 'Where are you from? Where did you play?' What if somebody tries to call New Jersey and finds out nobody's ever heard of us?"

"So, what're we gonna do, tell him not to score touchdowns?"

"Of course not," Rose Marie said, "but just what if somebody tries to do that? What'll we say?" She got up to get a cigarette from the drawer beside the sink, the drawer where she also kept matches and string and rubber bands and shopping coupons. Then she remembered she was trying to cut back on her smoking and abruptly sat again.

"I don't know," Sal said, pushing the photographs away from him across the table as if they were an argument to be rejected. "We'll tell 'em I'm a rocket scientist on a mission for the government or something, and make 'em swear to secrecy. But they're not gonna do that, Ro. Anyway, his picture's in there now," Sal said. "There's nothing we can do, so we might as well enjoy it."

Rose Marie smiled wistfully. She said, "You're right, I guess. I just want to be proud of him without worrying about it."

By Monday nothing had happened, and Rose Marie's tension eased. The game was part of their brief history. It was something they could share, talk about and savor, a useful memory, not part of that discarded past that had to be kept hidden.

Sal junior came in after Monday's practice and disappeared into his bedroom to change clothes. Joe and the two varsity players who were with him went straight to the refrigerator. They were spearing slices of cheese and bologna onto a plate when Sal followed them in from the driveway, where he'd been washing one of the cars. "Jeez, what savages," he said, picking up a piece of meat and eating it.

"Hey, Mr. ———." The kid gave Sal a hand slap. "How you doin', Mr. ———?" said the other, repeating the gesture. The boys were brothers, black, a year apart, and the younger one had stayed in the Polisis' spare bedroom at a time of difficulty with his parents.

"How was practice?" Sal asked.

"Light, man. Coach was still high from Friday night. We did some run-throughs, but nothin' heavy. He was like, rewarding us." Sal junior came in and started piling cheese and bologna into a sandwich.

"Hey, that was last week's game. You've got to win again this week," Sal said. Then, "Watch what you eat, son. Your mother's making baked ziti tonight."

Rose Marie entered the kitchen carrying a grocery bag and said, "There are four more in the car," and two boys went outside. She was glad to see football players in her home again. Sometimes she thought they just followed their noses to her oven. But they came for

more than her cooking. They liked the boys, they liked Sal's banter.
He did seem able to motivate them at the Thursday night team
meetings, and she took that as another sign that perhaps he really
was changed, after all. She enjoyed it, the embrace of her new
community, the acceptance it was showing all of them. It was an
open, nonjudgmental, unsuspicious place, where people took you at
face value. After her father died, she had volunteered for every job
a booster and parent could be asked to do. The therapy had worked.
She still was sad, but she had stopped crying at night because she
was simply too exhausted not to sleep. Now, emerging from her initial
period of grief, she felt at home. They all did. The boys were not
only popular, but leaders. Some of the other kids were even imitating
their baggy sweatshirts and their funky city look. Their neighbors
greeted them by name. Their roots were finding nurture. There were
six around the table for baked ziti that night, and Rose Marie thought
that if she had the time, she could spread the secrets of Italian
cooking into every corner of the state.

The boys had left for school the next morning when the phone
rang. Sal put his newspapers aside and answered. Jack's voice came
over the phone, the marshal sounding even more dour than usual.
"We got a problem," he said, before Sal could ask him if he'd seen
Sal junior's picture in the paper. "I'm coming to see you at one
o'clock." He hung up before Sal could ask him what the problem
was.

"Who was it?" Rose Marie called.

"It was Jack. He wants to come at one o'clock. Says there's
some kind of problem."

"Oh, my God, I knew it. All those stories." She came around
the corner from the living room to find Sal settling down again at the
breakfast table after hanging up the phone. His newspapers were
overflowing from the tabletop onto the chair beside him. She went
straight to the drawer beside the sink and rummaged for a pack of
cigarettes.

"He didn't say that," Sal said.

"What did he say?" She tapped out a cigarette, lit a match,
then hesitated and let the match burn out.

"He didn't. I don't know what it is."

He did know, though. The money he'd used to buy the kid's
Camaro had been in an account back East. It was his bail money,
refunded after he'd begun cooperating. Technically, of course, half
of it belonged to Phyllis, but she'd intended one of her three houses
for each child and Sal figured she could sell Rose Marie's to pay the
shylock back. Ralph was holding two deeds, but he'd rather have
the money.

Ralph. Sal laughed to himself. Right before they left Port Jervis,
Sal had gone to pay Ralph the interest on the bail loan, taking along
some phony papers showing he was selling the racetrack for big
money. The truth was he'd barely persuaded somebody to take over
the mortgage, but the papers persuaded Ralph to loan him another
forty thousand on a handshake. All the while, Ralph had been complaining about some guy who was beating him for a mere five grand.
It's driving me nuts, he moaned, cradling his belly. I'm eating everything in the house. And Sal thought, Ralph, you better chain the
fucking refrigerator shut because I've got your forty and you ain't
ever gonna see me again. Serve the greedy bastard right for making
Rose Marie pay under the table to get the bail loan. The agents with
Sal thought so. He'd been wired, they heard the conversation and
they didn't even care.

So it wasn't that that had Jack coming for a visit. It must have
been the bail money.

"What do you think it is, then?" Rose Marie said, emphasizing
the word "think." She lit another match and touched it to her cigarette, looking at him closely.

"I think it's nothing," Sal said. "I think we oughta wait till Jack
gets here before we start to worry. What're you doing? I thought you
were trying to quit."

. . .

Rose Marie was a wreck by one o'clock. She was down to her
last pack of cigarettes and had emptied the ashtray in the kitchen
three times. When the doorbell finally rang her hand jumped so she
spilled her coffee, and while Sal went to the door she fumbled for
another match.

Sal talked excitedly as he led Jack into the kitchen. "Hey, did you see the kid's picture in the paper? Read about his game last weekend? It was something, wasn't it? Player of the Week!"

"Yeah," said Jack, "I read about it. Saw his picture, saw your name all over the place. I guess that's the good news."

"Coffee, Jack?" Rose Marie offered.

"No thanks." The marshal sagged into a chair and looked at Rose Marie and then at Sal, his toothpick working furiously. Then he tucked his face down, adding to the number of his chins, and said, "The bad news is, Washington knows about the transfer."

Sal spun away and took a little walk. I knew it, he thought. He'd been not only greedy but impatient. He'd wanted to make their new life so attractive he'd been careless. It was part of his old urgency, the need to be in control, to show he was on top, with his own set of rules. Who could live on fourteen hundred a month, anyway? he thought, beginning to rationalize his act as Rose Marie and the marshal waited for him to respond. Shit, he'd made fourteen hundred a day dealing heroin after he got out of prison. He'd hated the business, no challenge to it like a hijacking. But Jesus God, the money. He'd made a thousand or two a week just holding the heroin and changing money for Jackie Donnelly and Dominic Cataldo, taking the crumpled fives and tens that smelled of smack and sweat and changing them for nice fifties and hundreds. He'd charmed enough bank tellers to change a hundred thousand a week and Beans and Dominic would pay him two percent. The huge amounts of money hooked him. You could take a nine-hundred-dollar ounce of heroin, already cut, cut it some more and sell it by the gram for—who could believe it?—eight thousand, four hundred. It was irresistible, even when you had to sneak and hide what you were doing from certain other mobsters like John Gotti, even though addicts died in the park across the street where your kids could find them, even though your brother-in-law ignored your advice to treat it strictly as a business (although Phyllis had told Rose Marie that Lenny was getting straightened out). No, there had been too much money in it. He'd talked to Andy Bruno about greed. He thought it was behind him. But you got used to having money. And that bail money had been sitting there back East, it would take the government too long to wash it and get it to him safely, without a paper trail. And he didn't want to dip into his stash of diamonds and Krugerrands. So he'd moved the money from the old name to the new one. He didn't think they'd catch it.

Rose Marie said, "What transfer?"

Sal said, "Never mind." To Jack, he said, "Yeah, so?"

"So you're traceable." Jack sat back and crossed his legs, resting an ankle on his other knee. He studied Sal and coolly chewed his toothpick.

"Yeah, well, that doesn't mean anybody's gonna trace us," Sal said. He was leaning with his back against the counter, hands gripping the counter's edge. He was vaguely aware of Rose Marie exhaling a column of smoke.

"You don't understand how this works, do you?" Jack said.

"You tell me. How does it work, now that you know about this transfer?"

"It's a breach of security. A breach of security, doesn't matter what it is, a paper trail like you've created here, a visit to the danger zone, contacting your old pals, makes no difference, you've got to start over. You've got to go into the program all over again. Otherwise, there's no way to guarantee your safety."

Rose Marie broke in, her voice quavering. "What do you mean, go into the program all over again?"

"The whole enchilada, Mrs. ———. New names. New ID. New home. Maybe even another nice trip to Washington." Jack broke into a smile. "See, Mrs. ———, because your husband here couldn't wait for us to get him this money he had stashed away, you got to go through it all again. That's for the Marshal Service to keep you in the program."

"Go through the whole thing . . ." Rose Marie started to ask the marshal if he was really serious, but Sal's voice drowned her out. "What are you, a crazy man?" he shouted. "Are you sick? Are you crazy outta your mind. You read the sports pages, right? You saw my kid in there. You think I'm gonna ask him to move again now? After this?"

"It's not a question of asking," Jack said. "It's what you got to do if you want to stay in the program. If you don't relocate, you'll be terminated."

"Terminated?" Sal spoke sarcastically, and made a face. "Now you want to terminate me, too?"

"From the program. You know what I mean."

Rose Marie felt an overwhelming, helpless anger. They had done everything right, she thought. Transferring money seemed like such a little thing, when you knew the all of what they had left behind back there. You needed money. Who could live with the marshals' rigid rules? She was angry with Sal for not telling her, and she faintly suspected it was money to which Phyllis was entitled, but that could wait. Now her anger went toward Jack. "That's not fair," she said indignantly. "The kids are just getting settled. They're getting their identity, doing their thing now and enjoying it and getting friends. And now to say, 'Drop everything and start over'? We don't have the right to do that to those guys."

Jack shrugged. "You're going to have problems down the road," he said, "but it doesn't make any difference to me. I'm just telling you what the rules are. Think about it. Let me know what you're going to do."

When the marshal had left, Rose Marie lit another cigarette. "What transfer?" she demanded.

"Just some money," Sal replied. "It doesn't matter now."

"Damn you, it does matter." She was cursing and shouting. Not like her, not for a long time. "Are we going to have to move again? I can't do it. They can't do it. We can't ask them to do it. You can't ask me to do it. How can you say it doesn't matter?" Suddenly her anger dissipated into exhaustion. "You're right," she said, sighing, crushing out the cigarette and watching the waste smoke spiral and disappear. "It doesn't matter. What are we going to do about it, though? I think we should leave it up to them."

"To the marshals? You've gotta be joking." Sal was about to start shouting now.

"No. No. To the boys. If they're willing to take a chance on staying, we should go along with what they want to do."

• • •

I took the handoff, the guard pulled and I followed him through the hole, which was just where it was supposed to be. They always were, in practice. Wheeling around to head back toward the scrimmage line, I saw the Camaro stopping at the edge of the practice field. Dad got out and stood along the sideline watching.

Whenever I saw him like that, for the last month anyway, I flashed on the story he'd told me about Johnny Dio and his trip to Florida, the guy I'd never given a face to twisting on the pool table, the part of him I did see bloody, hacked and incomplete, the sac where it wasn't supposed to be. Still expanding and contracting? I wondered, and the thought gave me a sudden chill under the autumn sun. Only a solitary man, such as the one who stood alone and watching, could do a thing like that, I believed, but now he moved down the sideline, greeting our defensive backfield coach. They shook hands, laughed. Their friendly voices carried on the wind to me.

Our unexpected win the previous weekend had erased much of the lingering ugliness of the scene he had described to me. He had not told me any stories since that night. There were more, I knew. Maybe he had wanted to confess away a small fraction of his burden. Although I didn't see what difference it could make; his mountain of sins was as high as the Staten Island landfill, where once I had gone on a class field trip to view this mountain of garbage under wheeling flocks of gulls. Maybe he thought that if I still could love him after that (and I did), he was safe and free from sanction. In any case, in the afterglow of victory it didn't seem to matter much. Pieces of our new life were piling up and covering the old.

Practice ended. Dad was waiting when I came out of the locker room. Joe had finished freshman practice, and we got in the car and headed home together. I drove. Joe rode in back. We had just pulled out of the school drive when Dad said, "We've got a problem I need to talk to you two guys about."

"What problem?" I asked. The natural thing to think of was the picture and all of the publicity. But I hadn't been able to shake the idea that the guy Johnny Dio had sent my dad to see was out there somewhere.

"Well, you know there are a couple of reasons we've got some money now . . ."

"Krugerrands. And ice," Joe said from the backseat, sounding a little like a wiseguy type. Dad had shown us the contents of his attaché one rainy afternoon. But Joe hadn't seen the way Dad's forehead was knotted in the middle, so he didn't know whether he was serious. Dad was joking a lot of the time; you had to pay attention.

Dad swung around. "Hey, this is serious, now. Let's talk serious," he said. Joe was like, oh, excuse me, and Dad continued. "There's another reason, too. I transferred some money out here, from the old name to the new one."

I thought, uh, oh. Joe said, "So?"

"So Jack came today and said the marshals know about it."

"What does that mean?" Joe again.

"He said we've either got to move again or leave the program."

We were all quiet for a minute. The road from school to the house went up and down over slight hills and through several stoplights. You passed the big apartment complex, the garden store and the shopping mall where Mom bought groceries. Then there was a right-angle turn and another into the development where we lived on our curving street of patched asphalt. It hadn't been that long, but we knew the way and it was familiar. The thought of leaving, hitting me suddenly like a splashing with cold water, left me without the breath to speak. Finally Joe said, "Say that again, Dad."

"Move again or leave the program."

"Why? What'd we do?" Joe was up between the seats almost.

I got my voice back. "He said he'd transferred money, Joe. Or some dumb thing." Out of frustration I floored the Camaro and burned rubber leaving a stoplight. On the other side of the intersection I passed on a yellow line and wrenched the wheel to put us back into the right lane just in time.

"Oh, yeah, kill us now so the mob won't have the chance," Dad yelled, throwing me a look.

"What's the difference?" I shot back.

Joe was leaning up between the seats again. "Jack said we were gonna have to move again?"

"Or leave the program," Dad replied.

"Why, Dad?" Joe said helplessly. "Why'd you do that? With the money? We just got here. I don't want to move again. You screwed up again, Dad."

"Hey, both of you. It was my fault, okay? I'm sorry. I just thought we'd need the money."

"Well, why didn't you just sell Krugerrands?" I said. "Or diamonds?"

"Aw, I didn't know the dealers here, who to go to. Anyway, I didn't think the marshals would find out about it, but they did. Now we gotta deal with it."

There he was, sliding over the mistakes as usual, pushing us on to whatever their consequences were. But what if you cared about your life? What if you didn't want it to be an adventure? What if you just wanted to be a normal kid? That's what he had promised us.

I said, "Joe's right, Dad, that's what you said last time. You made a mistake and got arrested, and you said it was a mistake, but if we moved away and gave up everything things would all work out and they'd be great. And we did that, Dad. Didn't we, Joe? We did, and it's like, things are fine here. I didn't like it at first, but now I do. I'm playing football, and Joe's gonna play varsity next year, and now you're telling us we have to move again. No way, Dad."

Joe said, "Yeah, that sucks."

Dad switched into his manipulation mode. "Hey, let me live, you guys. Okay? We don't have to move. We can stay here. We just won't be in the program."

"Well, how're we supposed to be protected, then?" Joe asked.

"Let me tell you something," Dad said. "You know what kind of protection you get? You get Jack coming around, okay. And you get a phone number you can call in case of an emergency. You know what you get when you call that number? Huh? You get an answering machine. It says leave a number and we'll get back to you. What kind of protection's that?"

I said, "But what about the money? Could somebody figure out where we are now?"

"They could, I guess. The marshals say they could. That's why it's a breach of security. It's not like going back to Ozone Park and hanging out with your old buddies, but it's the same thing to the marshals. It makes us, what do you call it, traceable. They could. But probably they won't. Who's gonna do it, anyway? The judge?"

I turned into the driveway of our house. Mom was cooking something. I could smell the marinara sauce when I walked in the door. Home smells like marinara sauce to me. Mom was stirring the sauce and smoking a cigarette at the same time, flicking the ashes in the ashtray on the counter by the stove. We called her Alice the Alarmist just for fun, because we knew she worried, but she'd smoked a lot less since our lives became more settled. Her smoking meant that she saw another crisis in our lives.

Dad insisted we decide right then. He made us all sit down around the kitchen table and said, "Okay, I made a mistake. Everybody knows it. I admit it. So we have to move again or leave the program. What does everybody say?" He looked at me. "You're the one who's most affected by it, son. What do you want to do?"

I thought about doing it all again. The thought just wore me out. I was sore from practice. Football season was three months of soreness: bruises, scrapes, muscle pulls and aches, little cuts that never heal until the season's over. But moving again, meeting new people, having to explain myself again, trying to remember another new name—how many names could you remember to answer to in your lifetime?—shading our background, all that stuff of a life built on lies weighed on me like a bar of weights across the chest. I couldn't think of lifting it again. I said, "I don't want to move."

But then I thought, am I being selfish? How dangerous is it if we stay? Because I felt the danger was more to him than the rest of us. It came down to a choice between his safety and my future, mine and Joe's. Should we take the chance, sacrificing his safety for our opportunity? Or should Joe and I throw away football and our chance to go to college in order to draw away from danger?

I knew what we would do, suddenly, and I felt afraid. Maybe somebody would come after us, but I didn't know who. Dad hadn't even testified against the judge yet. You can't just keep running from what you think might happen. "I don't think we should move," I repeated. "I think we should stay here."

"Me, too," Joe said.

Mom said, "That's the only fair thing."

And so we began to live without the protection of the marshals and without the money they were giving us, the fourteen hundred a month. But the money Dad had transferred took care of that, and for a time we experienced what seemed to be a greater freedom.

• • •

Their neighbor across the street who was always pruning shrubs and watering his lawn was the first to notice Sal's departures. Sal would leave early in the morning and return a day or two later, never carrying more than a Samsonite briefcase and an overnight suitcase, always casually dressed. If Sal saw the man he would wave and say, "Headed out of town. Business." Finally, the man said, "Just what do you do?"

"Oh, I'm in the jewelry business," Sal said. "I've still got a place back in New Jersey. Most of the time it takes care of itself, but now and then I've gotta go check up. Like with the holidays coming up, you know."

"That's a relief," the man said. "I was beginning to think you were in the Mafia or something."

In fact, events in New York were sending irresistible ripples to lap at the Polisis. Brennan's trial was approaching. Sal was traveling to New York to prepare to testify. At the same time, federal prosecutors in Brooklyn were assembling their racketeering case against John Gotti and six codefendants. But this had nothing to do with Sal. Not then.

The football players noticed Sal's absences, too, since they were always at the house. "Hey, where's your dad?" they wanted to know.

"Aw, he had to go back to New Jersey on business."

They would have let it go at that if the talk had not turned one day to cars. It was after football practice, they were hanging out in the parking lot, not quite ready to go home, and one kid was either bragging or complaining that the car he drove cost his folks nearly three hundred dollars a month in payments.

"What about you, ———?" somebody asked Sal junior, who had his hands jammed into his jacket pockets and was polishing the Z-28's front fender with the seat of his no-rivet jeans. "What're the payments on your car?"

Car payments? Sal had walked in and paid cash for the Camaro. Sal junior didn't realize until that moment just how unusual that was. He said, "Nothing. We don't make any payments."

The kid acted like it was a joke. "Right. What do you mean, you don't make any payments? Everybody makes car payments."

"No, I mean it's paid for."

"Come on, it's a new car." Everybody knew a new car was never paid for.

Sal junior gave a little shrug, like, what was going on here, what was the big deal? "Yeah, so?" he said.

"So how did your dad pay for it?"

"I don't know. He just paid for it."

"You mean he just went in and bought the car and paid for it?"

"Yeah. Didn't he, Joe?" Joe said, yeah, again like it was no big deal.

One of the kids said, "I never heard of that."

Another took it up. "Yeah, where does your dad get the money to do that, just go in and buy a car?"

A chorus. "Yeah, and what's he going to New Jersey all the time for? I bet he's not really in the jewelry business. I bet your dad, he's in the Mafia, and he goes back to New York to see the godfather." "Yeah." "Yeah." Everybody laughed, but sort of waited, too.

"Oh, boy, you guys have really been watching too much TV." Sal junior turned to Joe and the brothers exchanged a glance that showed just how crazy it was, these warped ideas people had.

Joe said, "Just 'cause we're Italian, you think everybody Italian's in the Mafia." Their new name was indeed Italian, a common one; they had all decided that no one would buy them as the Joneses or the Smiths. "Just like you think everybody in New York gets mugged when they go outside their door. That's crazy."

"No, no," the chorus continued, "your dad's in the Mafia. He goes to see the godfather."

Sal junior remembered something his dad had said. "You can't change your past, but you can laugh about it." He said, "Yeah, okay, you're right. He goes back all the time to see the Columbuses and the Gambidinis. And he visits the Banana family. That's how he gets all the bananas we use to buy the cars."

Joe picked it up, remembering scraps of talk from Sal. "That's right. Our dad's a big criminal. He's wanted in New York for felonious haberdashery."

"In the third degree," Sal junior added. "And don't forget malicious mopery."

"Yeah, sure," somebody said, disappointed that the joke had turned. "No kidding, how'd you get the car?"

"We had sixty-five acres in New Jersey. We just sold it, and Dad used some of the money on the car. He didn't want to pay the finance charges."

Looks all around. Shrugs. The talk drifted back to football, and nobody noticed the look Sal junior and Joe exchanged across the roof of the Camaro as they climbed in for the drive home.

• • •

I was walking down the hall in school one day and somebody called, "Sal." I turned around, and then had to pretend I'd dropped a quarter to account for it.

Mostly, though, things were going pretty well. It didn't seem much different in the program or out of it. Sometimes before I went to bed, I'd peek out from a corner of the shade and watch the shadows, but they never moved.

The game coming up was for the championship of our local area. We had never won it, even though the team had gone to the state play-offs the year before. The night of the game, it was pouring rain. While we were suiting up, I saw Dad huddled with Coach, talking to him with their heads together. Coach was loose about that kind of thing, and Dad would take advantage of it. He even walked around the sidelines during games, like he was one of the coaches or something. Coach let him do it because Dad had team meetings at our house.

When we had suited up and were waiting to go out onto the field, Coach shifted his chew to the side of his mouth and addressed us. "I probably don't need to remind you guys that this is kind of a big game," he said. "We've never won this thing before. I'd like to do it this time. How about you guys?"

We roared back a big "Yeah!"

He talked to us some more and we said a prayer, and as we were clattering toward the door that led to the field Coach slapped me on the butt the way coaches do, to send you off. He said, "We're gonna be expecting a lot from you tonight, ———. Go out there and do a job."

Waves of rain obscured the floodlights in the stadium and made the field a muddy swamp. The wind slashed the rain and drove it under the tightest kind of collar. I thought the local fans would come out in any kind of weather for a football game, but the dismal stadium was empty. Only the hardiest had come, and they were huddled underneath the stands. The rest had stayed home to listen to the radio broadcast of the game.

The game was a lumberous affair. If that's not a word, it still describes it. By the second quarter everybody was covered with mud. You couldn't see a number on a single jersey. You could hardly tell which team was which. They were ahead 5 to 0 at the half, a score as weird as the night. By the third quarter we were like sea monsters, trailing grass and muck. Running was like running in quicksand; you had to pull half again your weight.

Sometime along in there, late in the game and toward our end of the field, I took a handoff and like a miracle there was a hole that somebody hadn't slipped down and blocked. I roared like a mudball into the secondary. Angling toward the sideline, I found some room to run and outslogged everybody I could see. The yard markers were obliterated, but I passed a bench and knew I'd passed the fifty. I was getting heavier and heavier, laboring. The goalposts appeared through the sweeping rain but I got no closer to them than the sight because somebody tackled me from behind and sent me face-first into the soup. It was the first time I could remember that anybody had caught me from behind.

It was a fifty-five-yard run. I scored a couple of plays later. Then we recovered a fumble and scored again. We ended up winning the game 15 to 5, and sagged off the field to celebrate our victory.

We rolled into the locker room just like it was a sunny day.

There was excitement there, congratulations and high fives and a lot of sloppy hugs, like wet dogs romping around in a small room. Nobody figured us to win the championship, which made it that much sweeter. And I was excited for another reason. It was something that was a part of me, a piece of my new history that had nothing to do with the secrets we had left behind. It was more than a victory, more than a championship, more than the almost 150 yards I gained. It was another league of distance between the present and the past.

Next Monday after practice, Coach took me aside and said, "Son, your dad told me all about it."

"All about what?" I asked. I felt my face go red.

"About your situation. I just want you to know that it don't make any difference to me. It makes me respect you more, is all, 'cause you've gone through a lot and you're doing a good job in spite of it. I don't know what went on back there, but you've got good family values now. Better than just about anybody in our program. Your secret's safe with me, son."

Standing there, exposed for what we'd been, I realized it wasn't my father's past that would haunt me forever. It was his ego. It would always insist on telling who he was. I could run a thousand yards a game and I'd still be colored by the light he cast. I wondered what more I needed to know than that about him.

• • •

The Brennan trial was docketed for November 18 in U.S. District Court in Brooklyn. As the date approached, Sal began to think about his car shop days, because that was what led him to Judge Brennan in the first place, the auto fraud case that he'd paid to make disappear. The Saturday before the trial, as he and the boys were sitting in front of the television, eating popcorn and speculating about the football bowl bids, Sal sat up in his chair and said, "Hey, you guys remember Paulie Artale?"

"Sure," Sal junior said, "Paulie, from the car shop. Guy talked funny."

"Yeah, because he had a harelip. That's the guy." Sal shook the bowl of popcorn and reached in for a handful.

Joe said, "Didn't he used to go with us on karting trips?"

"Right," Sal said, "and drove the van back. But he worked at the car shop, too, and one time I made him the president of Noto Classic Cars."

Sal had three garages in one block under the Liberty Avenue el, outfitted with electric doors. Two of them were chop shops, where stolen cars were disassembled faster than General Motors could put them together, the identifiable parts crushed and the rest sold to John Carneglia at Fountain Auto Parts, who had a standing order with Sal for as many Chevy "packages"—front and rear bumpers, doors, front fenders, hood and trunk—as he could deliver. Four doors were a special order. So were specific colors.

Not all the stolen cars were broken up for parts. At least not right away. You could tow in a wreck that needed a front end and a wreck that needed a back end, legitimate cars, then steal a car to match and cut it in half. You'd have two cars with legitimate numbers you could sell. Or if that was too much trouble (which it almost always was), you just took the Vehicle Identification tag off a wreck, put it on your stolen car and sold it. That was called a tag job. All you had to do was steal it back before the Queens Auto Squad caught up with the fact that somebody was driving a car that was supposed to have been totaled, and that the Vehicle Identification Number that seemed legitimate really wasn't after all. Without the evidence they couldn't do a thing.

Sal had beat them to the punch on every car but one. He'd chased a car all the way to Maryland and back to Connecticut. He'd sold an El Dorado to a cop and stolen it back six hours later from in front of the station house. The one was the '77 Monte Carlo he'd given Rose Marie to drive, and he'd been so busy tracing other people's cars he'd forgotten all about it. That was the one that got him busted.

Noto Classic Cars, the only one of Sal's three garages with a sign, fronted for the chop shops. It was supposed to be a legitimate restorer. Sal stuccoed the black plastic Old English–style letters into the side of the building and instructed his Jewish secretary from Brooklyn to answer the phone, "Noto Classic Cars," with an English accent. He wanted to give the place a little class.

"Paulie was the president? You're kidding," Sal junior said. He fished in the bottom of the bowl for a handful of kernels and said, "Hey, Joe, go in the kitchen and get us some more popcorn."

Joe said, "The season's over, you get lazy." But he went.

"Well, see," Sal continued after Joe returned, "it was after your mom got stopped for driving that tag job I had given her, and then Lenny in another, and they both traced back to Noto Classic Cars. Mike Coiro told me I couldn't be identified as part of the corporation, so I needed somebody to say they were the owner and general manager."

"But Paulie?" Joe was shaking popcorn from a paper grocery bag into the bowl. Some was dribbling on the floor.

"Well, Paulie was a little slow. He had hung around there forever. He'd do something stupid, and I'd fire him, but he'd always come back. Once I told him he oughta pay me fifty dollars a week to let him work there and he said, 'Where'm I gonna get fifty dollars?' He thought I was serious. So now I'm looking around, wondering who I can get to do this, and there's Paulie, sweeping up."

Sal junior and Joe looked at each other with amused foreknowledge. Both leaned toward the popcorn bowl.

Sal continued. "I said, 'Paulie, look around the shop here and tell me, if you had your dream, what car would you own?' And he points to this sixty-two Corvette convertible, white, the last year before they made the Stingray. It was gorgeous. He said, 'I love that car.' And I said, 'Paulie, that car is yours if you just do one thing for me.' His eyes got wide and he said, 'Really? What do I have to do?'

"And I said, 'How would you like to be president, vice president and general manager of Noto Classic Cars?'

"He said, 'What do you mean?'

"Well, I didn't lie to him," Sal said, stretching and picking some popcorn debris from the front of his sweat suit. "I told him, 'Look, I got to make somebody president of this company because the cops, they want to arrest the person in charge. So all you got to do is say you're the president, vice president and general manager. They'll take you to jail for like half a day. I know you've never been arrested, but I'll come and get you out.' "

Sal junior said, "Oh, boy, poor Paulie."

"Right," Sal said. "He said, 'When can I have that Corvette?' And I said, 'Just as soon as you get out of jail.'

"So Monday, the cops come. I'm there, dressed a little dirty, but I told Paulie to wear something nice, and told my secretary to make him out a check for like five hundred, he's been on the books for years, but he just got a promotion. And Paulie's sitting there at my desk, rocking back and making the chair squeak, happy as a clam. The cops ask my secretary where's the manager, she says, 'Back there.' They come in, Coiro's there, and they say to Paulie, 'What's your position with this company?'

"And Paulie, just like I told him, he says, 'My name is Paulie Artale, president, vice president and general manager of Noto Classic Cars, and I don't want to say anything else.'

"The cops are moaning, saying, 'Give me a break. We don't want you. We want that cocksucker Polisi, he's been stealing cars all over the city.'

"But Paulie just said, 'I don't know anything about that. My name is Paulie Artale, president, vice president and general manager of Noto Classic Cars.' Man, he wanted that Corvette. So they took him off to jail.

"We get him out, he gets a two-hundred-and-fifty-dollar fine and I give him the car. You had to see him. He was so happy, driving all over the neighborhood in that Corvette. Later when I got a big Lincoln and blew like a quarter million in the stock market, he was my chauffeur. But after that he got in the life and went to jail for real. Poor Paulie. Anyway, that was the end of Noto Classic Cars. 'My name is Paulie Artale . . .' "

Sal junior said, "How was it the end?"

"The auto squad was all over me by then, on account of those tag jobs. It was auto fraud, possession of stolen cars, all that. I got us out of it, but it was pretty much the end."

Joe rummaged in the bowl for a final piece of popcorn. "That was when you bribed the judge for real?" he asked.

"Well, I gave the money to Coiro, five thousand here, ten thousand there. I never saw him hand it to the judge. But that's what it was. And that's what I told John Limbach after I got busted for

cocaine. So here we are." Sal leaned back in the recliner with the
footrest up, and began to focus once again on the TV.

"Do you think he'll be convicted?" It was Sal junior again.

"Brennan? Sure. Bruno's gonna testify, and he was the bagman
for all those years."

"Who's gonna be mad at you, besides the judge?"

"Nobody, I hope."

Andy Bruno broke down and cried the night before he testified
against his friend Judge Brennan. Dan Russo, who was with him that
night at dinner in Scotch Plains, New Jersey, believed Bruno never
would have broken if Brennan had returned his frantic phone calls
in the days after Bruno was arrested. Bruno's testimony was subdued
and emotional. He said he still considered the judge his good friend,
and was testifying to protect his wife.

Sal described his approach to Bruno and their meetings, and
transcripts of the tapes he'd made were passed around the courtroom.

The betting ticket the FBI found in the Brunos' bathroom wastebasket, photographed, enlarged and placed upon an easel, was the
prosecution's star exhibit. The ticket, with the scribbled notes that
came from Sal's drug case file checked out to Brennan's chambers,
was vital circumstantial evidence linking Bruno with Brennan. Nobody in Brennan's office would admit to checking out Sal's file, but
the notation on the check-out slip was also introduced.

Organized Crime Strike Force head Ed McDonald, the first man
Sal asked to meet with when he decided to cooperate, was in the
audience when Sal testified. With him was Diane Giacalone, the
assistant U.S. attorney for the Eastern District who was preparing
the racketeering case against John Gotti and his codefendants. They
both thought Sal made a decent witness.

Brennan was convicted on December 12 of all twenty-six counts
of taking bribes, attempted extortion, fraud and racketeering. The
cases included Sal's drug case, and cases of gambling and attempted
murder. Sal was in Grand Rapids, Michigan, where he'd flown to
meet with Giacalone and John Gleeson, who also was working on the
Gotti racketeering case. The two young prosecutors learned of the

verdict when they called back to the office to say they'd missed their flight and were driving from Detroit to Grand Rapids. They told Sal as soon as they saw him. For the rest of that day and the next, Friday the thirteenth of December, 1985, they asked about the times he'd spent with Gotti.

Three days later, "Big Paul" Castellano, boss of the Gambino crime family, and Thomas Bilotti, Castellano's recently appointed underboss, were shot dead at the height of the evening rush hour as they stepped out of a Lincoln to attend a family sitdown at Sparks Steak House on East Forty-sixth Street in Manhattan. The papers soon announced that John Gotti had taken over as head of the Gambino family.

S I X T E E N

News of Big Paul Castellano's murder and John Gotti's elevation didn't attract that much attention in our town. There weren't any headlines, just items buried in the news digest on page two of the local paper. For most readers, they were just part of the gruesome fairy tale of life in faraway, depraved New York City.

We noticed them, however. Dad spent what seemed like hours on the phone with Dan Russo, but so many other things were happening that our fears slipped into the background.

The big news where we were, as usual, had to do with football. My team had lost in the first round of the play-offs, to finish the 1985 season at seven and four. It was a decent year by most standards, with our local championship and all. But football was more than just a pastime here. I mean, whoever said it was a way of life was serious. So for the team, the year went down as being only passable. I averaged close to a hundred yards a game, and Coach said major college scouts were going to be keeping an eye on me next year. The local paper named me its Arrival of the Year in high-school football. That was what they called the outstanding newcomer in town. A columnist wrote that our backfield had "given new meaning to the term power sweep, power football, pretty much power anything." Dad cut the story out and put it in the new scrapbook he was keeping, to replace the clippings we turned over to the marshals. My picture was in again, but to everybody's relief at home, that first big surge of curiosity was over.

Mom grew sad with the approach of Christmas. It was a familiar sadness. It wasn't just being cut off from her family, but that she had no outlet for her generosity. So what she did, she started baking. Our neighbors started answering their doorbells to find Mom standing *on the doorstep with one of her chocolate swirl cheesecakes. We used to hear people in Port Jervis say they'd kill for just another bite of one. Giving out her cheesecakes made Mom happy, but sometimes Joe or I would catch her just staring out the kitchen window, lost in some other zone of thought or memory.*

Dad was not so sad as he was restless. He was used to throwing money around at Christmas and then sitting back while people dropped their jaws at his extravagance, lapping up the praise that everybody lavished on him. He gave presents like Scrooge after his visit from the ghosts. None of us had ever forgotten the race-car bed he bought one year for little Albert, or the little motorcycles he gave me and Joe long before we were old enough to drive them; he and Foxy rode them, chasing each other around the little playground, the park across 88th Street there in Ozone Park. In Dad's salad days, he spent money on champagne and twenty-dollar tips, diamond pinky rings and plane trips to Las Vegas, cars and ten-grand football bets and stock options, not to mention the gold pants for our midget football team. But he said he never felt as good as he did when he was buying Christmas presents. This year he had his transferred money—six figures, he said, minus the Camaro. It must have been burning a hole in his pocket.

Last Christmas seemed about a hundred years ago. Now, instead of Rockefeller Center and the bustle of Manhattan and streets rich with the smell of roasting chestnuts, we had shopping malls with plastic trees and Santa arriving in a helicopter. I remembered buying Linda the sweatshirt with OH, BABY *on the front in hot pink letters and the sudden vision of her twisted my heart. The ID bracelet she had given me, well, she had no way of knowing an ID bracelet was not the perfect gift that year. I let it slip out of my hand into Niagara Falls when we stopped there on the way back to Cheektowaga from a Toronto Blue Jays baseball game. Tom Seaver had been pitching for the White Sox. We knew by then what was going to happen. The afternoon light on the boiling mist made me want to do something dramatic. As dramatic as a first love lost forever. Can you stand it? I had already written Linda the last letter I ever wrote to her, but I didn't think I needed to explain; she would have understood. I just* took the bracelet off and let it slip into the stream. If I hadn't, the marshals would have gotten it. There was a new girl I was dating now, but I thought of Linda anyway.

Joe was moping around, too. It was looking like we would all be in a funk for Christmas.

I guess we were hoping that the mood would lift, because we waited until Christmas Eve before we even thought about doing any shopping. We had a tree up at home. It was decorated and all, but it seemed naked without presents all around it. The mantelpiece, which should have been filled with Christmas cards, looked bare with the few we'd received from our new friends. The smells of Mom's baking were the main evidence of Christmas cheer.

Finally we had no choice but to go out shopping. We were wandering listlessly through a shopping mall, hearing the tinny lilt of carols and the jangle of Salvation Army bells, when Dad said, "Wait a minute." He pulled us over to a bench in the middle of the mall and said, "What's wrong with everybody? What's wrong is, we've got nobody to give presents to this year. Is that right?" We agreed it was. He said, "So let's buy some clothes and take them out to that boys' home."

"What boys' home?" we said in unison.

It turned out he'd read about the place somewhere, probably in his early morning survey of the papers. Or maybe he'd seen it on TV. Anyway, it was one of those places that has kids from eight to eighteen, who got the short end of the stick in the parent department and now they were in a home trying to learn that life could be something decent after all.

"Yeah, why not?" we said. "It sounds like a good idea."

It must have been, because all of a sudden we were having fun. Mom and Dad went around piling socks, underwear and T-shirts into a shopping basket. Joe and I went off to pick out a few sweatshirts and athletic shorts. Joe dumped his load into the basket and disappeared into the crowd. A minute later he reappeared and beckoned to me. "Hey," he said, "come here a minute. I want to show you something."

He led me through the crowds to the sporting goods department,

down an aisle past a display of ski equipment and to some shelves
against the wall. He picked up an expensive genuine pigskin football
and tossed it to me. "Let's get 'em some of these," he said.

"They've probably got all that kind of stuff," I said.

"Not like these," he said. "These are better."

I looked at the price tag. They sure were. We talked about it
for a minute and he made me see the light. "That's a good idea,
————," I said. "You know, sometimes you're smarter than you
look. I bet someday you can even feed yourself."

"Why don't you go play with some weights?" he said. We each
picked up two of the footballs and went looking for Mom and Dad
at the check-out counter.

"But that's over a hundred dollars," Mom objected.

"Okay. Okay," Joe said. "Here's what we decided." He looked
at me, and I said, "We talked about it." Joe leaned in like he was
talking in a huddle. "You didn't buy anything for us yet, right? And
so, if you just buy us one less thing apiece, it would almost even
out. Because we've got lots of clothes and all. We've still got all that
stuff we bought with the marshals' money. We've got stereos, we've
got TVs, we've got Walkmans, so we don't need so much. Besides,"
he added, "we would've spent that much on little Albert."

"That's very generous, you guys," Mom said. She looked real
proud, but it was really just a matter of momentum once we had
gotten in the spirit. It was like we finally figured out what to do and
just went ahead and did it. There wasn't even any illusion about it.
We knew we were doing it as much for us as anybody.

Dad said, "Why not? It's Christmas."

We didn't even wrap the stuff when we got home. We left it in
the shopping bags, all but the footballs, which Dad and Joe and I
kept picking up and smelling and tossing from hand to hand for the
smell of fresh new leather. We exchanged our presents that night,
as usual. We got one gift from outside the family. After we moved
in Coach had looked around our house and said, "I've never seen a
house without somebody's name. You need one thing with your name
on it." He and his wife gave us a cookie jar with our new name
stenciled on the side.

The next morning we got up and went to church, all of us together, for the first time I could remember. But not Catholic. It was one of those all-purpose churches where people sway when they sing and everybody's happy all the time. Then we drove out into the country to the boys' home.

We found the place, and turned in between a couple of brick posts with a sign arching overhead. The drive wound uphill between rows of cottonwood trees. It led to a parking lot in front of a brick building where a sign said, ADMINISTRATION. Behind that about a hundred yards, across a dip in the landscape, you could see, like, dormitories scattered around, some playing fields, a bigger building like a gym and an empty swimming pool. It was cold, not a morning to be out. The place looked pretty much deserted on a Christmas morning. Mom said, "We should have called. It doesn't look like anybody's here."

But Dad raised somebody at the administration building. He came back out to the car and got in, rubbing his hands and blowing on them. He said, "Look, we don't need to see anybody. Why don't we just drop the stuff off here? I mean, it's not like we have to see the kids who live here."

It wasn't like Dad to not want credit for his generosity, but there was something about him different this morning, not quite right. He had stood up earlier in church when the preacher asked the people moved by the spirit to stand, and you could have knocked any one of the rest of us over with a feather. Mom thought he was going to do something embarrassing, and almost pulled him back down by the waist of his pants. Her hand moved in that direction, but he just stood there quietly, and she brought her hand back to her lap. Now he said, "They don't need to know about this, but maybe I can come back and speak to them sometime."

Mom said, "What are you talking about?"

He said, "I've been thinking. Kids like this, they need direction. I could tell 'em what it's like to lead a life of crime, and maybe they'd think twice about it."

Shock radiated over Mom's face like the pulse of an earthquake. My face might have looked the same. She clearly thought he had gone insane. "Are you crazy?" she said. "You want to stand up in front of people and tell them who you are?"

"I don't want to tell them who I am," he said, "but I could tell them who I was. I wouldn't even have to tell them where I'm from. I could be from out of town somewhere. I bet these kids, they're intrigued by a life of crime and drugs and violence, and they've never even heard what it's like from somebody who's really been there. It'd be a powerful message. I could tell 'em to try to find the love in their families, just like we've got here, and stay away from all that other stuff. I bet they'd listen."

Joe and I were quiet. I could see Dad and hear him, talking to a bunch of kids. They would laugh and they would listen, he was absolutely right. It was an idea that sounded good for everybody but us. But Dad hadn't thought that far. He was building up one of his enthusiasms, and it would be hard to put him off the idea.

Mom said, "I don't believe what I'm hearing. You talk about love? We're already out of the program. You've gone and told Coach who we really are. And now you want to jeopardize your own children by getting up in public and telling people who you are? I can't believe you'd even think about it."

Dad drew back like she'd slapped him. Which she looked as if she felt like doing. She was really mad, a kind of bleeding-under-the-skin mad, that his mind had gone off on this weird tangent. Here we had come out on Christmas morning to do something nice for somebody, and he was talking about doing something worse than what had gotten us kicked out of the program. He didn't even see what she objected to. Or maybe he did, because he slowed down and said, "You've got to admit it's needed, though."

"Of course it's needed," Mom said, "and you'd be good at it. You were good at those Thursday night team meetings at our house. But my God, you've got your own family to think about."

"It wouldn't have to be here," he said. "I could do it somewhere else. There's homes like this all around the country."

"It would still be dangerous," she said.

"Aw, Ro, you have to pay a price for everything."

"No more," she said. "We're not paying any more."

"But look at all the kids who don't have what these guys have."

"I don't know whether it's worse to have a crazy father or no father," she said. "But it doesn't matter what I say. You'll do it anyway. You'll do what you want to do and I can't stop you, but you can't do it here. I don't care where else you do it. Just promise me you won't do it here. Promise all of us." She looked past him toward the administration building of the home. "Who's that?" she said.

Dad screwed around in the seat and looked at the tall man with sideburns who was walking toward us, bundled up in a dungaree jacket with a sheepskin collar. "Oh, that's the guy I told we had some stuff for them. I promise, Ro. Come on, kids. Let's get the merch."

Joe said, "It's not merch anymore, Dad, it's presents."

We got out of the car and took the shopping bags out of the trunk. The tall guy's eyes got wide when we kept pulling the bags out. We carried everything up the hill to the office. Joe said, "It's mostly clothes, but we brought some footballs, too." He pulled one out to show, proud of his contribution to the gift.

The tall guy nodded and kept nodding, looking around at all the stuff. Then he said, "Let me get your name, Mr., uh . . ."

Dad said, "No, we don't wanna leave no name. We just wanted to drop it off and wish you a Merry Christmas."

"But it's tax deductible," the guy said.

Dad laughed, kind of chuckled. "That's okay," he said. "Just put down 'anonymous.' Okay? Okay, we gotta go. Merry Christmas, then, okay?"

We all said, "Merry Christmas."

The guy said, "Well, okay, Merry Christmas."

We were quiet driving back home through the countryside, which in winter was the color of wheat and faded canvas and tree bark. Each of us was thinking his own thoughts.

. . .

The last day of February 1986 was a Friday, and Sal was in a snit. He'd been looking for something to put his money into, had his eye on a pool hall in a little shopping center. He was going to have to make some money sometime. But the deal had fallen through that morning and for the first time in a long time Sal felt like having a

Heineken. He looked at his watch: eleven-twenty. Well, so what, it was afternoon somewhere. He spied a Bennigan's restaurant and pulled into the parking lot.

Double doors at the entrance led into a vestibule, then another set of doors opened into a reception area, with the bar on the right and the dining room to the left. Sal went through the second set of doors and turned toward the bar. Three men looked up from their conversation; perhaps they were expecting someone. Sal saw them and stopped cold. Their appearance was the first thing that registered, the slick suits poorly concealing beefy bodies, the brushed-back, shiny pompadours. But that was only two of them. It was the third man, casually dressed in dark sports clothes, who transfixed Sal. As the man raised his head and turned toward the door, Sal found himself looking into the eyes of Alphonse Persico.

Allie Boy Persico was the brother of Colombo family boss Carmine Persico. Carmine, known as "the Snake." Allie Boy had been the crime family's acting boss when his brother was in prison. When he'd disappeared on a Monday morning in June 1980, on his way to be sentenced on a loan-sharking conviction, he'd been *consigliere*, third in command. The feds had been looking for him ever since. Sal would know him anywhere, the black, wavy hair, the handsome, slightly pockmarked face, the impressive stature. They had been in the joint together in the middle seventies, at West Street in Manhattan when Sal was back and forth between jail cells in New York and Lewisburg. They had even shared a cell. Allie Boy would have been in his fifties now.

Their eyes held briefly. Neither said a word. Sal tried to hide the shock of recognition, but it felt branded on his face. He turned around and walked out of the restaurant.

Don't run, he thought, as the door closed behind him and left him alone on the sidewalk. He was grateful that an early lunch crowd had started to arrive. Two cars had just pulled into the lot. People were walking across the parking lot, heading toward the entrance where he stood. Don't run. Don't panic. Safety in numbers. What was Allie Boy doing there? Had he by incredible coincidence lammed it to the same town the Witness Protection Program had sent Sal and his family? Had he been here all along? Even a gambler like Sal wouldn't have taken odds on that one. And who were the men he was talking to? If it was Allie Boy, and there was no doubt about it in Sal's mind, the word would reach Colombo family circles in New York by that afternoon that Sal had been spotted. It wouldn't take a family sit-down to decide that Sal should be hit, not the way he'd used Joey Cataldo to get to Bruno, not the way he'd spilled his guts about gambling and loan-sharking and hijacking and selling heroin and every damned thing else when he was talking to Ed McDonald and Gleeson and Giacalone. It was just something that was understood, Polisi gets whacked whenever the opportunity arises. Oh, Jesus, who were the men Allie Boy was talking to?

Sal walked around the corner of the building and waited. If he sees the car, he thought, he'll know I'm not just passing through. Give it ten minutes. Now give it five more. Let the clock move toward noon, bring more lunch trade to the parking lot. Sal finally ran back to the car, dove inside and drove away. He passed a gun shop and almost did a U-turn.

He thought about it all weekend. On Monday, after the boys had gone to school, he poured one more cup of coffee than he was used to, and told Rose Marie, "I saw somebody from the old life on Friday."

Rose Marie covered her mouth with the back of her hand. "Who?" she said. "Where?"

"Allie Boy Persico. At a Bennigan's. I was going for a beer after the pool hall deal fell through. I walked into the bar and he was there talking to two other guys. I practically ran into them."

"My God," she said. "Did he see you?"

"I'm afraid so."

"That means he knows we're here."

"Maybe not. I turned around and left, but I didn't go right to the car. I went around the corner and waited. He probably didn't see the license plate."

"Are you sure he recognized you? Maybe he didn't know you," she said hopefully.

"We were in the joint together, ———. At West Street. He looked at me, I looked at him, and we knew we knew each other."

"And he'll tell people in New York."

"Sure. It's a close tie with the Cataldos. We gotta think about what we're gonna do."

"We have to tell the boys," she said.

"That's right, in case we have to lam it."

Sal called Dan Russo the next day.

Russo was at his desk, set off by low partition walls, when the secretary said that Sal was on the line. Even in the vast bullpen of the FBI's Manhattan headquarters, Russo had managed to personalize his space. He'd already framed and hung next to his desk an eight-by-ten-inch photograph of the betting ticket his search team had found in Bruno's wastebasket. He was proud of that find; from his investigator's point of view, it was the missing link that had brought the case together. It seemed to Russo as if he was always taking calls from Sal. The month before, after Brennan had been sentenced to five years in prison and fined two hundred and nine thousand dollars by U.S. District Judge Jack Weinstein, Sal had called full of indignation.

"Five years? I thought he would have gotten more," he'd said. "Didn't Dearie ask for more?"

"He asked for close to the maximum on racketeering," Russo had replied, speaking of the U.S. attorney's sentencing memorandum to the judge. "That would have been twenty years." He could hear the newspaper rustling at Sal's end. "Is that *The Times* you've got there?" Russo said. "Did you read the editorial? They called it 'a slap on the wrist.' I think his age had a lot to do with it. He was sixty-eight."

"Yeah, but wait," Sal said, "what about this? Here it is. The judge called Brennan 'casually corrupt' and 'amiably dishonest.' That's the same as being halfway pregnant, isn't it?"

Russo had laughed. Sometimes he couldn't believe the nerve. Now Sal was calling him again. Sal was Russo's burden since he'd breached his security and gotten booted from the witness program. He reached for the phone.

"What's up?" the FBI agent said.

"We might have a problem," Sal said. He was flat and abrupt. Russo sat up and brought his notebook close. Usually it took five minutes to get to the point with Sal, if there was a point; sometimes, during football season, for example, he would call Russo with reports of Sal junior's football games. And there was something in his voice that Russo hadn't heard before: an unmistakable edge of fear.

Sal related his story about seeing Persico.

Russo asked all the questions Rose Marie had asked. Yes, Sal was sure it was Allie Boy, they'd shared a cell at West Street. Yes, Allie Boy had seen him, and recognized him. Russo wrote it all down in his notebook. "He's been on the lam for like five, six years," Sal said. "Maybe he lives here. Wouldn't that be a boot in the ass?"

"What do you want to do?" Russo asked.

"I don't know. Maybe we ought to think about going back in the program."

"Give it some time," Russo said. "Think about it. Maybe it's a false alarm. I'll try to get out there in a few weeks and we can talk it over."

Russo waited two months before he made the trip. In the interim the Gambino family racketeering trial of John Gotti and his brother Gene, John Carneglia, Anthony "Tony Roach" Rampino, Wilfred "Willie Boy" Johnson, Nicholas Corozzo and Leonard DiMaria had begun and been postponed after Gotti's newly appointed Gambino underboss, Frank DeCicco, sat down in a Buick that then exploded. Jurors suddenly couldn't be found who hadn't heard about the case and who weren't intimidated. Judge Eugene Nickerson adjourned the trial till August. By then the defendants had been reduced by three; Charles Carneglia and Armand Dellacroce had gone underground, Dellacroce after pleading guilty. His father, Aniello Dellacroce, the former underboss, had died of natural causes. The day before Russo arrived on May 14, Gotti's bail had been revoked for intimidating a refrigerator mechanic with whom he'd had a run-in. The mechanic had been foolish enough to file a complaint.

Sal picked up Russo at the airport. Russo noticed that as he drove Sal was more fidgety than usual. "I'm worried about this, Dan, I don't care what anybody says," Sal said, his eyes darting between the rearview mirror and road. He said he'd reported seeing Persico to the U.S. marshals, and had called up Ed McDonald at the Organized Crime Strike Force.

"All they say is that everybody's seen him," Sal complained, "but nobody knows where he is. He's been on the lam for like six years, and he's been reported in most of the fifty states and half a dozen foreign countries. McDonald even said he thought he'd seen him once, in a federal jury pool in Brooklyn, for Christ's sake. He told the marshals and they thought he was crazy."

Sal slowed the car and pulled into the right-hand lane, waited until a Buick with a rental sticker passed and eyed it sharply until it disappeared in traffic. Russo thought he seemed relieved when he left the freeway for the smaller local roads that carried lighter traffic.

"They say there's no indication he's in this part of the country," Sal said when he and Rose Marie and Russo were sitting together in the kitchen, talking about what to do. "But I think that's bullshit. I mean, there's no indication he's anywhere, or else they would've caught him. Why couldn't he be here?"

"I guess he could," Russo said. "They're saying that it's just not likely."

" 'Not likely' isn't gonna do me any good when I go out to start the car and it blows up. Or she does, or the kid." Sal kept rubbing his face with his hands in agitation.

Sal usually brushed off danger warnings. The closer to the edge he got, the happier he seemed. Russo remembered that Sal had been ecstatic when he'd gone off to meet with Andy Bruno, knowing Bruno was going to be looking for a wire. Now Sal was showing real concern. Russo placed a finger to the side of his nose and rubbed it thoughtfully. "So have you thought any more about what you want to do?" he said.

"Maybe I should just prepare myself."

"What does that mean?"

"Get some guns. A couple of thirty-aught-sixes, three-by-nine power Weaver scopes, maybe a Winchester thirty-thirty. Whatever I need, and a couple of pistols. Head for the hills and tool up for an onslaught of the wiseguys. What else am I gonna do?"

"Oh, my God, Sal," Rose Marie interjected.

"Whoa, whoa, now you're talking crazy," Russo said. "If you want to talk about me sponsoring you to go back in the program, we can talk. If you want to talk about buying weapons, you don't want to talk to me."

"Okay," said Sal, "let's talk about the program. If we did it, it would mean breaking up the family. The kids have their lives here. They could stay, somehow, and just the two of us would go. Or the three of us, and leave Sal junior here to finish high school."

"Have you talked to them about this?"

"We've mentioned it. They say they could handle it. It doesn't make them happy."

Russo looked at Rose Marie. He knew her great attachment to her children. He knew what separation from his own children would do to him and worse, what it would do to Mary Beth. He raised his eyebrows in a silent question. Rose Marie said, "I don't know, Dan. It would kill me to be away from my children. I could take it, I guess, if I knew it meant a better life for them. If it would make them safer. But my God . . ." She paused to take a breath. "My God, it would kill me."

"The point is, would you violate?" Russo said.

"You mean, would we visit them?" Sal asked.

"Yes. Any contact would be a violation, and you'd be back out again."

"We could only see them at a neutral place, set up by the marshals?"

"You know the rules, Sal, better than I do. That's the way it works. That's what you'd have to agree to. So let me ask you again. Would you violate?"

"Probably."

"Well, then, you don't want to go back in. I wouldn't sponsor you again."

Russo left Sal and Rose Marie still fearful, still ambivalent about reentering the program.

• • •

Dad seeing Allie Boy Persico was a reminder of our old life that dropped down like bird shit from the sky.

It caused a low-grade kind of fear that you couldn't quite forget. I took to looking out from my darkened room every night before I went to sleep, just to see if anything was there. Or I'd have my earphones on, mixing and scratching music on my turntable when I'd sense a need to stop and take the earphones off and listen. There was a feeling things could change at any minute, but we were at home by now, and didn't want to leave, so we plowed ahead as best we could.

I was dating steadily, a clear-skinned little honey-blonde who stopped my traffic, I mean, cold. Once that summer we went floating down a river on inner tubes, and she said her father was on the lam for something, maybe it was drugs, like marijuana. Joe and his girl were along. He and I looked at each other across the water, and he said, "On the lam? What does that mean?" I forget what she said, but we had a little fun with it; the girls couldn't make us out; they didn't know what we thought was so funny. We splashed them, finally, to show them we were kidding. My girl climbed into my inner tube with me and we forgot the whole thing then, because this girl, in a bathing suit, man, she could make you forget anything.

When I thought of Linda, I thought, I guess you're not really in love when you're sixteen, the way you thought you were.

Dad kept his promise about not speaking at the boys' home, but once when he was off talking to some government lawyers, he met some people from a home for kids in the Midwest, and he went off there to speak. He said he was doing it "to touch kids' lives," that he wanted to tell them they "had to break the cycle, the way you guys did."

Practice came, and then the season, and I welcomed the chance to lose myself in football. I felt more than ever the joyous freedom of the run, the sheer physical escape of it. You could let the sweat and fatigue bubble up and submerge you so that when you called it up again, the effort you needed to perform, it was a pure act, an unthinking, animal act where instinct outweighed thought, and I loved it because thought was what I wanted to avoid. Without thought, I was without care and the future was certain, it was as far as you could get without being tackled, not some uncertain blur that lay out there somewhere.

*We won our first game. I gained eighty-nine yards and scored
two touchdowns. We won our second game and I gained ninety-five
yards. The letters from colleges started to arrive. They came from
schools in the Big Eight, Pacific Ten, Southeastern and Southwest
conferences and a few big independents. Dad took more pleasure in
reading them than I did.*

*We lost our third game. One of the teams we'd beaten last year
had been laying for us all this time. Their defense rose up and we
couldn't crack the end zone. Sometime—maybe it was late in the
first half, I really don't remember—one of their guys nailed me with
his helmet in the thigh. I could feel it all the way to the bone, the
shock, then numbness, then I got the feeling back and it seemed to
be okay. I was able to finish out the game, for all the good it did. I
gained close to a hundred yards running and forty receiving, but it
was all between the twenties.*

*The thigh bruise was worse than anybody thought. It deepened
and hardened. The blood mass began a slow descent. I took anti-
coagulants and waited on the bench for it to go away.*

*And then we were plunged full force back into reminders of the
old life, because now Dad was in New York to testify against John
Gotti.*

• • •

Sal was the lead witness in the Gotti trial, which had reconvened
in August. Jury selection took over a month, and opening arguments
a few more days. As Sal's appearance date approached, Diane
Giacalone and John Gleeson led him through intense debriefings.
Over and over, Sal described his life of crime, and his associa-
tions with John Gotti and the other defendants in the racketeering
trial.

Giacalone called Sal at his motel the day before he was scheduled to appear. The prosecutor said she wanted a final preparation
session. More grilling. More dicing of Sal's past. More footsteps
through the garbage.

Sal said no.

"Don't give me that," said Giacalone. "We've got to prepare."

"I'm prepared," Sal said. "I'm ready to go. All I have to do is recount my whole life. I just don't want to talk about it anymore. I just want to go in there and get it over with."

He called Rose Marie, fuming. "I don't want to listen to this stuff no more," he shouted on the phone. "I don't live that life no more." The FBI agents in the adjoining room could hear his shouting through the walls.

Dan Russo had to call him from Connecticut, where he was working another investigation, to calm him down.

Sal rose on the morning of October 2, 1986, dressed casually in slacks and a striped sweater, and rode with his protective escort to the federal courthouse in Brooklyn. He blinked in surprise when he entered the courtroom. The fuckin' place was packed. It was like the whole world was in there. It looked like half the mobsters in New York, lining the rows at the back of the room, decked out in their designer jogging suits. In front, there were two or three rows of reporters; he would be a star. The Gotti trial was a spectator sport. Then Sal focused on the shorter distance, where to his left and in front of him he met the lethal gazes of men he'd once called friends.

Gotti sat at the end of the L-shaped defense table closest to the witness stand. His disdainful smile and impeccable suit betrayed nothing of his four-month stay in jail, nor of worry that he might lose the case. He looked older, the aura of power brighter than when Sal had seen him last, in the summer of '84 when Sal had gotten out of Rikers Island and was starting to work undercover for the government. He'd seen them all that summer around Ozone Park: Gene Gotti, Tony Roach, Willie Boy, Carneglia. He still owed Carneglia fifteen grand; he'd been wired when Carneglia told him to forget the juice, what the hell, we're friends, nobody's looking to blackjack nobody. He'd do worse than that, now, Sal thought. The other two, Corozzo and DiMaria, he didn't know so well. The defendants looked back at him with smirking contempt. They talked in stage whispers at his appearance. The defense table where they sat buzzed like the warning of a rattlesnake.

Sal sat back and proceeded to get comfortable.

"Tell us your name, please," said Diane Giacalone.

All that day and for two days of the following week, Sal told the story of his criminal life. He told of becoming a gambler and a loan shark, of pretending to be crazy, of being shot by the policeman and opening the Sinatra Club. Asked his occupation at the time, he said, "professional thief." He described the magnetism of John Gotti when Gotti was released from prison and began gambling at the club. He recounted closing the Sinatra Club and hanging out at the Bergin Hunt and Fish Club after his bank robbery arrest. He told of the robberies and hijackings he plotted and committed, of selling the merchandise through Gotti and Cataldo, of meeting John Carneglia in Lewisburg, of selling drugs and opening the chop shops and fixing the auto case and ending the drug business and opening the halfway legitimate jewelry stores, of finally moving from Ozone Park to try to revive the kart track near Port Jervis, of failing and returning to the drug business with the loan from John Carneglia. And of finally being arrested and cooperating with the government.

He returned to the witness stand the next day for cross-examination. Gene Gotti's lawyer went first. Jeffrey Hoffman was tall and youthful-looking, with striking blue eyes. He was deceptively pleasant. He asked if Sal had met with government lawyers to prepare for cross-examination. Sal said they had met the day before for seven hours.

"Did it take seven hours just to tell you to tell the truth?" Hoffman asked.

For the next three days, October 14, 15 and 16, Sal saw the ugliness of his life tossed back in his face before the courtroom audience. Every prank, every challenge, every complicated job was stripped of its glamour and humor and adventure and turned against him by the defense attorneys. And it was true, all of it was true. And he could not escape it. He heard about it in his motel room at night on the Cable News Network and New York's Channel 2. He called Rose Marie, enraged, and then woke up to read about it in the papers.

Sal spoke one day about his future prospects. He said, "The consequence of being a witness like myself today, is to be killed out there, to get killed if you become an informant, a witness or testify. The price you pay is [to be] dead."

His testimony was broken while lawyers approached the judge for a sidebar, a discussion beyond the hearing of the jury. Sal let his eyes wander the courtroom as he waited. The dangerous buzz rose up from the defense table. Sal looked at last upon John Gotti, closest to him. Gotti gave Sal an icy smile. He dropped his right hand below the tabletop, alongside his right leg, where it was invisible to everyone but Sal. Gotti pointed his finger like a pistol, cocked his thumb and dropped it like a hammer going down.

Sal felt a coldness wash from his heart outward to his fingertips.

Gotti's lawyer had the final crack at him. Bruce Cutler, burly, balding, was Gotti's ideological and sartorial twin. He dressed as expensively as Gotti and exuded as much distaste for Sal. "How many lies have you told in your life, Mr. Polisi?" Cutler asked.

Sal couldn't say. "An untold amount of lies," he answered.

"How many drugs have you sold, if we piled them up in the witness stand how high would it go?"

"I'm not sure."

"How much money have you stolen in your life?"

"Millions of dollars."

Cutler went on and on. How many policemen have you corrupted? How many women have you abused? Sal, trapped on the witness stand, wished with all his heart he could take Cutler on outside the courtroom. He wanted to explain himself. He wanted to say all that was behind him. He wanted to say he had really changed—none of which Cutler was about to let him say.

"How many people have you stuck up in your adult life, sir?"

"Many."

"How many people have you defrauded in your life, sir?"

"Many."

How many drug couriers have you employed? How many cars have you stolen? How many prostitutes have worked for you? The sordid catalog of his life rained down on Sal.

"Do you recognize the name Victor Cassatti?" Cutler asked.

"Yes, I do." Victor, from Sal's heroin days. You tried to find good dealers. The good ones were the ones who didn't use. They were just in it for the money. Once a dealer started using, forget about it. He'd waste the stuff, he'd skim some for himself and once he couldn't pay for his habit out of the profits he was making, he'd skim some more. Like poor Victor. Victor started out okay, a good, strong, loyal kid who got fucked up. He skimmed a little here, a little there, to feed his habit until Sal beat him bloody. He'd get clean and come back and beg to work for Sal again, and Sal would let him and Victor would get on the stuff again, over and over. It got where Victor knew Sal was going to beat him; he'd even hand him the little nightstick that he used to do it, and let Sal beat him, like a dog. It was a double loss, because Victor was also a good car thief.

"He's dead, he overdosed," Cutler was saying. Or was he asking, "You don't know that he's dead?"

Sal hadn't known. But it was a business. You couldn't feel responsible for that. You couldn't. Victor, dead?

Cutler kept flaying Sal. "Your father-in-law died and you didn't go to the funeral, did you? You wouldn't let your wife go either, would you?"

Wait a minute. "She . . ."

"Her own father's funeral. Did you let your wife go to her own father's funeral, yes or no? That's all I asked. Not any explanations."

"No."

Giacalone did her best to rehabilitate her witness. She asked "Are you proud of the way you played your life in the last twenty years?"

Sal said, "For the people I was associating with and what I was doing, I almost thought it was normal at the time."

"And now?"

"Now, I think it's completely un-American and I'm ashamed of the way I lived my life."

The swarming buzz arose from the defense table, the sarcastic, agitated hiss. When Cutler rose again and swaggered onto center stage, he asked, "When did you get this new religion, this elixir? Tell us, Mr. Polisi, who gave you this elixir? Did you receive an elixir from the government to become a new man? Did someone give you some injection? Tell us so we could free the jails, so we could free the jails of the lowlifes in there like you."

Finally it was over.

Sal returned home purged and empty. If he had needed punishment, he'd gotten it. If he had needed to confess, he would have handled it another way. But it was out of him at last. A part of him wished the boys had been there in the courtroom, watching him be punished. If they could have seen him having to eat Bruce Cutler's shit, they would have understood how changed he was. If they still loved him after knowing all that he had been, he would have an easy mind.

· · ·

Dad was on the Cable News Network it seemed like every night, his name and a goofy sketch of him on the witness stand in a pullover shirt. Nobody could have recognized him. They had his round face right, but the details were off and they drew his head a little small. Seeing it, hearing our old name, was just another way that other life was dogging us. It wouldn't stay behind us. It was right there in our living room.

The recruiters were calling at the same time, and I was desperate to get back in the lineup. After two weeks, I guess it was, I was working out again. My first day back at practice, I twisted the ankle on my other leg.

Lying there after it happened, I had to bite my lip to keep from crying. It wasn't the pain. It was having come so far to have this chance, this little spot of time in which to do good and seeing it all crumble. Damn my shitty ankle. Damn my clumsy step. Damn the kid who fell in front of me. Damn the very ground I tried to run on, it wasn't smooth enough. Damn, damn, damn everything. I beat my fists into the ground as the other players gathered until I heard Joe saying, "Maybe it's not bad." I rolled over and the trainer had a look. It was bad.

As I was leaving practice, Coach said, "Don't worry, son, you'll be straightened out in no time." Talking to me like my father. What a joke.

I left with crutches and heavy tape and an attitude. I didn't go home. I didn't call. I went to my girlfriend's house. I felt sorry for myself. I wanted someone to feel sorry with me, and I wanted comfort like I couldn't get at home.

I limped to her door with a crutch under one arm. She took one look at me and said, "Oh, baby." We drove out of town to the river where we'd been tubing back in the summer. The gravel parking lot that was full then was empty now in fall, at sunset, and at the end of the lot was a dirt track that wound another hundred yards or so and ended on a low bluff that overlooked the river. You had to keep to the left to stay out of the ruts, but you could make it. The river came in dark from above us, moving slowly and turning itself over, glistening like a seal. In front of us against the sun it rolled like a spool of copper wire and then angled slowly out of sight, reappearing for stretches until the sun left and took the light from the water.

I said, "Nothing's gone right. It's been such a shitty year."

"Don't talk," she said. "It's okay now." Her one hand pulled me toward her and the other drew a line of fire up my leg. "Here," fumbling now at the front of my jeans, "here, we'd better get that out of here." For a time there was just the back of her blond head in my lap. After that we threw caution out the window. I was on the other seat and she was on top of me, facing me, her fine sleek legs drawn up on either side of me, fingers biting into my shoulders, my hands cupping her ass, pulling her against me. Forget my ankle, we banged our elbows and knees on every piece of metal in the car. I could have died right then and there, her body was a streak of silver, flashing between the flaps of her unbuttoned open shirt as we moved against each other. I licked her skin and tasted her scent and the salt of our exertion. Each taste was better than the last. We were hungry and then we were hungry again and then again. Beyond us in the night the river flowed and glinted like the metal of a gun.

We slept at last. I woke up to the dull ache in my ankle, and it was a minute before I realized the tape around it was all I was wearing. I'd been clutching my sweatshirt to keep warm. She was wrapped up in my letter jacket, and we both were curled against each other. When I tried to wake her up, she pressed against me harder, shivering. I loved her, I thought. She had taken the poison

out of me. Both of us were just looking for warmth on a cold night.
It was a shame there was so little I could really tell her.

It was after midnight when I got home. Lights were blazing in
the house. Mom was outside in the driveway before I could get the
car door open. "Where have you been?" she cried. "My God, we've
been so worried. I called Coach, he said you'd gotten hurt again. I
didn't know what to think. I was about to call the police." She leaned
into the car and put her arms around me.

It was the weight of our unique aloneness that I finally couldn't
bear. I broke down and cried against her shoulder.

• • •

The season ended in a rush. Sal junior's was not the only injury;
the tailback was sidelined and the coach brought in Joe Polisi who
scored a twenty-two-yard touchdown in a late season victory. Sal,
who kept charts of both boys' performances, was excited by Joe's
progress. At fifteen, the sophomore was six-one and weighed one
ninety. He ran a forty-yard dash in 4.68 seconds and could bench-
press two sixty.

Sal junior's injury kept him out the rest of the year. He continued
to be recruited nonetheless, making weekend trips to college games.
He and Sal were always alert to television cameras.

Sal returned to New York in mid-November to testify against
the Leonards in the bomb case he'd made with John Limbach. On
November 18, a federal court jury in Brooklyn found Julius Leonard,
the Rebel, guilty of conspiracy and the sale of pipe bombs. Doris
was found guilty of possession of pipe bombs. Cynthia and Danny,
their children who were also charged, were acquitted.

On January 8, 1987, Julius was sentenced to a year and a day
and Doris was sentenced to probation.

Meanwhile, the Gotti trial continued.

On March 13, the federal jury in Brooklyn acquitted Gotti and
his codefendants on all counts. After eight months, the government
had not been able to prove their crimes were part of a criminal
enterprise. The jubilation in Brooklyn, and later in the neighborhoods
of Ozone Park and Howard Beach as Gotti and his pals returned to
their old haunts, was matched by concern in the Polisi home.

"What now?" Rose Marie said.

"Let's get the kid through high school, then we'll see," was Sal's reply.

He had a date in New York one month later to be sentenced. Sal, facing up to fifteen years on the federal drug charge that he'd bargained for with his cooperation, returned to court with high expectations. He'd had the sentencing judge, Jack Weinstein of the Brennan trial, showered with letters from the youth homes where he'd spoken. The letters extolled Sal's recently discovered Christian charity in dealing with young people. He expected the judge to recognize his turnabout and praise his transformation. But Weinstein looked down upon him sourly.

"The government says you've cooperated, and that's all I'm concerned about," Judge Weinstein said. "As far as all these letters, Mr. Polisi, that's between you and God." Sal looked stunned, like a little boy who craved attention, but had been rebuked instead. The judge sentenced Sal to five years on probation.

Sal returned to New York to testify once more, this time in May in a racketeering case against Bonanno family boss Joseph Massino. Unknown to the FBI, he flew in a day early and rented a car. He drove from the Newark Airport through the Holland Tunnel to Manhattan, and made his way across the Williamsburg Bridge to the Brooklyn-Queens Expressway. He got off at Queens Boulevard and drove toward Ozone Park.

The air was balmy with springtime. Tulips bloomed in window boxes. Sal wanted to see how he felt, that was all. He wanted to test the tug of his old life. The Queens Boulevard hangouts passed without effect, the place he'd had the jewelry store he called the Great Atlantic and Pacific Gold Co., the diners, the apartments he'd used to hide in and cut his heroin. Deeper into the old neighborhood, along Atlantic Avenue, he passed where the Sinatra Club had been, a few blocks later the Club Diner where he'd been arrested, then the Club 93 where he'd warned Eddie Provato about the FBI and laid the groundwork for his own arrest. Doubling back, he drove west on Liberty Avenue, under the el, past the corner garage where Noto Classic Cars had been, now an auto air-conditioning shop. A jog north took him to 101 Avenue, and he drove through the heart of

Ozone Park, past the delis and small Italian restaurants and past the storefront that housed the Bergin Hunt and Fish Club next door, now, to a nail salon. Nothing. He felt nothing. He felt detached and disconnected, a stranger in a familiar land. Until he passed the Cross Bay Oval where he'd first coached his sons at football, he didn't feel a thing.

EPILOGUE

It was a proud moment when I signed my football scholarship at the kitchen table with Mom and Dad and Joe
all there. I wrote my new name in a strong, bold hand. Mom and
Dad had to sign the papers, too, and the whole thing had to be
notarized.

We went out to dinner that night to celebrate. We went to an
Italian restaurant with red-checked tablecloths and candles stuck
into the necks of wine bottles dripped all over with wax. Dad drank
a glass of red wine. He made Mom get a glass of champagne, and
we all clinked glasses.

"You know, the last time we were together like this was at the
Cornucopia," Dad said.

"Oh, my God, don't bring that up," Mom told him.

"It's not," Joe said. "We ate in restaurants for about a year."

"I mean at a celebration," Dad said. He had a glow about him,
like he'd gotten the scholarship, not me. "Anyway, why not bring it
up? Look how far we've come from that night. We've got a lot to
celebrate. Our kid's going to college. I told him I'd give him a Porsche
when he got his scholarship . . ."

"Yeah, Dad, where's my Porsche?" I asked.

"Maybe you'll have to settle for something a little more modest,"
he said.

That was fine with me.

Dan Russo arrived the day after Dad got back from his last trial.
He was like a member of the family now. When his wife Mary Beth
had had their fourth child, we had all gone shopping for a present
and all gone together to put it in the mail. I liked him even though
I blamed the government in some way for all that we'd been through.
They used Dad like a piece of meat. They had that leverage on him.
He always had to do something else, and there were a lot of times

I wondered, Where is it gonna end? When is it ever gonna stop?

Now, even though Dad had been sentenced and testified for the last time, we renewed the debate about reentering the program. There was still that underlying fear. We laughed about John Gotti. We called him Get-Outta-Here, but we didn't know what he might do.

Russo wasn't for it or against it, our going back into the program. He was like an arbitrator, considering all sides.

"Are you in more danger now, with Gotti acquitted? I don't know," he said, between bites of Mom's chocolate swirl cheesecake. "The threat was there before you testified in that trial anyway. And it's still there. The spotlight's not going to fall on Sal junior"—he still used my old name, said he didn't want to know the new one—"the way it did in high school. Unless he becomes a major star, or wins the Heisman Trophy."

"I won't," I said.

"And even then, if anybody sees him, will they recognize him?"

We pondered that while Russo ate the last crumb of cheesecake off the plate. "Mmm, Rose Marie," he said, "that was really good."

"You want another slice, Dan? Sure you do. Come on," she said.

He accepted half a slice, took the first bite and continued. "The thing is, Sal, I've got to believe that people know too much about what you're doing. I don't know who you've told where you are, or who you've told who you are . . ." Mom looked at Dad, what you'd call a meaningful look. "But you're a little too loose, a little too free.

"Moving would undo a lot of your mistakes."

In the end, although Russo processed us and said we'd been accepted to go back into the program, we decided not to. Joe was just where I was when we moved the first time. His career would come together in the next two years. Coach had already said Joe could be his first great college player, but the marshals said Joe would never be able to play at a really good school, a visible top ten school like Notre Dame, say, if we were going to make it in the program. They wanted us to move to some place like Buffalo, Wyoming. We decided we were better moving on our own. We thought that way, we could be safe and still keep a little freedom.

Joe wasn't happy about leaving. We talked about it. "We don't

deserve to live like this," he said. We just wanted to live normal
lives. To go to school, play football, be successful. To live like
everybody else does. Not keep running because Dad did what he
had done for us. But it was for our safety.

By the first of August, we were almost ready. Dad went out and
rented a big van. We packed it full one afternoon. We just left
mattresses on the floor to sleep on, but we didn't get much sleep.
People were there until midnight. Coach came by and gave me a
game jersey, which he just never did. "You're gonna do well, son,"
he said. "And you," he said to Joe, "we're really gonna miss you,
boy. You change your mind, you come right back, you hear?" Finally
the house was empty and we went to sleep. Dad wanted to hit the
road at five.

The alarm went off at four, I guess it was. Lying there fogged
out, I thought that I heard voices. I heard silent footsteps through
the house and I heard my mom whisper, "Oh, my God." I got up
and joined her at the door and looked out upon candles burning in
our driveway and the movement of dark shapes. It took a moment to
realize it was our friends sitting out there in the dark. They were
having a good old time, talking quietly, drinking sodas, munching
this and that, like they were camping out or something while they
waited for us to wake up. Mom bit her knuckles hard, but she couldn't
keep from crying.

My girl was there. The moon was down but she outshone it
anyway. Joe's girl, too. Guys from the team. A few parents. Another
car pulled up as we walked outside, and two more kids from school
got out.

Mom was having trouble handling it. I mean, she wanted everybody to come inside and have breakfast. It didn't matter that the
refrigerator was empty and we had, like, a pot to boil water in and
that was it. Dad wandered out and said, "Hey, last-minute help.
You're the crew the moving company sent, right? Great." And so
everybody was enlisted moving mattresses into the back end of the
truck.

We were towing one car and driving the other. Finally the truck
was closed and the trailer hitched. Dad kept looking at his watch.
At five he said, "Okay, I'm starting." He went around giving hand-

shakes and good wishes. He told us where he'd be waiting by the roadside before the interstate, and to blink our lights to signal him.

God, it was hard to say all those good-byes there in the dark. I told my girl I'd fly her up for games, I'd come back to see her, everything, all those promises that I now knew were just to get you to a point where you could figure what to do. "I love you," I told her. She said she loved me, too.

Joe's good-byes were sad, leaving a team the way he was, but Mom's were saddest. She went from embrace to embrace, and everyone she hugged felt a gratitude they couldn't know the depth of. She was thanking people who two years before she'd never known, for giving her a life, for letting her be the real person that she was.

Finally she brushed one last tear from a corner of her eye and said, "We have to go."

We drove silently past homes with dark windows, past the entrance to the subdivision and out onto the road. You could just see the outlines of trees, heavy with their summer leaves, against the sky. We passed a patch of all-night restaurants, convenience stores and gas stations. Then we hit a stretch of dark road. At a spot where it widened I saw the U-Haul truck's reflectors winking in our low beams. I flashed the brights and slowed. Dad signaled to pull out ahead of us. The truck's broad back swayed onto the pavement and we fell in behind him into a cocoon lit by our headlights, while up ahead the road was dark and I searched for light on the horizon.